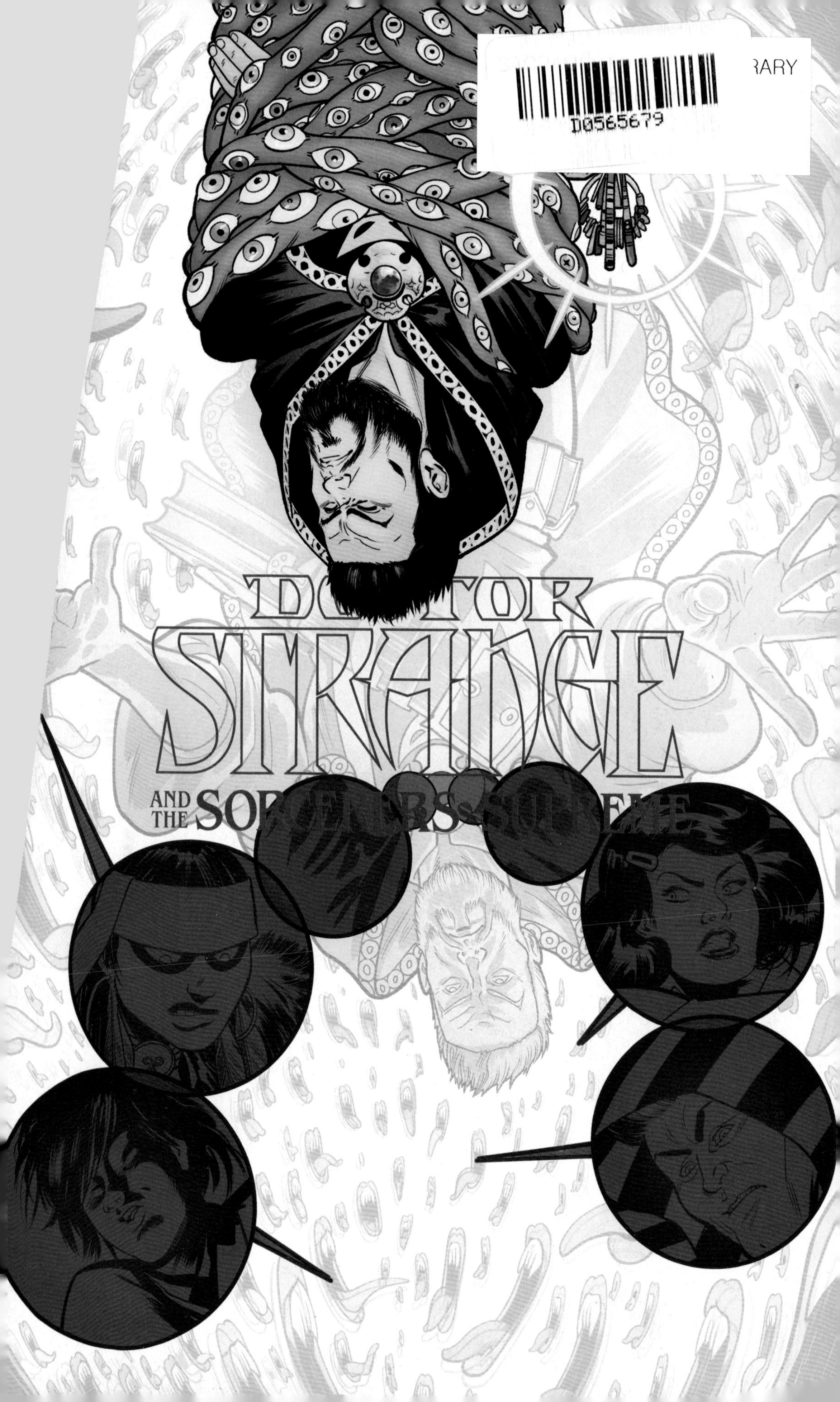
STRANGE
AND THE

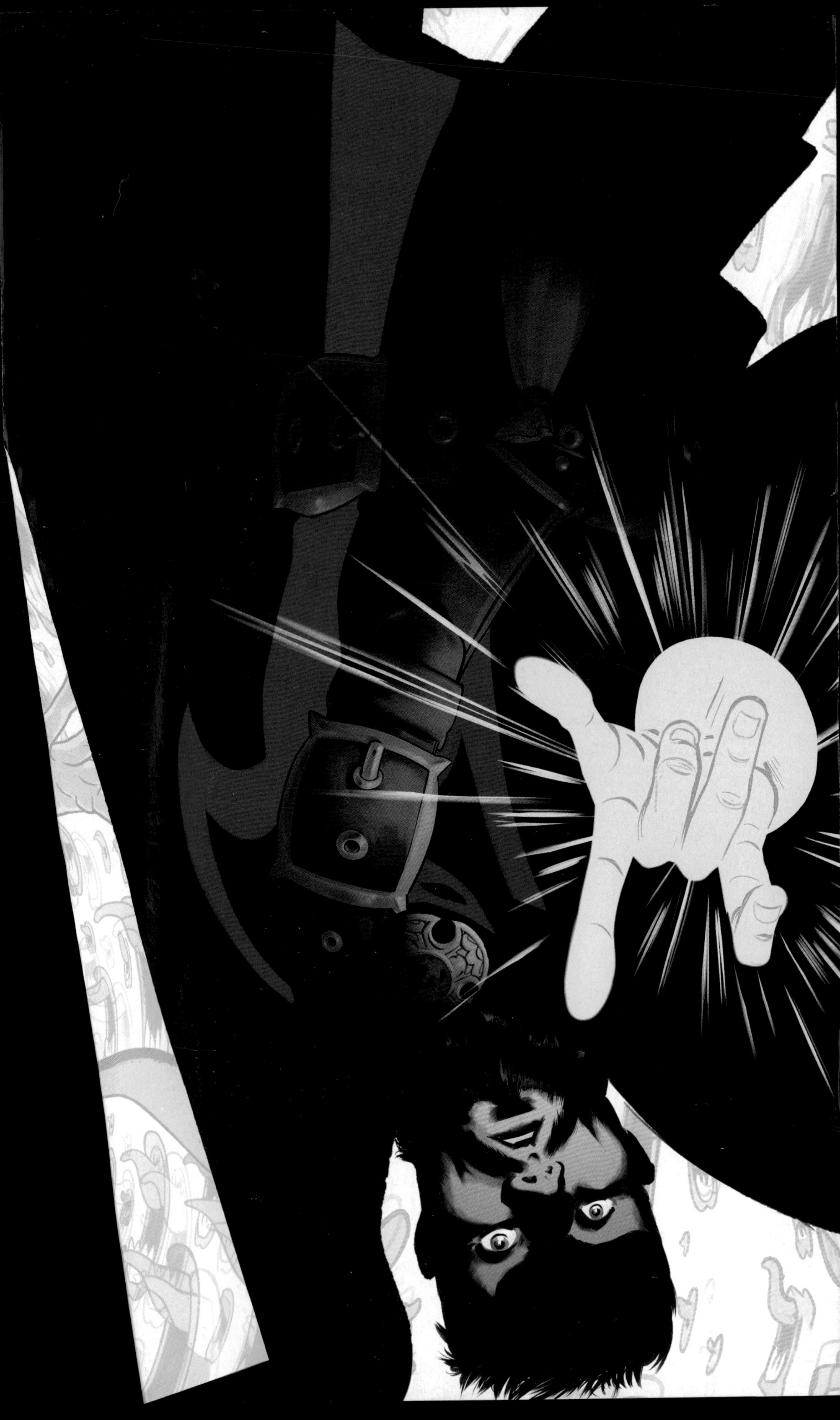

IN EVERY AGE, THERE IS ONE PERSON WHO POSSESSES GREATER MAGICAL SKILL AND POWER THAN ANY OTHER BEING.
THIS PERSON IS THE **SORCERER SUPREME**, AND THEY ARE THIS DIMENSION'S PROTECTOR AGAINST ANY MYSTICAL MAYHEM THAT THREATENS IT.

DOCTOR
STRANGE
THE
AND SORCERERS SUPREME

~ Out of Time ~

WRITER
Robbie Thompson

PENCILERS
Javier Rodríguez (#1-4 & #6) & *Nathan Stockman* (#5)

INKERS
Álvaro López (#1-4 & #6) &
Nathan Stockman (#5)

COLORISTS
Jordie Bellaire (#1-4 & #6) &
Tamra Bonvillain (#5)

LETTERER
VC's Joe Caramagna

COVER ART
Rafael Albuquerque & John Rauch (#1),
Javier Rodríguez, Álvaro López & Jordie Bellaire (#2 & #4)
and *Javier Rodríguez & Álvaro López* (#3 & #5-6)

CULTURAL ADVISOR, #3
Zainab Bradley

ASSISTANT EDITOR
Allison Stock

ASSOCIATE EDITOR
Darren Shan

EDITOR
Nick Lowe

~ DOCTOR STRANGE CREATED BY **STAN LEE & STEVE DITKO** ~

COLLECTION EDITOR: JENNIFER GRÜNWALD
ASSISTANT EDITOR: CAITLIN O'CONNELL
ASSOCIATE MANAGING EDITOR: KATERI WOODY
EDITOR, SPECIAL PROJECTS: MARK D. BEAZLEY
VP PRODUCTION & SPECIAL PROJECTS: JEFF YOUNGQUIST
SVP PRINT, SALES & MARKETING: DAVID GABRIEL
BOOK DESIGNER: ADAM DEL RE

EDITOR IN CHIEF: AXEL ALONSO
CHIEF CREATIVE OFFICER: JOE QUESADA
PRESIDENT: DAN BUCKLEY
EXECUTIVE PRODUCER: ALAN FINE

DOCTOR STRANGE AND THE SORCERERS SUPREME VOL. 1: OUT OF TIME. Contains material originally published in magazine form as DOCTOR STRANGE AND THE SORCERERS SUPREME #1-6. First printing 2017. ISBN# 978-1-302-90590- Published by MARVEL WORLDWIDE, INC., a subsidiary of MARVEL ENTERTAINMENT, LLC. OFFICE OF PUBLICATION: 135 West 50th Street, New York, NY 10020. Copyright © 2017 MARVEL. No similarity between any of the names, characters, persons, and/or institutions in this magazine with those of any living or dead person or institution is intended, and any such similarity which may exist is purely coincidental. **Printed in Canada.** DAN BUCKLEY, President, Marvel Entertainment; JOE QUESADA, Chief Creative Officer; TOM BREVOORT, SVP of Publishing; DAVID BOGART, SVP of Business Affairs & Operations, Publishing & Partnership; C.B. CEBULSKI, VP of Brand Management & Development, Asia; DAVID GABRIEL, SVP of Sales & Marketing, Publishing; JEFF YOUNGQUIST, VP of Production & Special Projects; DAN CARR, Executive Director of Publishing Technology; ALEX MORALES, Director of Publishing Operations; SUSAN CRESPI, Production Manager; STAN LEE, Chairman Emeritus. For information regarding advertising in Marvel Comics or on Marvel.com, please contact Vit DeBellis, Integrated Sales Manager, at vdebellis@marvel.com. For Marvel subscription inquiries, please call 888-511-5480. Manufactured between 3/31/2017 and 5/2/2017 by SOLISCO PRINTERS, SCOTT, QC, CANADA.

9 8 7 6 5 4 3 2 1

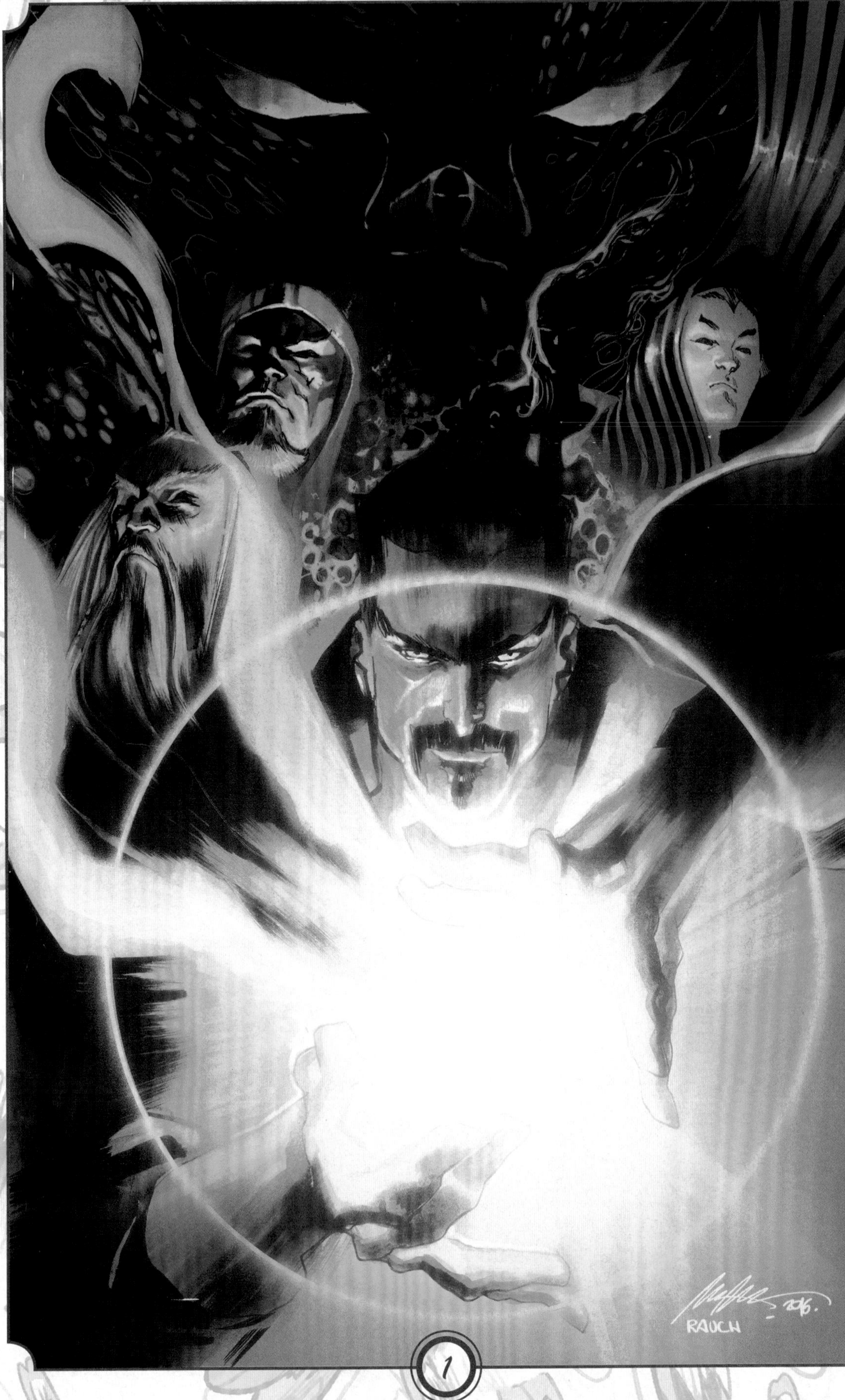
RAUCH
1

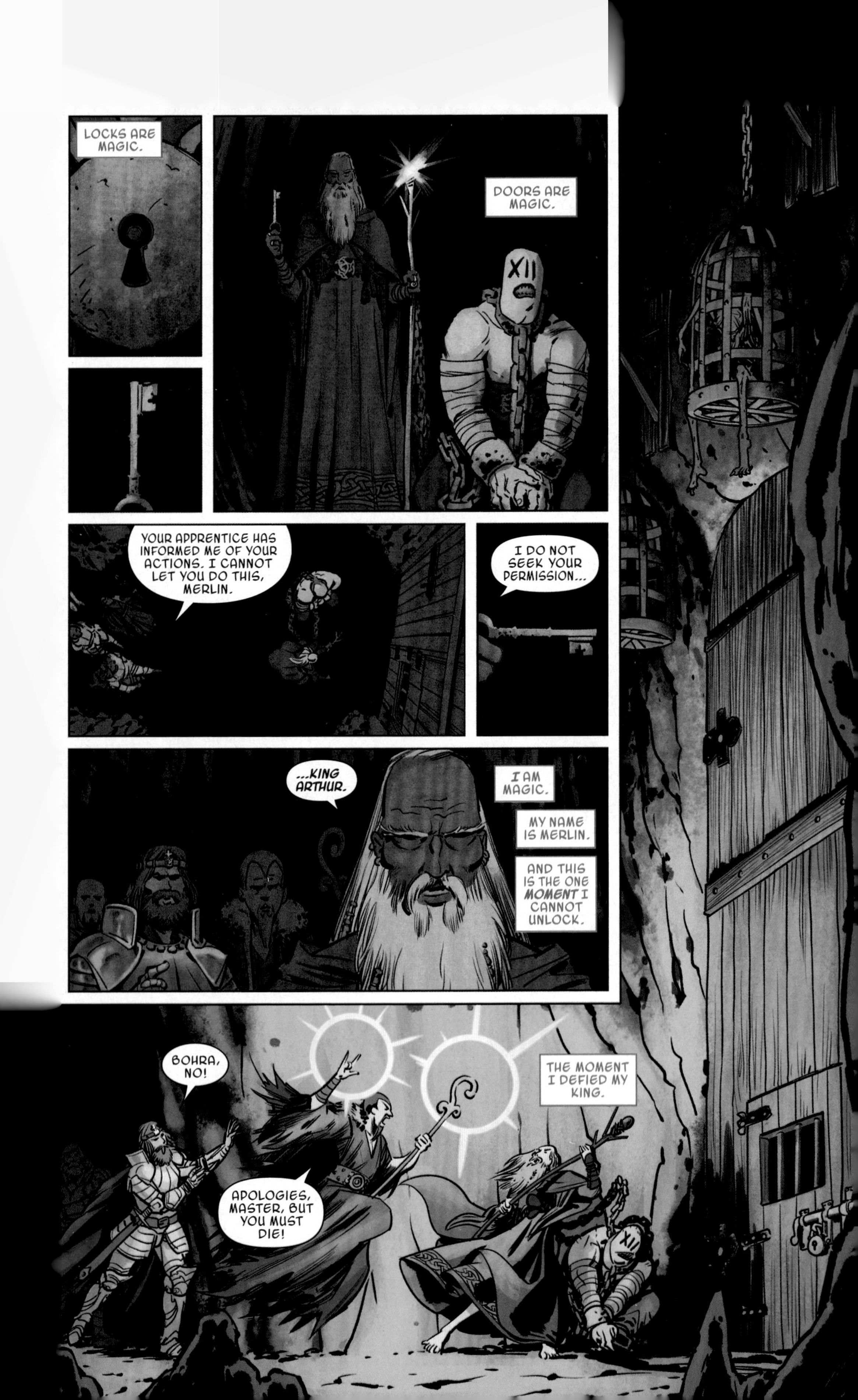
LOCKS ARE MAGIC.
DOORS ARE MAGIC.
YOUR APPRENTICE HAS INFORMED ME OF YOUR ACTIONS. I CANNOT LET YOU DO THIS, MERLIN.
I DO NOT SEEK YOUR PERMISSION...
...KING ARTHUR.
I AM MAGIC.
MY NAME IS MERLIN.
AND THIS IS THE ONE MOMENT I CANNOT UNLOCK.
THE MOMENT I DEFIED MY KING.
BOHRA, NO!
APOLOGIES, MASTER, BUT YOU MUST DIE!

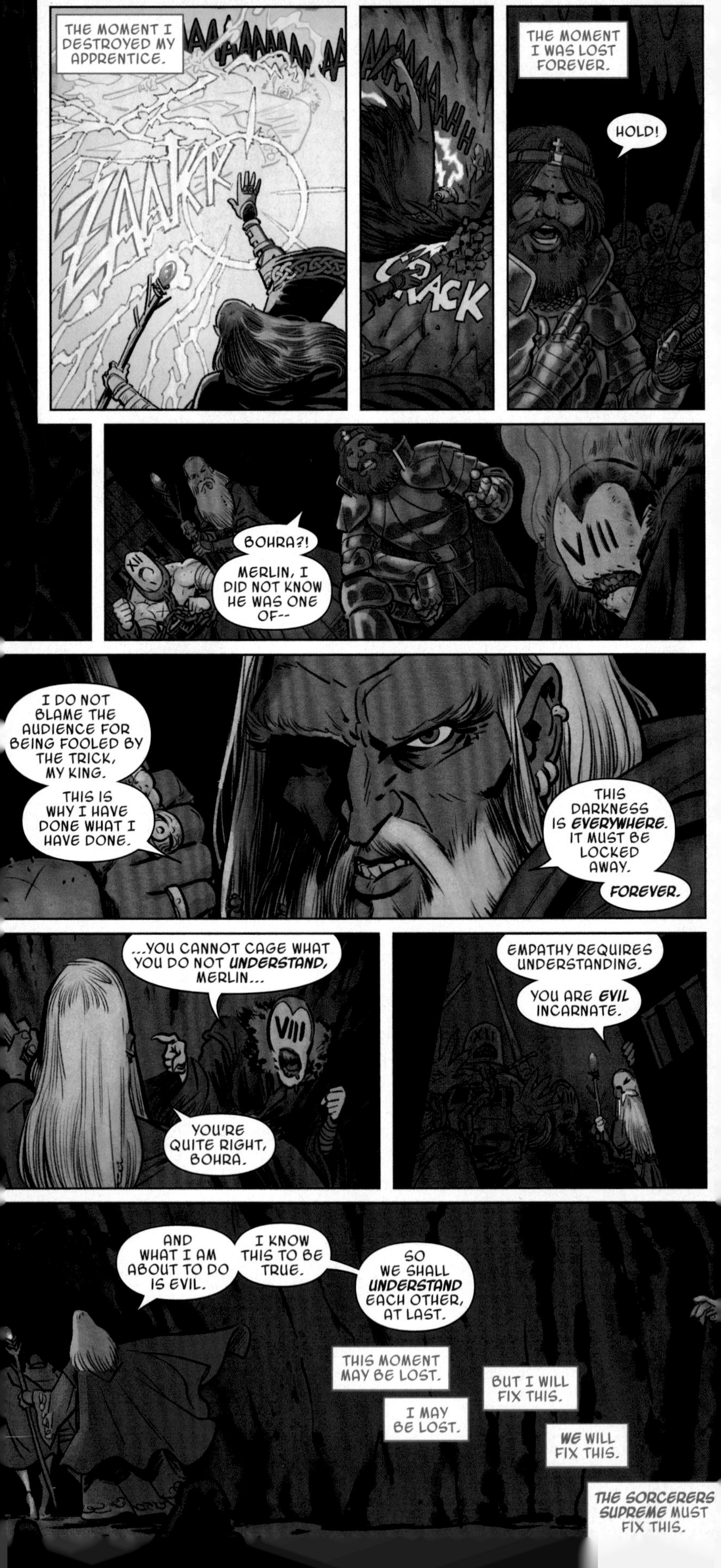
THE MOMENT I DESTROYED MY APPRENTICE.
ZAAKKR
AAAAAAAAAAAAAHHH
CRACK
THE MOMENT I WAS LOST FOREVER.
HOLD!
BOHRA?!
MERLIN, I DID NOT KNOW HE WAS ONE OF--
I DO NOT BLAME THE AUDIENCE FOR BEING FOOLED BY THE TRICK, MY KING.
THIS IS WHY I HAVE DONE WHAT I HAVE DONE.
THIS DARKNESS IS *EVERYWHERE*. IT MUST BE LOCKED AWAY.
FOREVER.
...YOU CANNOT CAGE WHAT YOU DO NOT *UNDERSTAND,* MERLIN...
YOU'RE QUITE RIGHT, BOHRA.
EMPATHY REQUIRES UNDERSTANDING.
YOU ARE *EVIL* INCARNATE.
AND WHAT I AM ABOUT TO DO IS EVIL.
I KNOW THIS TO BE TRUE.
SO WE SHALL *UNDERSTAND* EACH OTHER, AT LAST.
THIS MOMENT MAY BE LOST.
I MAY BE LOST.
BUT I WILL FIX THIS.
WE WILL FIX THIS.
THE SORCERERS SUPREME MUST FIX THIS.

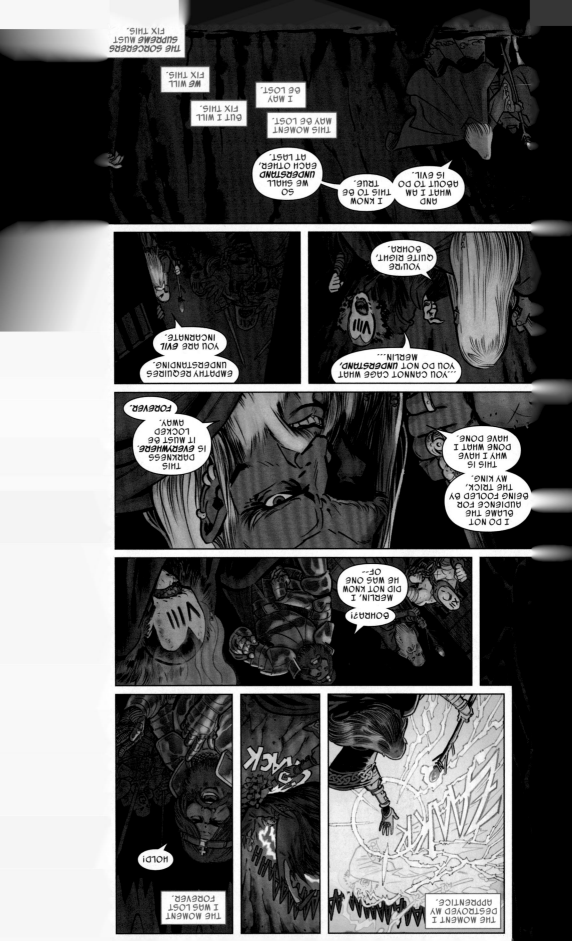

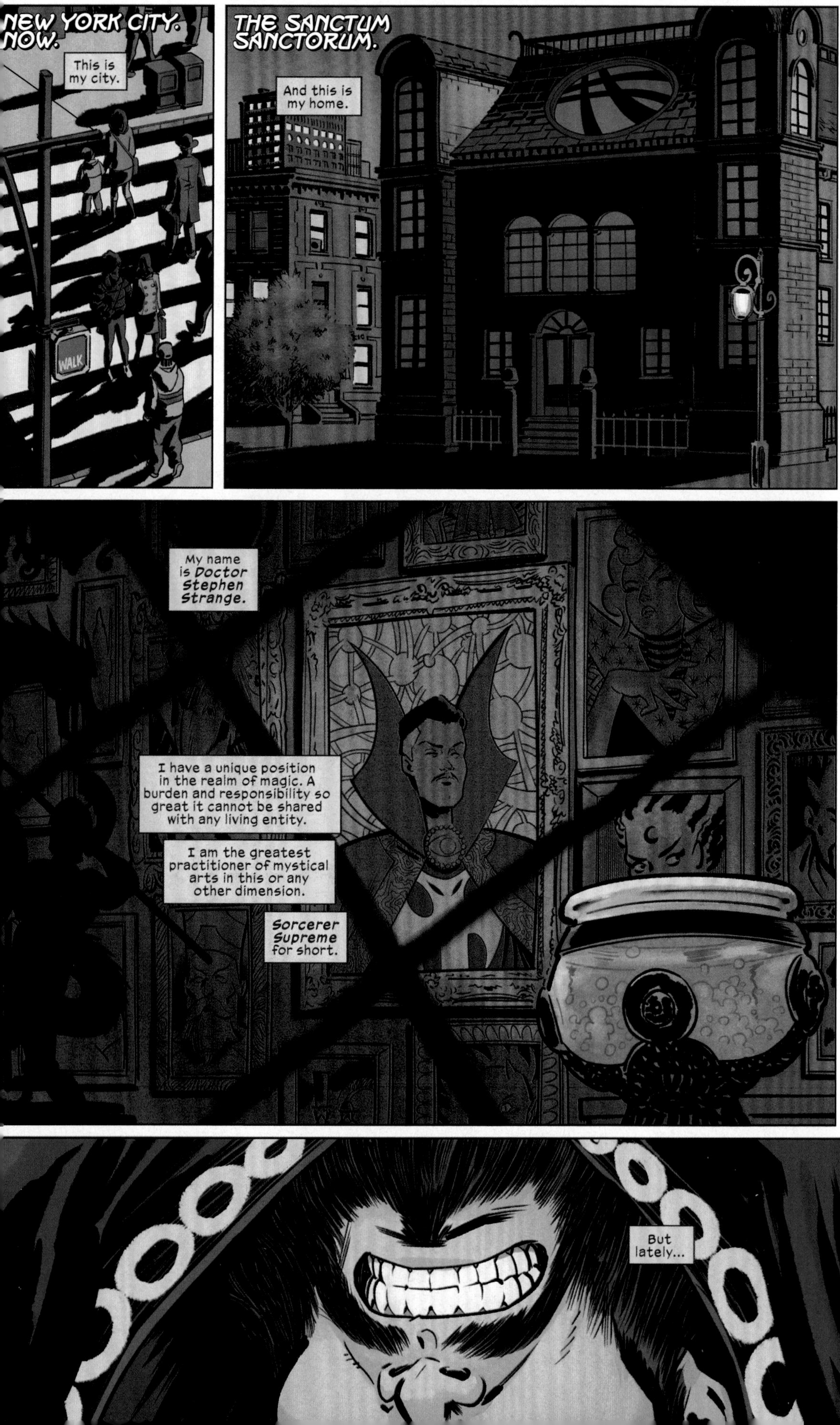
NEW YORK CITY.
NOW.
This is my city.
WALK
THE SANCTUM SANCTORUM.
And this is my home.
My name is *Doctor Stephen Strange.*
I have a unique position in the realm of magic. A burden and responsibility so great it cannot be shared with any living entity.
I am the greatest practitioner of mystical arts in this or any other dimension.
Sorcerer Supreme for short.
But lately...

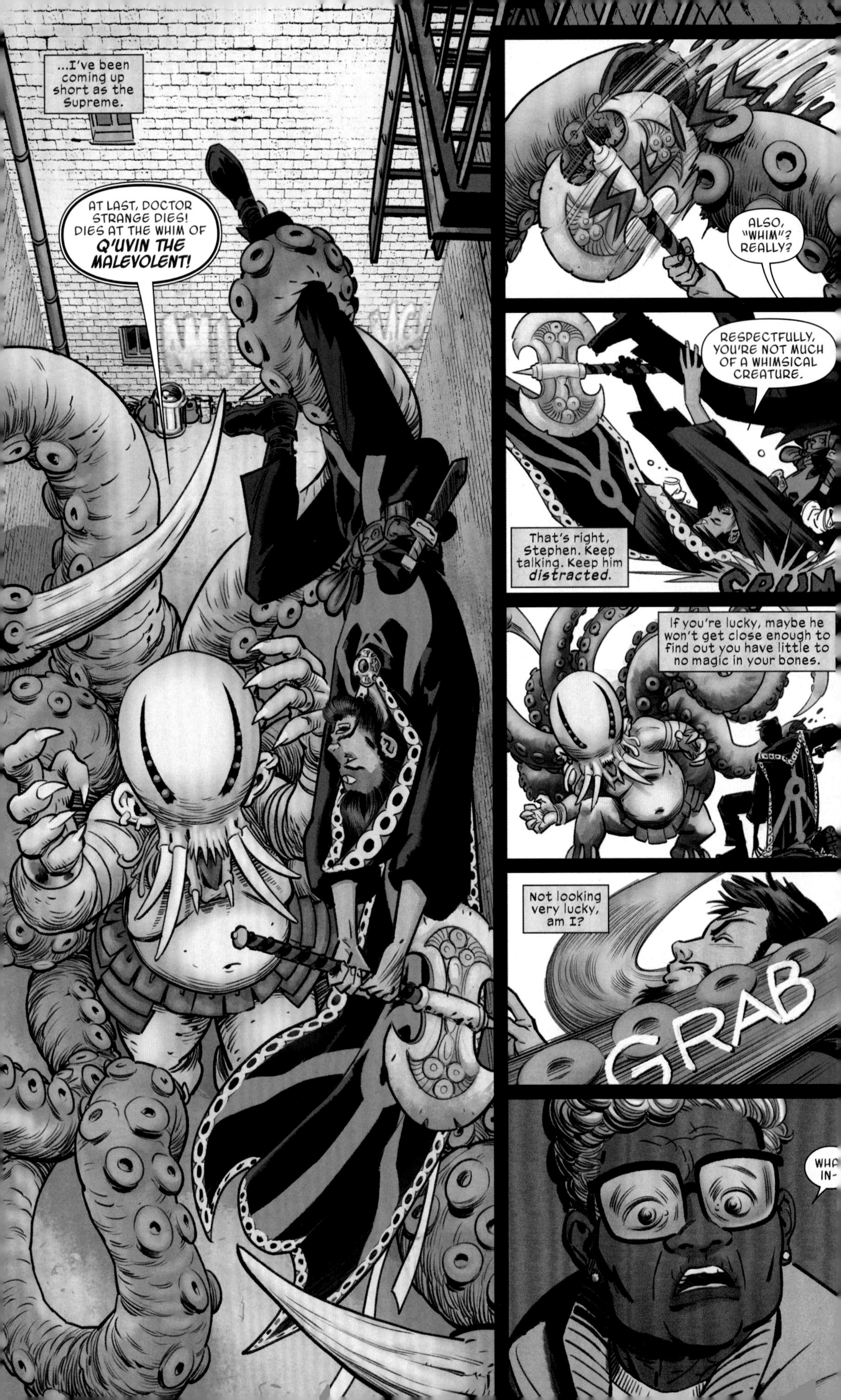
...I've been coming up short as the Supreme.
AT LAST, DOCTOR STRANGE DIES! DIES AT THE WHIM OF Q'UVIN THE MALEVOLENT!
ALSO, "WHIM"? REALLY?
RESPECTFULLY, YOU'RE NOT MUCH OF A WHIMSICAL CREATURE.
That's right, Stephen. Keep talking. Keep him distracted.
If you're lucky, maybe he won't get close enough to find out you have little to no magic in your bones.
Not looking very lucky, am I?
GRAB

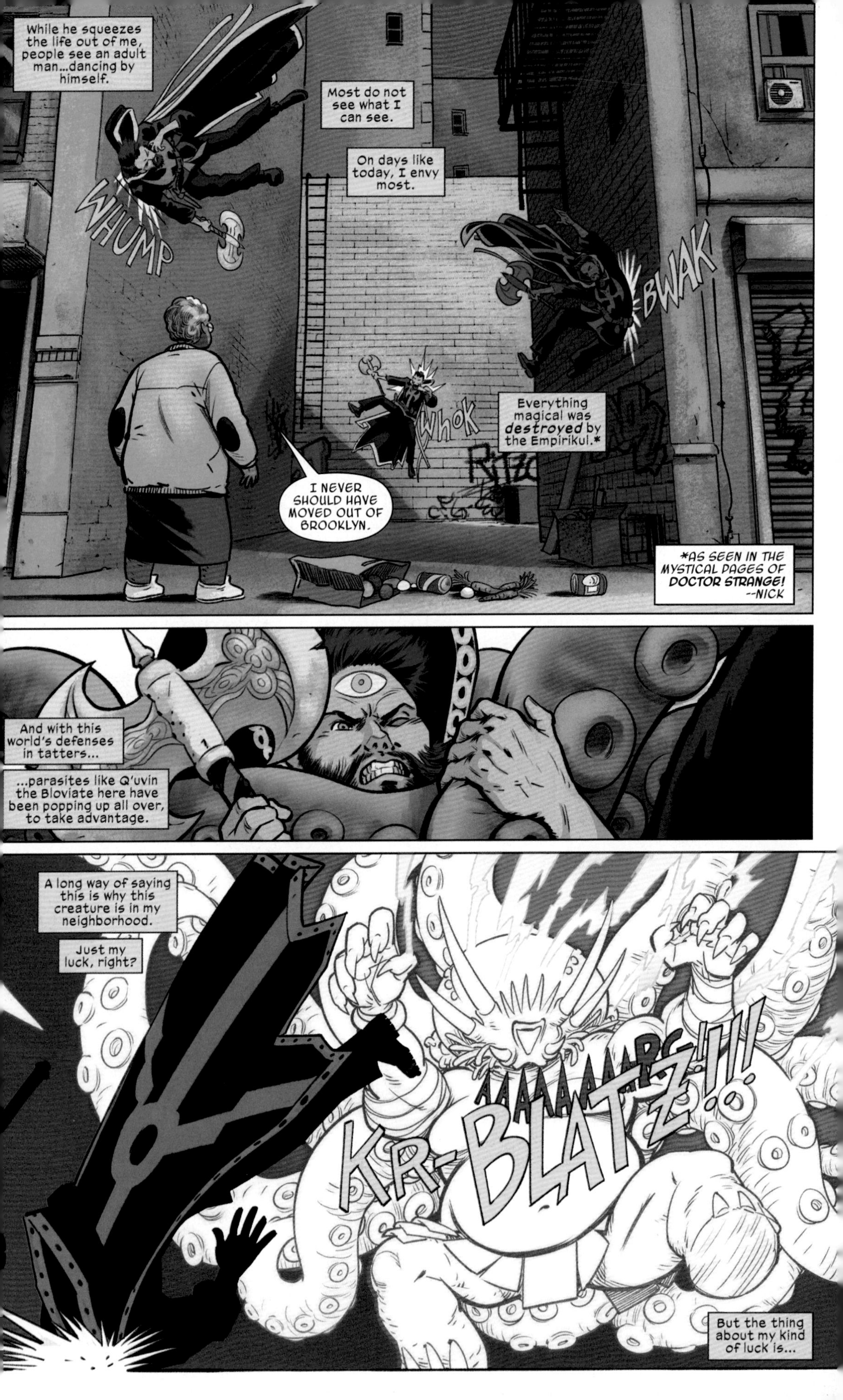
While he squeezes the life out of me, people see an adult man...dancing by himself.
WHUMP
Most do not see what I can see.
On days like today, I envy most.
BWAK
WHOK
Everything magical was *destroyed* by the Empirikul.*
I NEVER SHOULD HAVE MOVED OUT OF BROOKLYN.
*AS SEEN IN THE MYSTICAL PAGES OF DOCTOR STRANGE! --NICK
And with this world's defenses in tatters...
...parasites like Q'uvin the Bloviate here have been popping up all over, to take advantage.
A long way of saying this is why this creature is in my neighborhood.
Just my luck, right?
AAAAAAARG
KR-BLATZ!!!
But the thing about my kind of luck is...

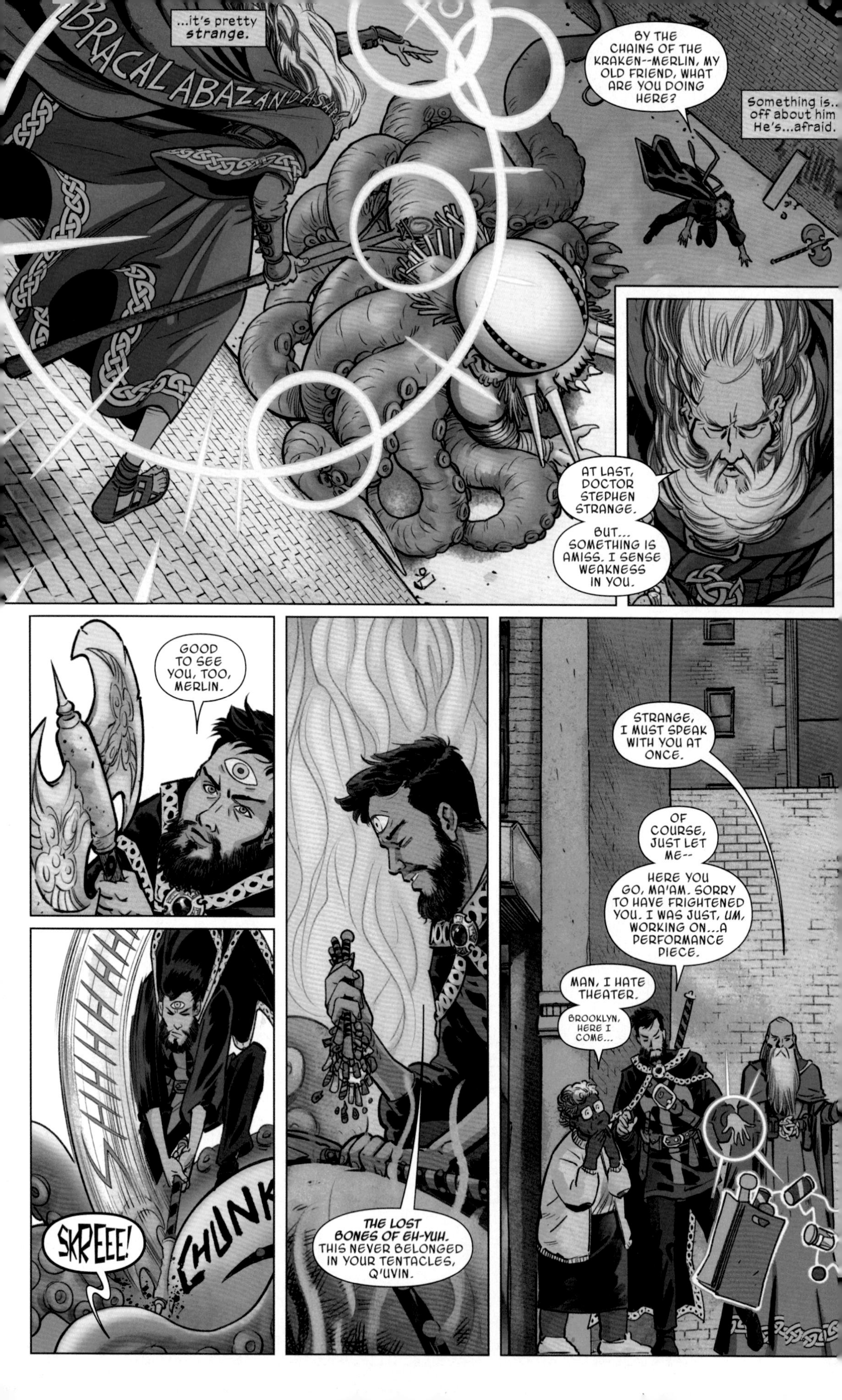
...it's pretty strange.
ABRACALABAZANDASAR
BY THE CHAINS OF THE KRAKEN--MERLIN, MY OLD FRIEND, WHAT ARE YOU DOING HERE?
Something is.. off about him He's...afraid.
AT LAST, DOCTOR STEPHEN STRANGE.
BUT... SOMETHING IS AMISS. I SENSE WEAKNESS IN YOU.
GOOD TO SEE YOU, TOO, MERLIN.
SHHHHHH
SKREEE!
CHUNK
THE LOST BONES OF EH-YUH. THIS NEVER BELONGED IN YOUR TENTACLES, Q'UVIN.
STRANGE, I MUST SPEAK WITH YOU AT ONCE.
OF COURSE, JUST LET ME--
HERE YOU GO, MA'AM. SORRY TO HAVE FRIGHTENED YOU. I WAS JUST, UM, WORKING ON...A PERFORMANCE PIECE.
MAN, I HATE THEATER.
BROOKLYN, HERE I COME...

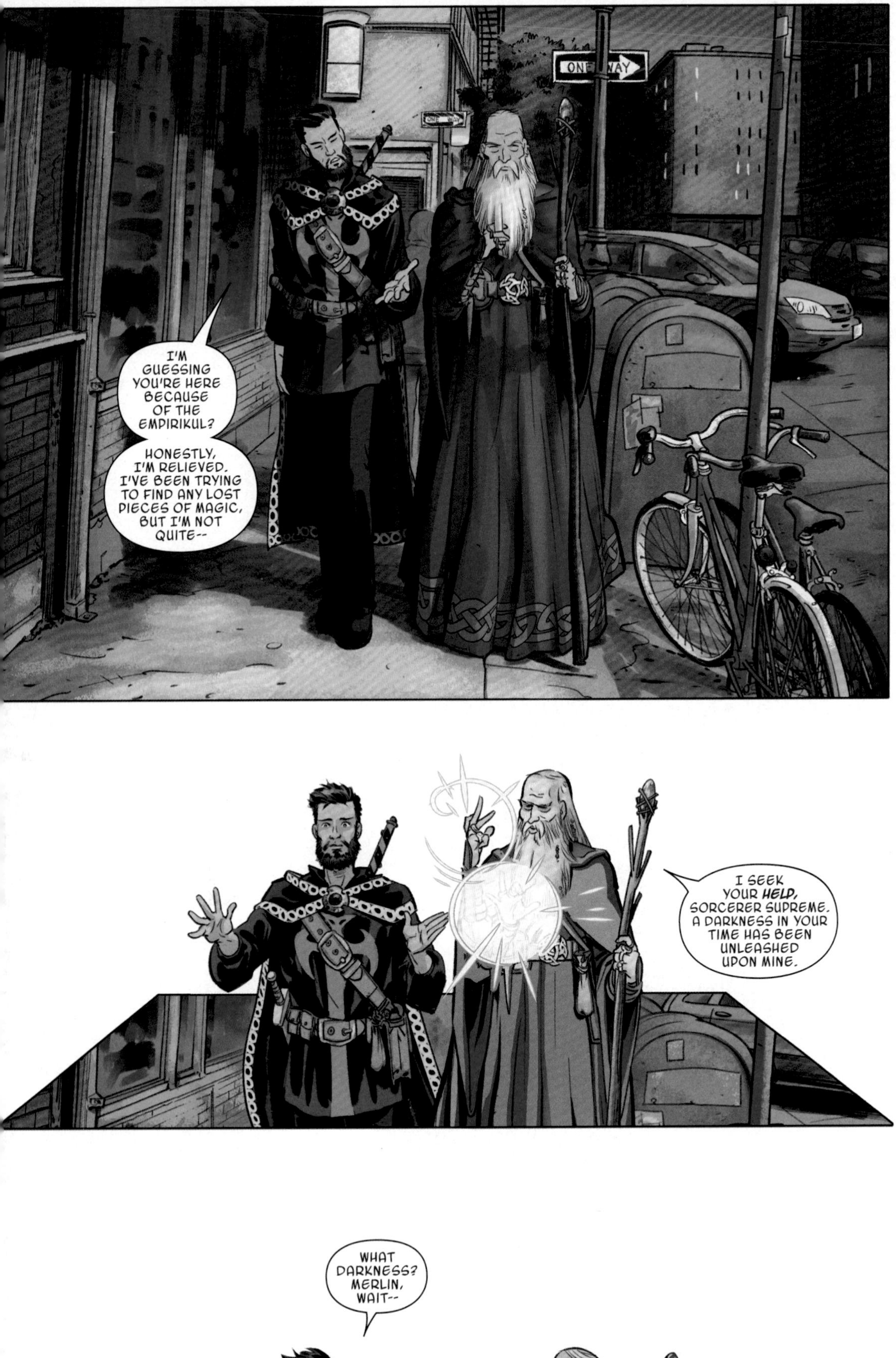
ONE WAY
I'M GUESSING YOU'RE HERE BECAUSE OF THE EMPIRIKUL?
HONESTLY, I'M RELIEVED. I'VE BEEN TRYING TO FIND ANY LOST PIECES OF MAGIC, BUT I'M NOT QUITE--
I SEEK YOUR **HELP,** SORCERER SUPREME. A DARKNESS IN YOUR TIME HAS BEEN UNLEASHED UPON MINE.
WHAT DARKNESS? MERLIN, WAIT--

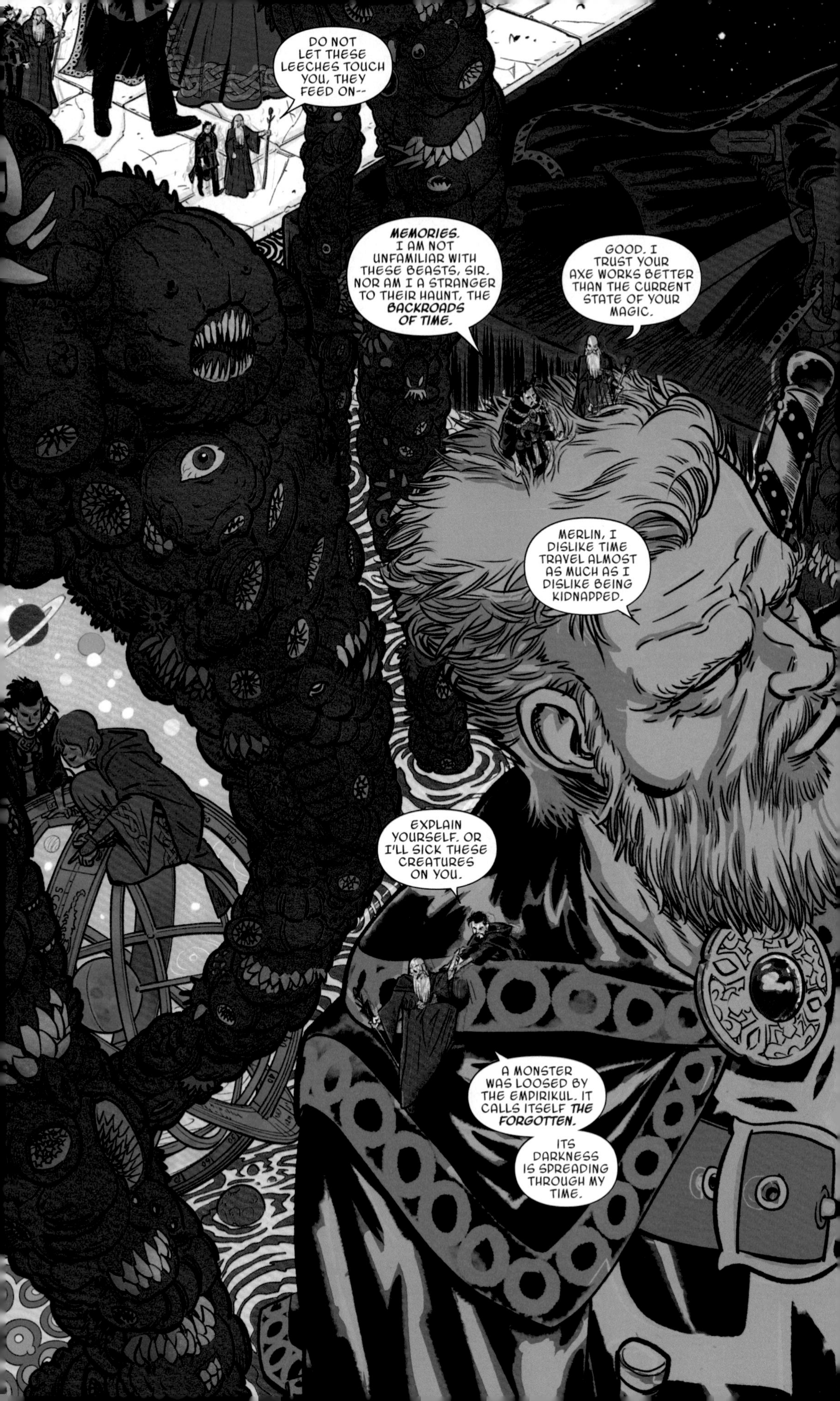
DO NOT LET THESE LEECHES TOUCH YOU, THEY FEED ON--
MEMORIES. I AM NOT UNFAMILIAR WITH THESE BEASTS, SIR. NOR AM I A STRANGER TO THEIR HAUNT, THE **BACKROADS OF TIME.**
GOOD. I TRUST YOUR AXE WORKS BETTER THAN THE CURRENT STATE OF YOUR MAGIC.
MERLIN, I DISLIKE TIME TRAVEL ALMOST AS MUCH AS I DISLIKE BEING KIDNAPPED.
EXPLAIN YOURSELF. OR I'LL SICK THESE CREATURES ON YOU.
A MONSTER WAS LOOSED BY THE EMPIRIKUL. IT CALLS ITSELF **THE FORGOTTEN.**
ITS DARKNESS IS SPREADING THROUGH MY TIME.

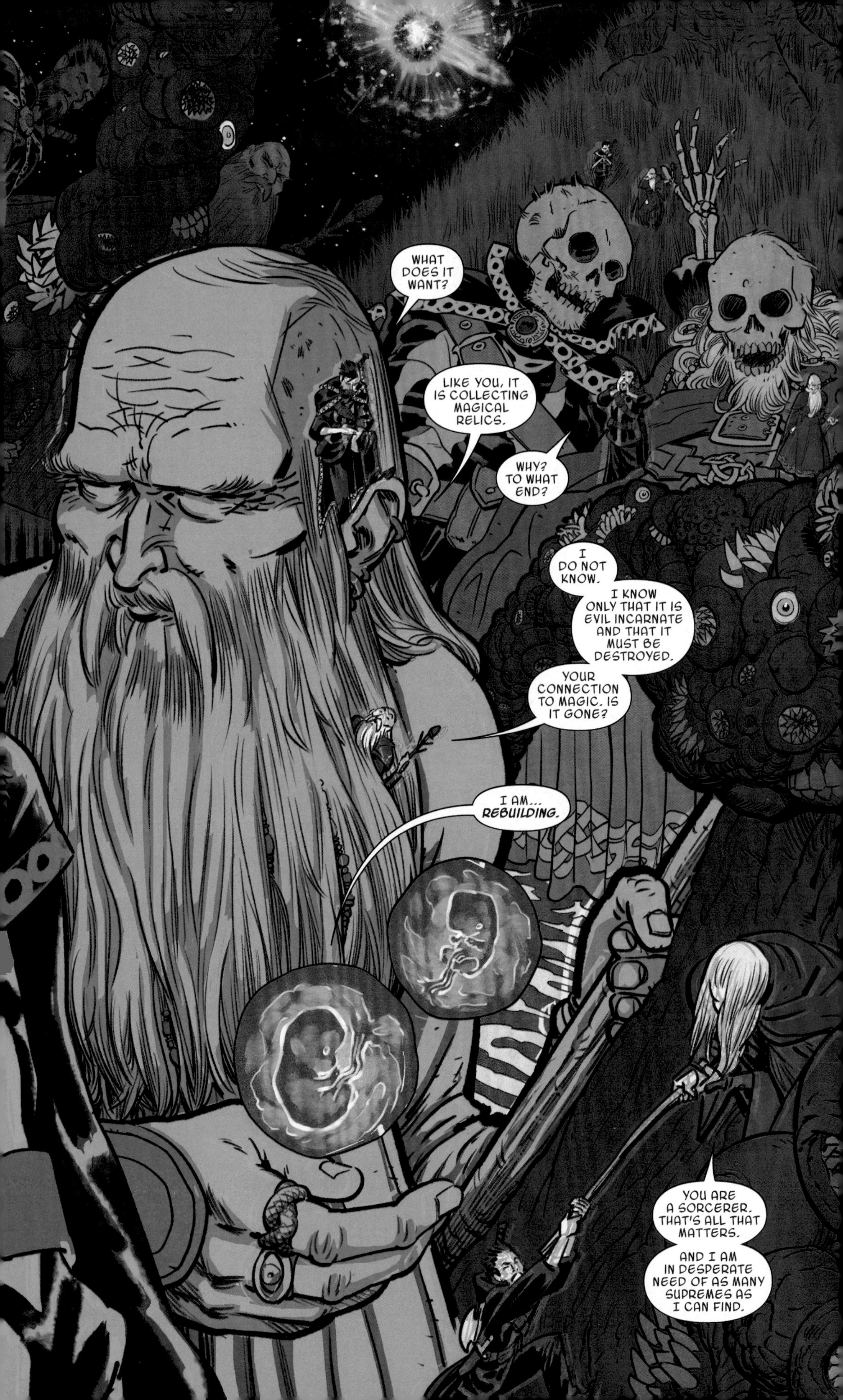
WHAT DOES IT WANT?
LIKE YOU, IT IS COLLECTING MAGICAL RELICS.
WHY? TO WHAT END?
I DO NOT KNOW.
I KNOW ONLY THAT IT IS EVIL INCARNATE AND THAT IT MUST BE DESTROYED.
YOUR CONNECTION TO MAGIC. IS IT GONE?
I AM... **REBUILDING.**
YOU ARE A SORCERER. THAT'S ALL THAT MATTERS.
AND I AM IN DESPERATE NEED OF AS MANY SUPREMES AS I CAN FIND.

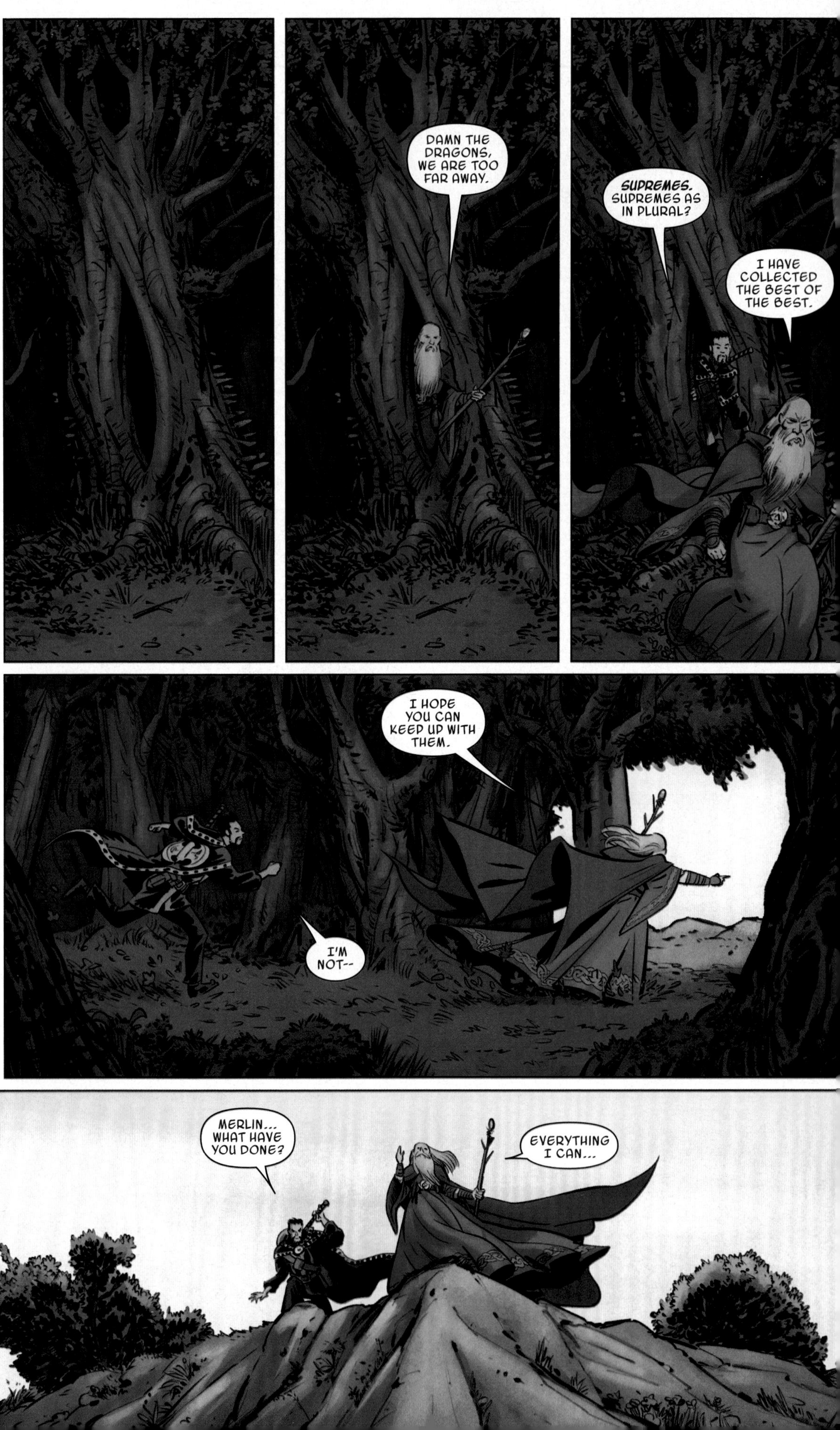
DAMN THE DRAGONS, WE ARE TOO FAR AWAY.
SUPREMES. SUPREMES AS IN PLURAL?
I HAVE COLLECTED THE BEST OF THE BEST.
I HOPE YOU CAN KEEP UP WITH THEM.
I'M NOT--
MERLIN... WHAT HAVE YOU DONE?
EVERYTHING I CAN...

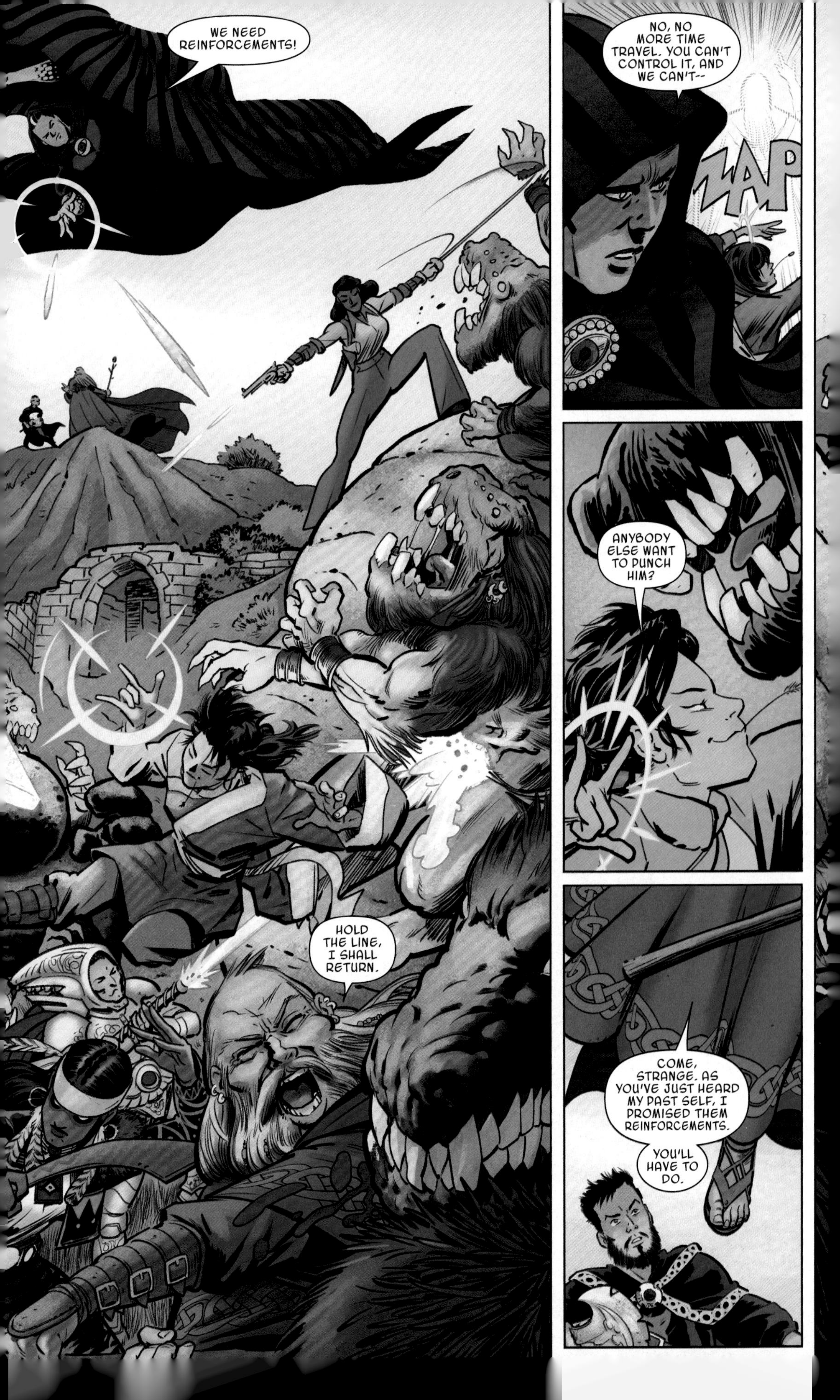
WE NEED REINFORCEMENTS!
HOLD THE LINE, I SHALL RETURN.
NO, NO MORE TIME TRAVEL. YOU CAN'T CONTROL IT, AND WE CAN'T--
ZAP
ANYBODY ELSE WANT TO PUNCH HIM?
COME, STRANGE. AS YOU'VE JUST HEARD MY PAST SELF, I PROMISED THEM REINFORCEMENTS.
YOU'LL HAVE TO DO.

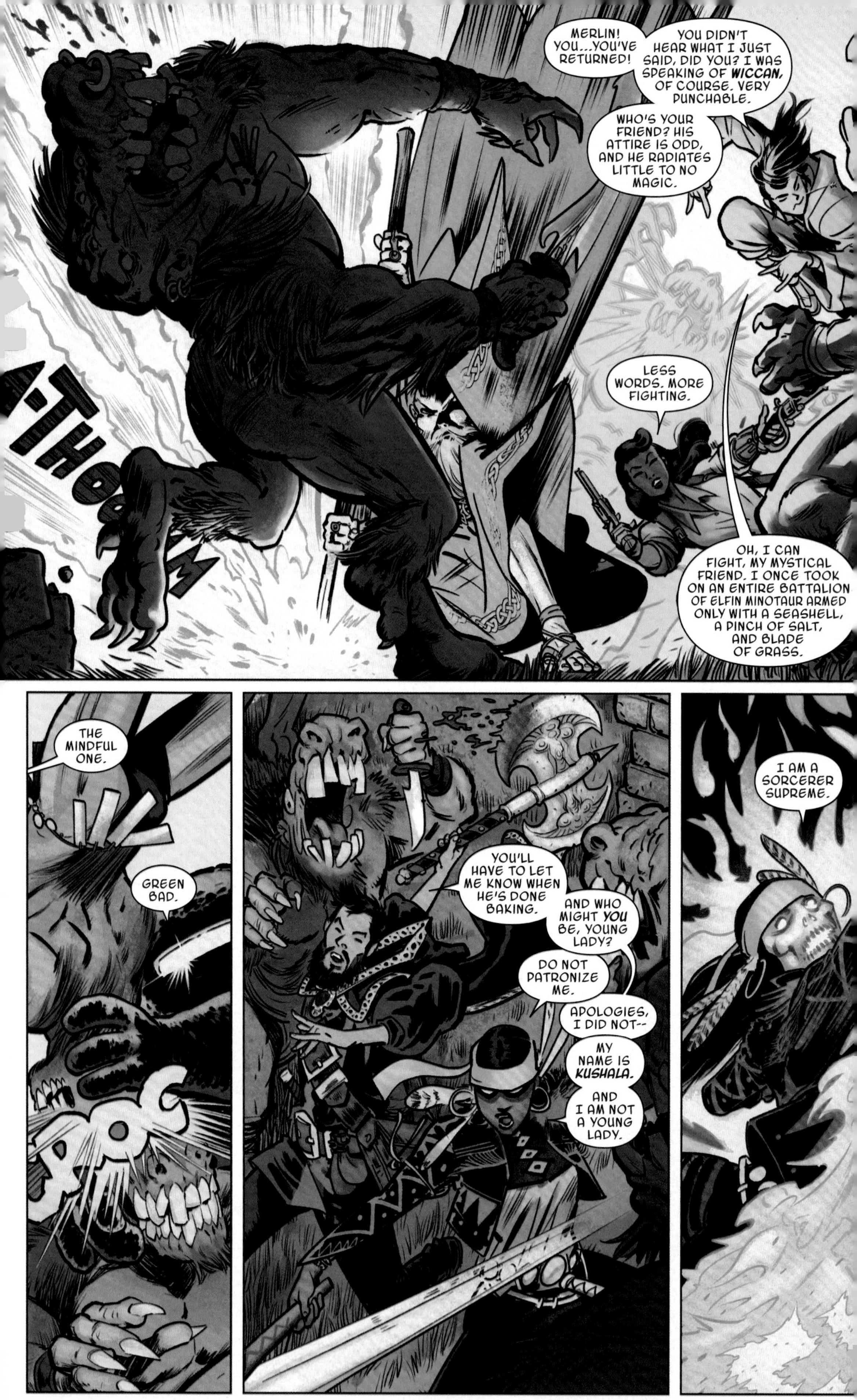
MERLIN! YOU...YOU'VE RETURNED!
YOU DIDN'T HEAR WHAT I JUST SAID, DID YOU? I WAS SPEAKING OF **WICCAN,** OF COURSE. VERY PUNCHABLE.
WHO'S YOUR FRIEND? HIS ATTIRE IS ODD, AND HE RADIATES LITTLE TO NO MAGIC.
LESS WORDS. MORE FIGHTING.
OH, I CAN FIGHT, MY MYSTICAL FRIEND. I ONCE TOOK ON AN ENTIRE BATTALION OF ELFIN MINOTAUR ARMED ONLY WITH A SEASHELL, A PINCH OF SALT, AND BLADE OF GRASS.
THE MINDFUL ONE.
GREEN BAD.
YOU'LL HAVE TO LET ME KNOW WHEN HE'S DONE BAKING.
AND WHO MIGHT **YOU** BE, YOUNG LADY?
DO NOT PATRONIZE ME.
APOLOGIES, I DID NOT--
MY NAME IS **KUSHALA.**
AND I AM NOT A YOUNG LADY.
I AM A SORCERER SUPREME.

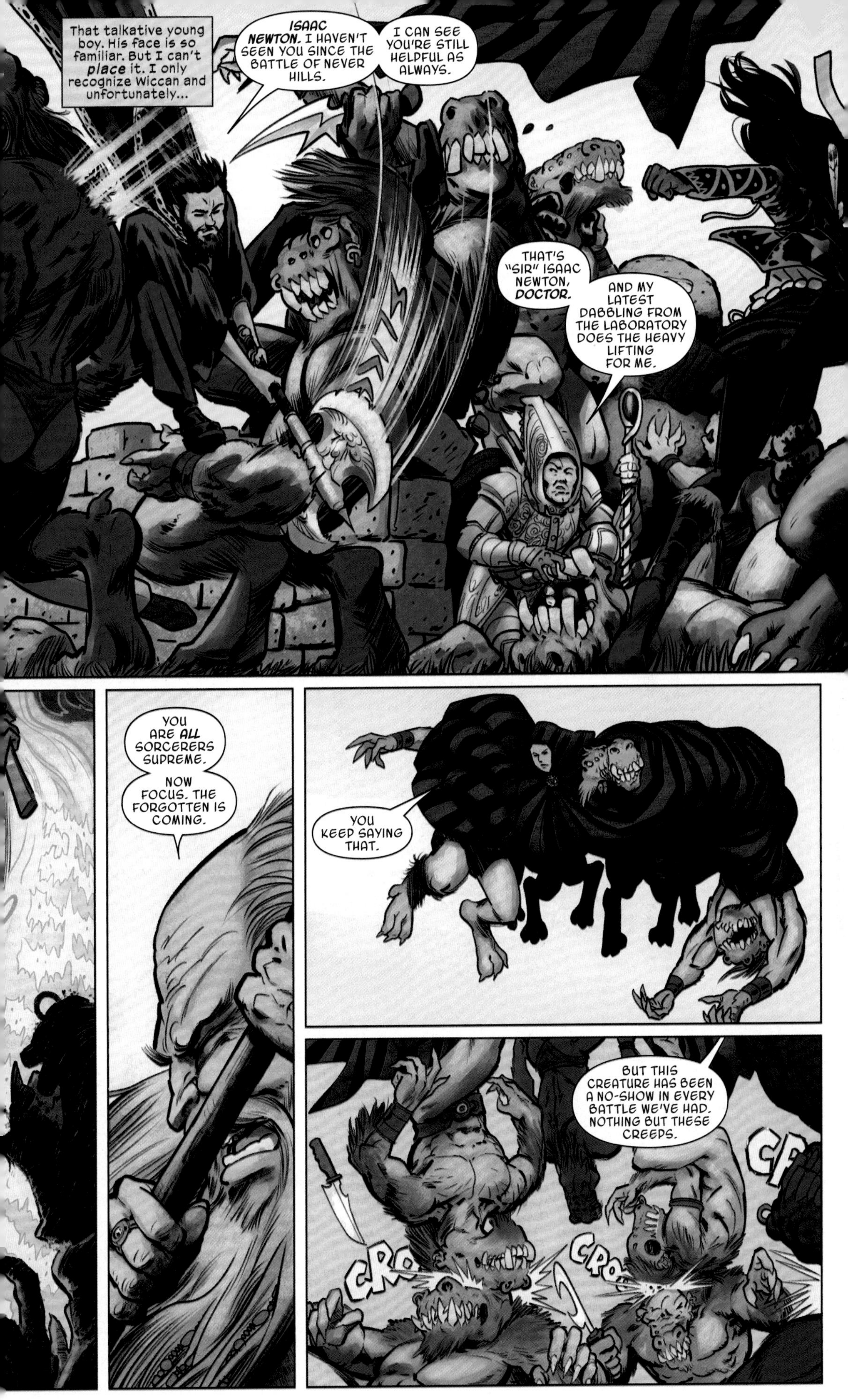
That talkative young boy. His face is so familiar. But I can't *place* it. I only recognize Wiccan and unfortunately...
ISAAC NEWTON. I HAVEN'T SEEN YOU SINCE THE BATTLE OF NEVER HILLS.
I CAN SEE YOU'RE STILL HELPFUL AS ALWAYS.
THAT'S "SIR" ISAAC NEWTON, *DOCTOR.*
AND MY LATEST DABBLING FROM THE LABORATORY DOES THE HEAVY LIFTING FOR ME.
YOU ARE *ALL* SORCERERS SUPREME.
NOW FOCUS. THE FORGOTTEN IS COMING.
YOU KEEP SAYING THAT.
BUT THIS CREATURE HAS BEEN A NO-SHOW IN EVERY BATTLE WE'VE HAD. NOTHING BUT THESE CREEPS.
CRO
CRO

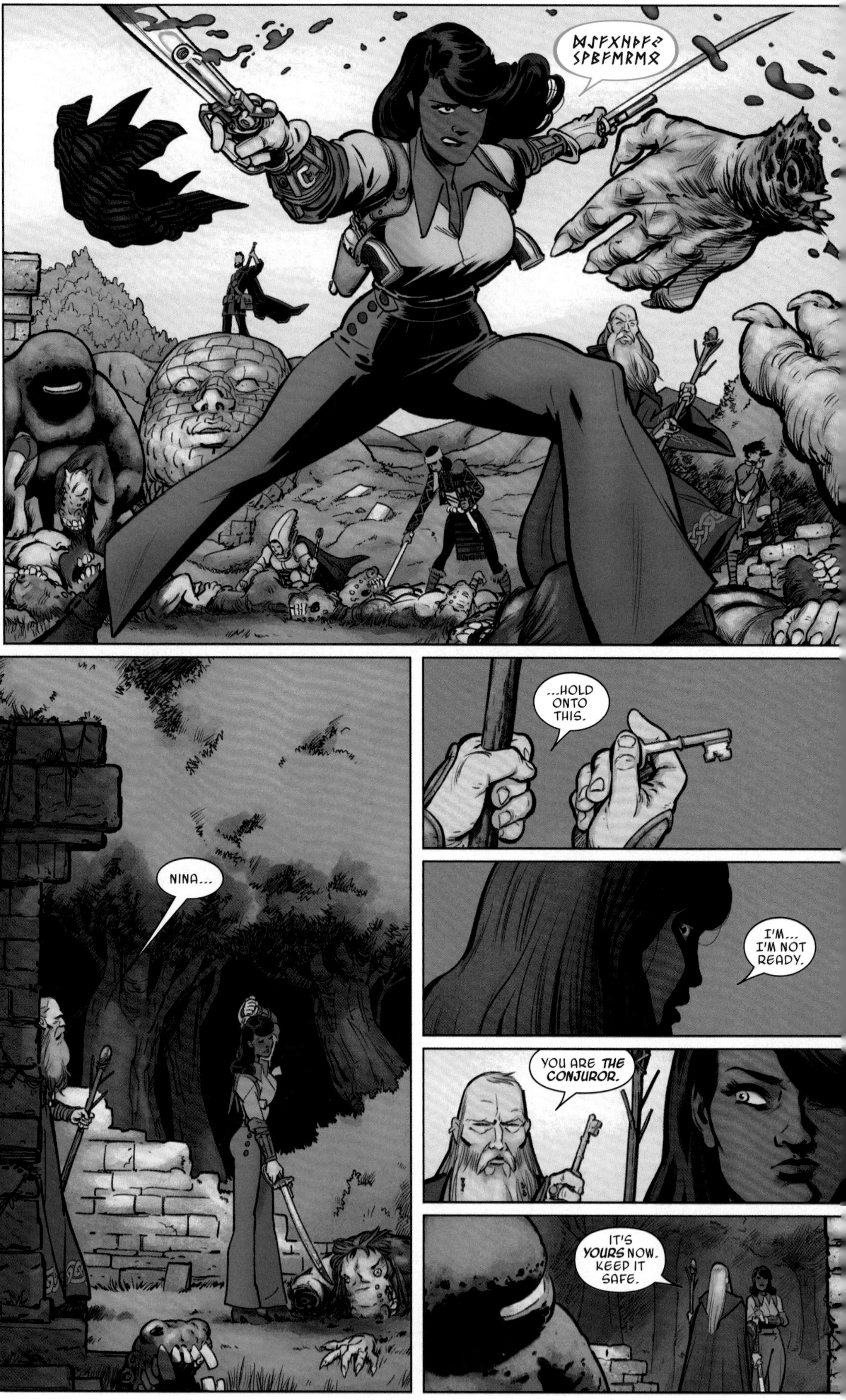
NINA...
...HOLD ONTO THIS.
I'M... I'M NOT READY.
YOU ARE **THE CONJUROR.**
IT'S **YOURS** NOW. KEEP IT SAFE.

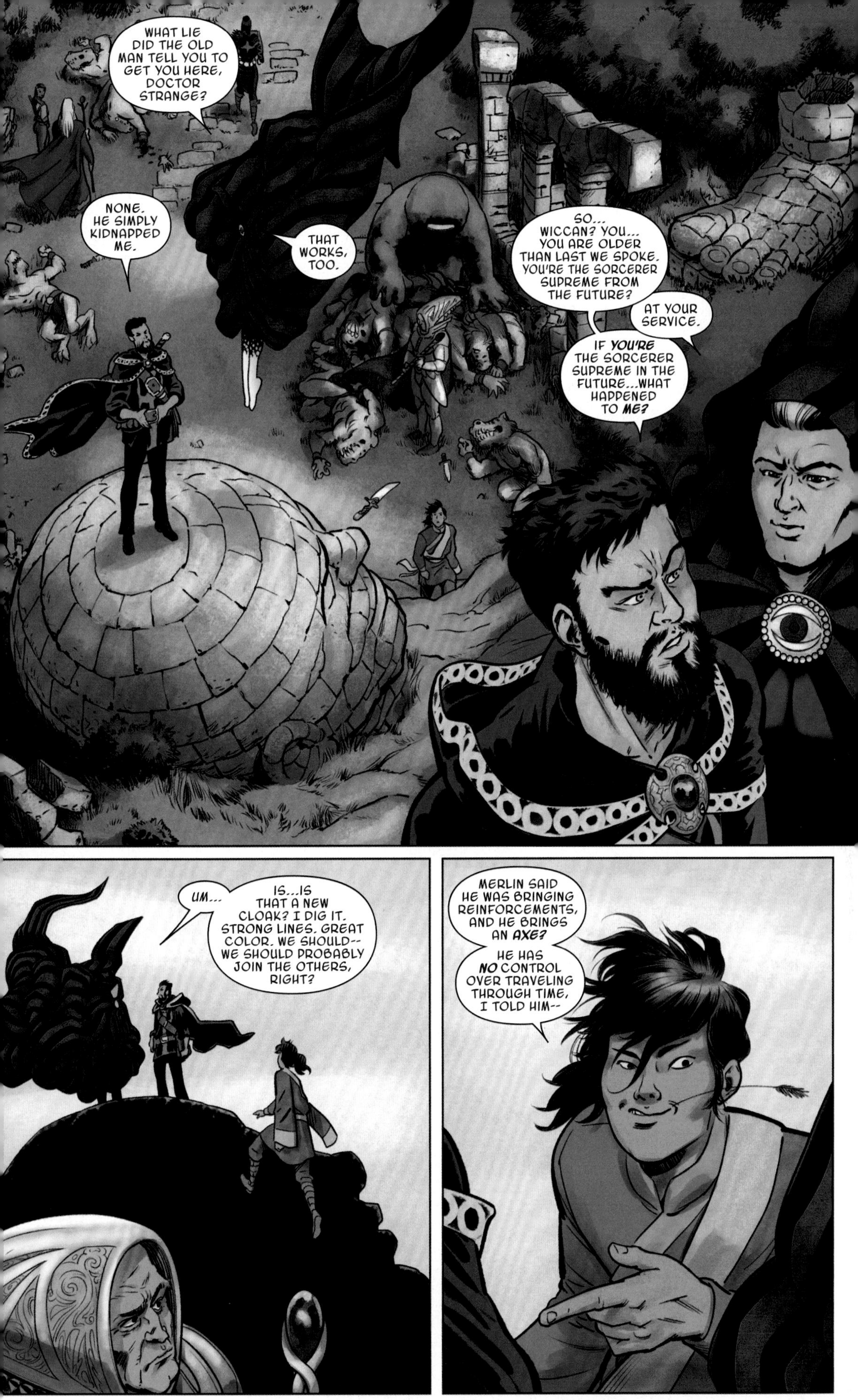
WHAT LIE DID THE OLD MAN TELL YOU TO GET YOU HERE, DOCTOR STRANGE?
NONE. HE SIMPLY KIDNAPPED ME.
THAT WORKS, TOO.
SO... WICCAN? YOU... YOU ARE OLDER THAN LAST WE SPOKE. YOU'RE THE SORCERER SUPREME FROM THE FUTURE?
AT YOUR SERVICE.
IF *YOU'RE* THE SORCERER SUPREME IN THE FUTURE...WHAT HAPPENED TO *ME?*
UM...
IS...IS THAT A NEW CLOAK? I DIG IT. STRONG LINES. GREAT COLOR. WE SHOULD-- WE SHOULD PROBABLY JOIN THE OTHERS, RIGHT?
MERLIN SAID HE WAS BRINGING REINFORCEMENTS, AND HE BRINGS AN *AXE?*
HE HAS *NO* CONTROL OVER TRAVELING THROUGH TIME, I TOLD HIM--

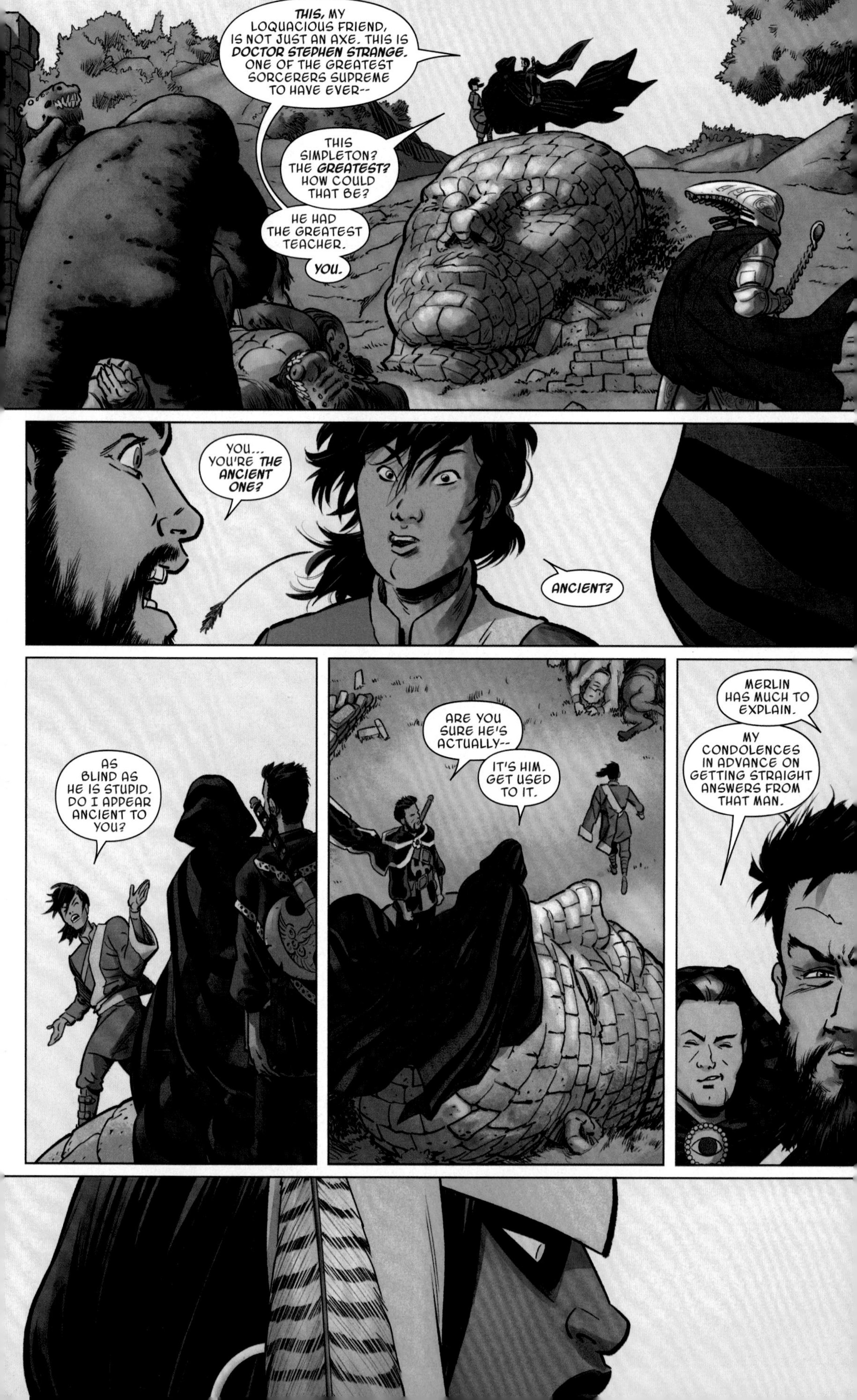
THIS, MY LOQUACIOUS FRIEND, IS NOT JUST AN AXE. THIS IS DOCTOR STEPHEN STRANGE. ONE OF THE GREATEST SORCERERS SUPREME TO HAVE EVER--
THIS SIMPLETON? THE GREATEST? HOW COULD THAT BE?
HE HAD THE GREATEST TEACHER.
YOU.
YOU... YOU'RE THE ANCIENT ONE?
ANCIENT?
AS BLIND AS HE IS STUPID. DO I APPEAR ANCIENT TO YOU?
ARE YOU SURE HE'S ACTUALLY--
IT'S HIM. GET USED TO IT.
MERLIN HAS MUCH TO EXPLAIN.
MY CONDOLENCES IN ADVANCE ON GETTING STRAIGHT ANSWERS FROM THAT MAN.

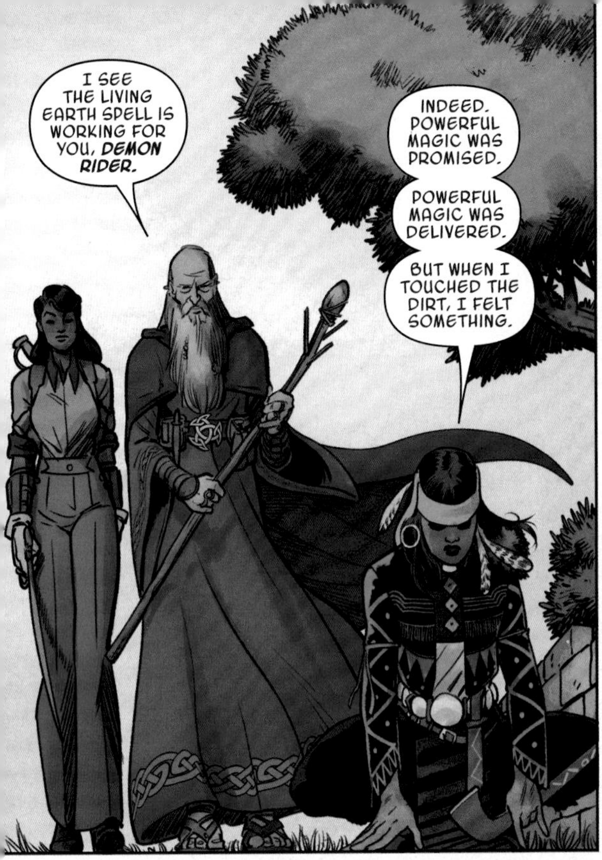
I SEE THE LIVING EARTH SPELL IS WORKING FOR YOU, *DEMON RIDER.*
INDEED. POWERFUL MAGIC WAS PROMISED.
POWERFUL MAGIC WAS DELIVERED.
BUT WHEN I TOUCHED THE DIRT, I FELT SOMETHING.

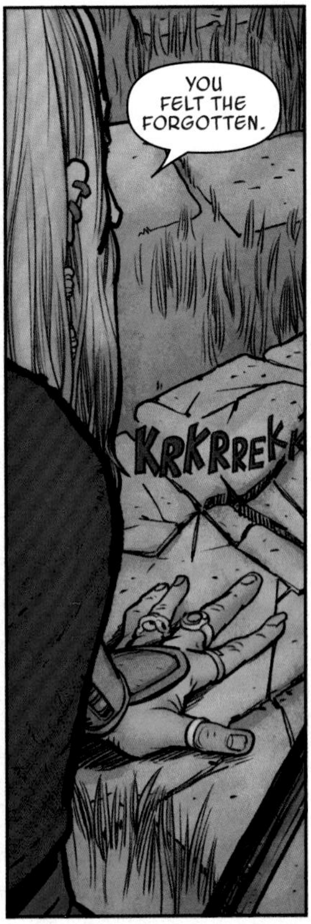
YOU FELT THE FORGOTTEN.
KRKRREKK

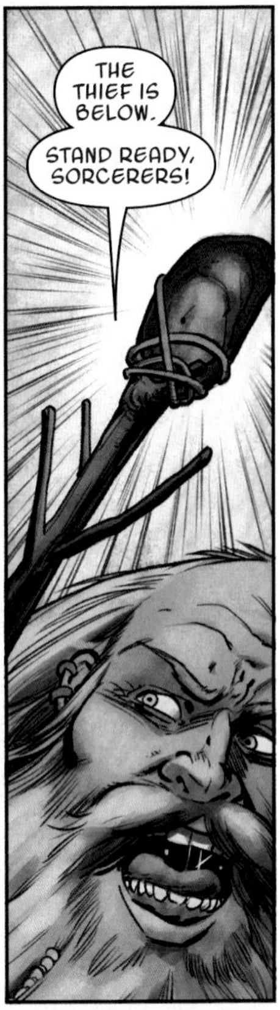
THE THIEF IS BELOW.
STAND READY, SORCERERS!

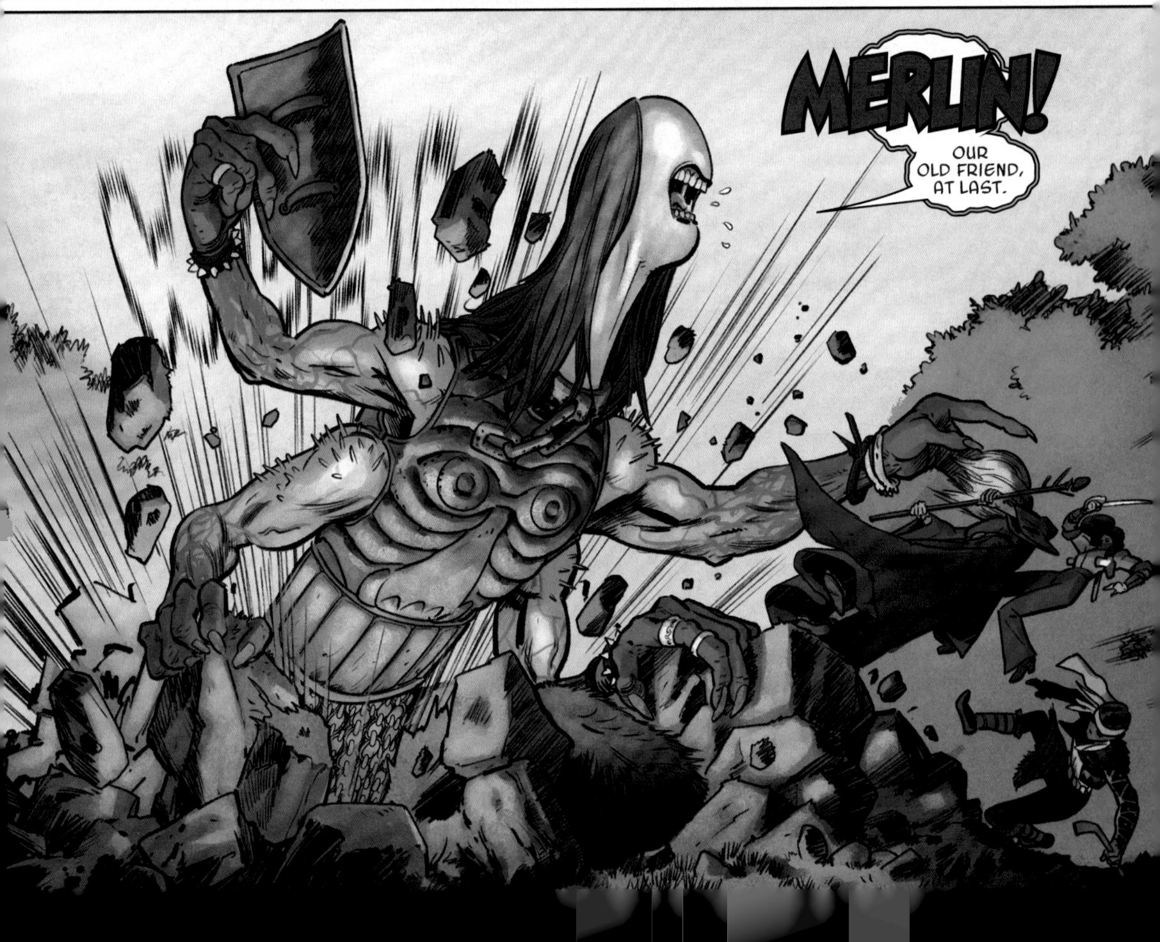
MERLIN!
OUR OLD FRIEND, AT LAST.

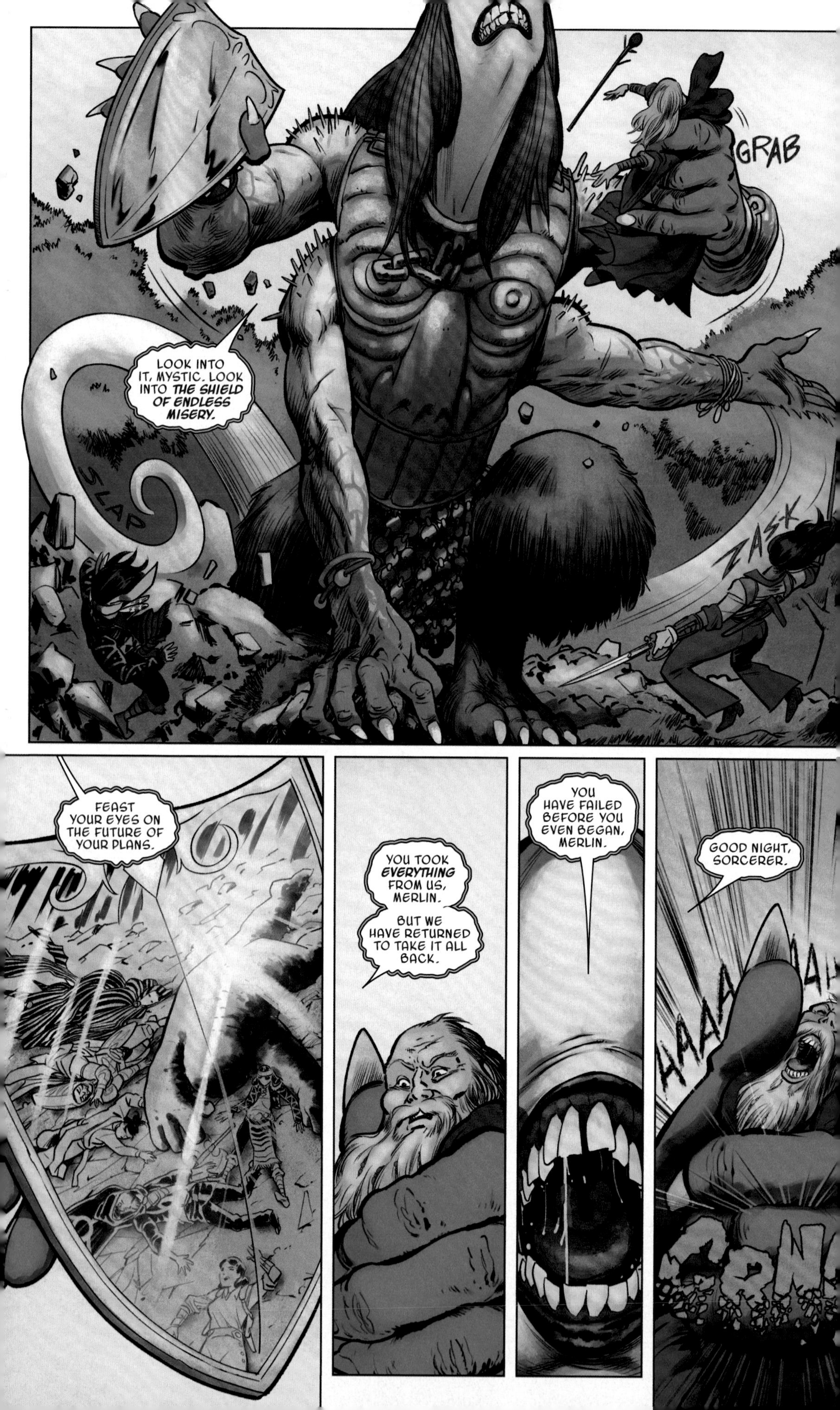
GRAB
LOOK INTO IT, MYSTIC. LOOK INTO THE SHIELD OF ENDLESS MISERY.
SLAP
ZAS-K
FEAST YOUR EYES ON THE FUTURE OF YOUR PLANS.
YOU TOOK EVERYTHING FROM US, MERLIN.
BUT WE HAVE RETURNED TO TAKE IT ALL BACK.
YOU HAVE FAILED BEFORE YOU EVEN BEGAN, MERLIN.
GOOD NIGHT, SORCERER.

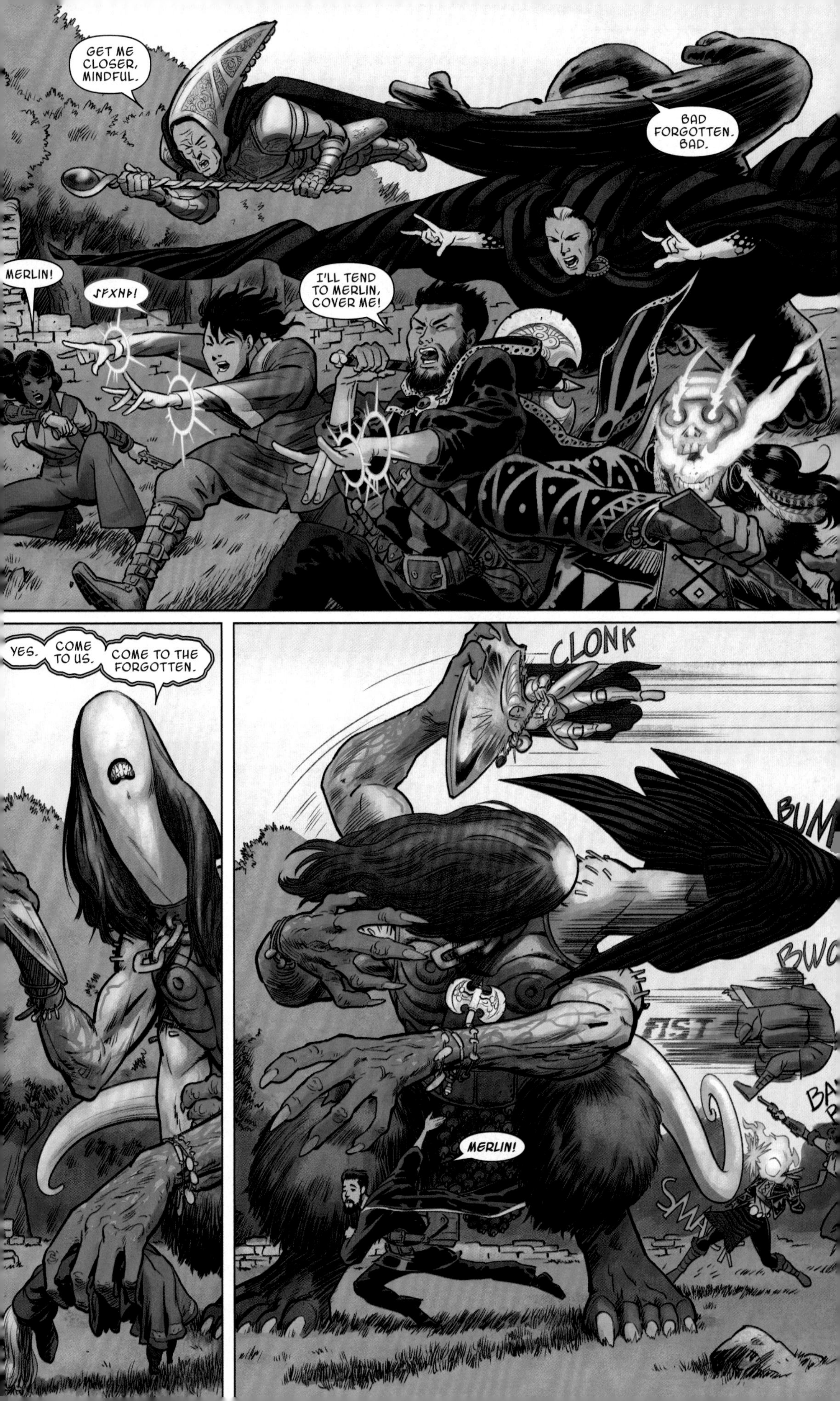
GET ME CLOSER, MINDFUL.
BAD FORGOTTEN. BAD.
MERLIN!
I'LL TEND TO MERLIN, COVER ME!
YES.
COME TO US.
COME TO THE FORGOTTEN.
CLONK
FIST
MERLIN!

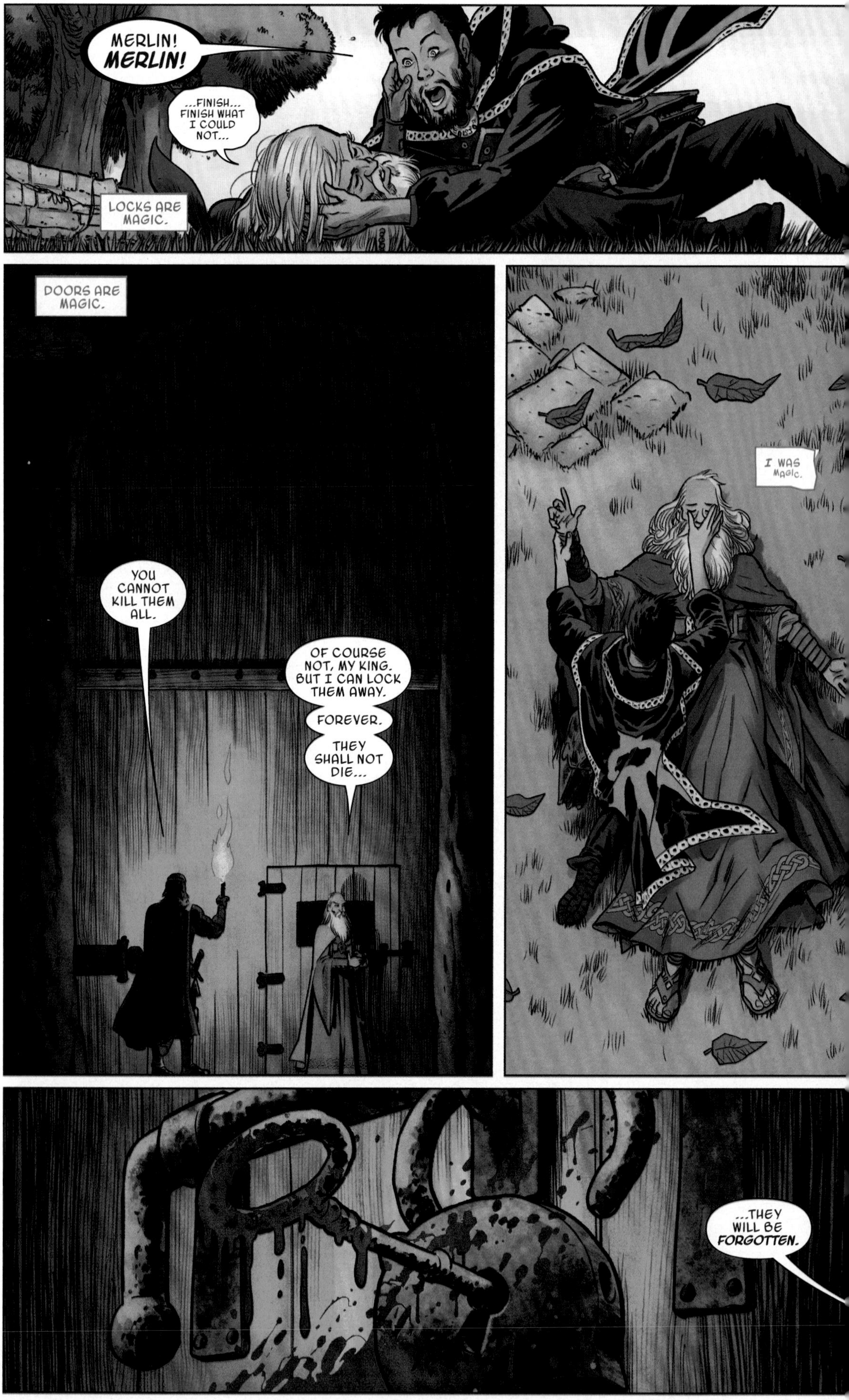

MERLIN! MERLIN!
...FINISH... FINISH WHAT I COULD NOT...
LOCKS ARE MAGIC.
DOORS ARE MAGIC.
YOU CANNOT KILL THEM ALL.
OF COURSE NOT, MY KING. BUT I CAN LOCK THEM AWAY.
FOREVER.
THEY SHALL NOT DIE...
I WAS MAGIC.
...THEY WILL BE FORGOTTEN.

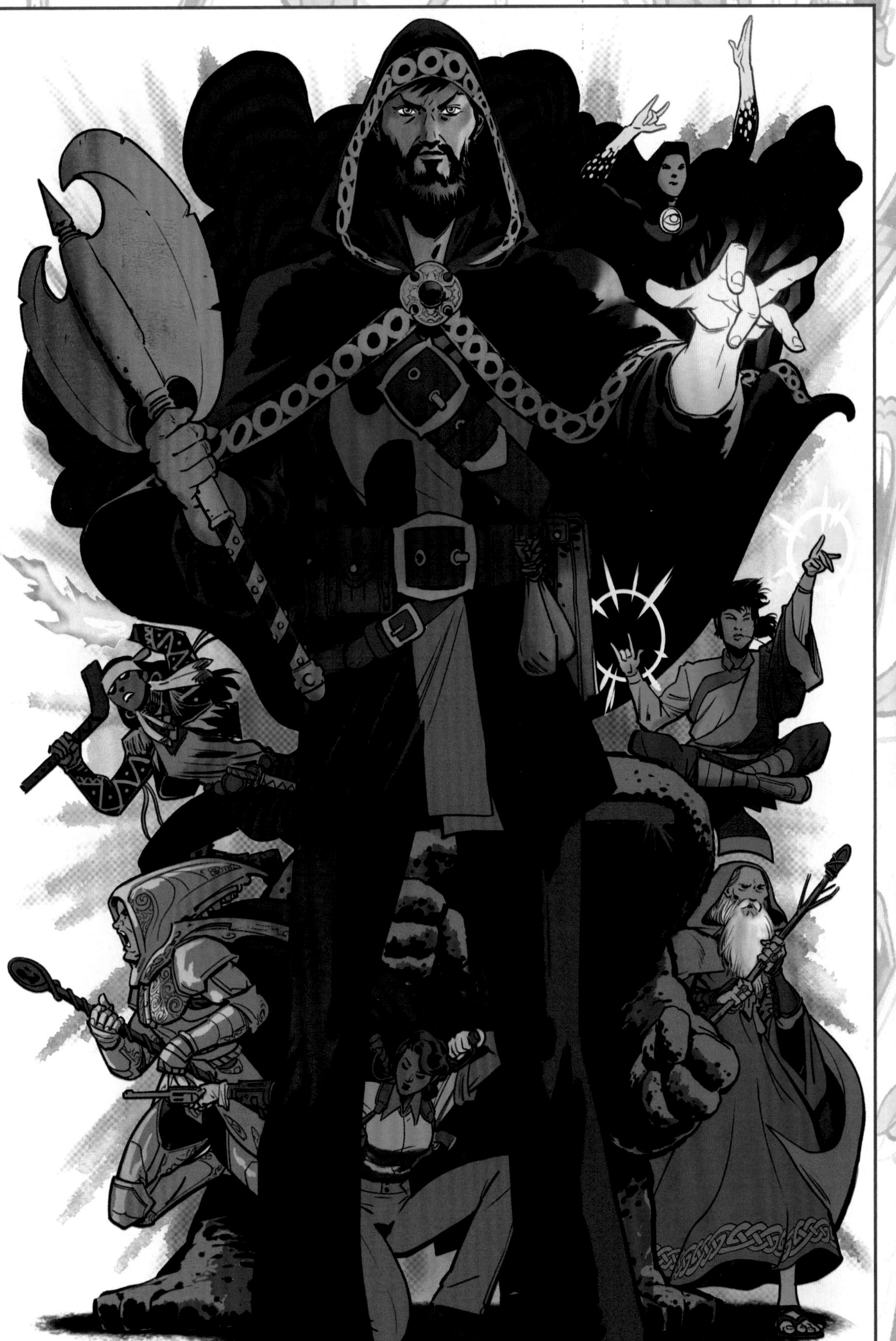

NO. 1 VARIANT BY **JAVIER RODRIGUEZ** & **ÁLVARO LÓPEZ**

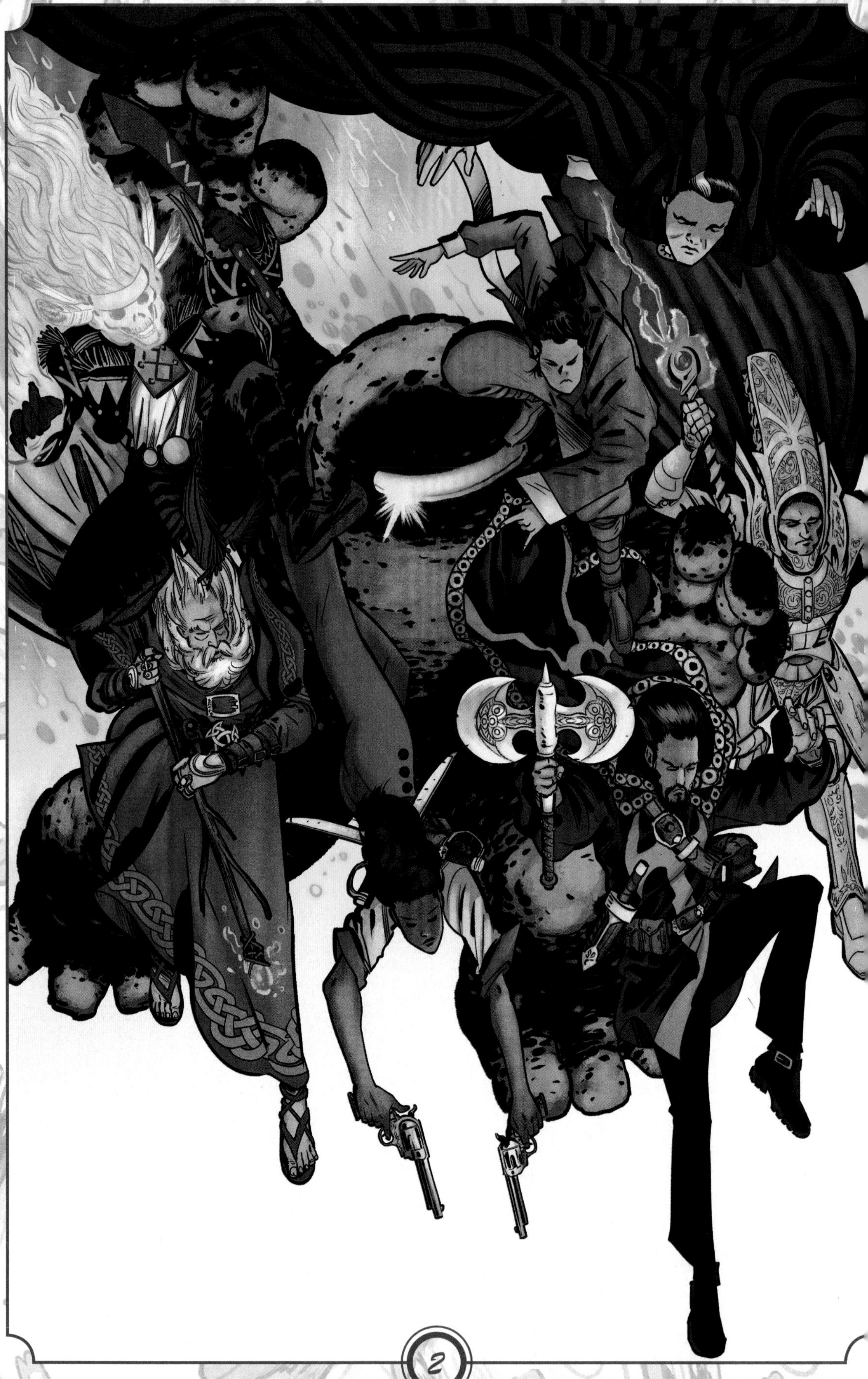

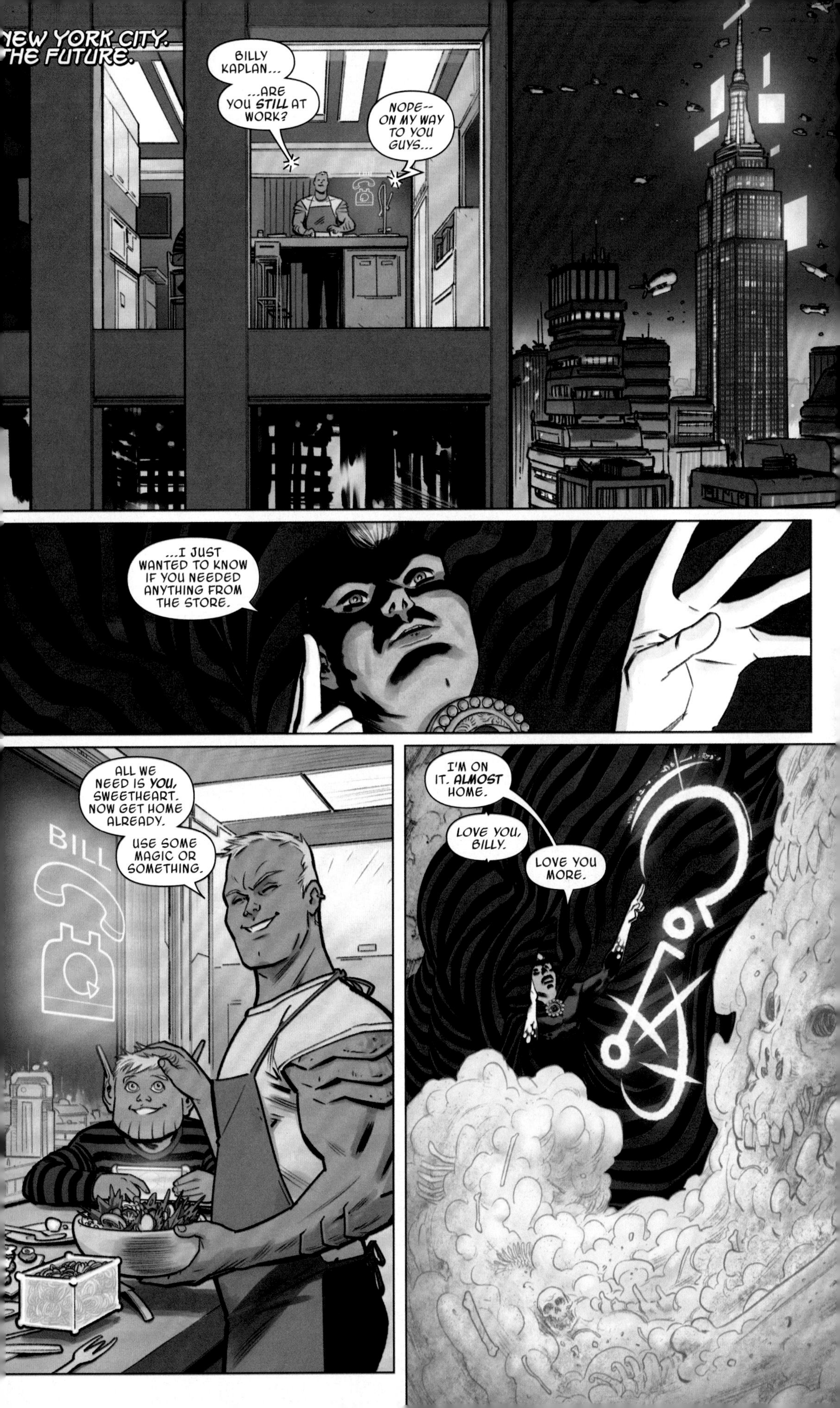
NEW YORK CITY.
THE FUTURE.
BILLY KAPLAN...
...ARE YOU STILL AT WORK?
NOPE-- ON MY WAY TO YOU GUYS...
...I JUST WANTED TO KNOW IF YOU NEEDED ANYTHING FROM THE STORE.
ALL WE NEED IS YOU, SWEETHEART. NOW GET HOME ALREADY.
USE SOME MAGIC OR SOMETHING.
BILL
I'M ON IT. ALMOST HOME.
LOVE YOU, BILLY.
LOVE YOU MORE.

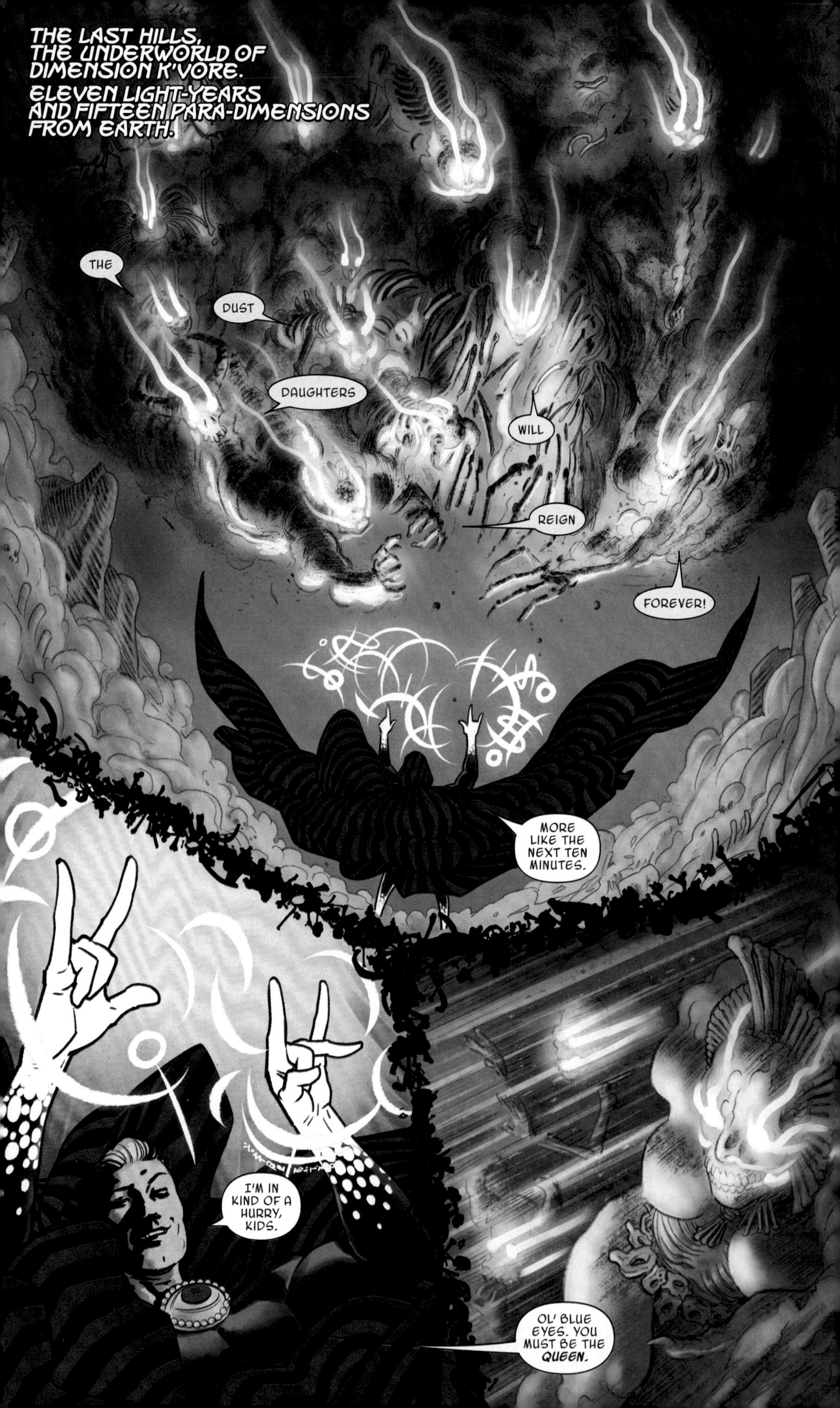
THE LAST HILLS, THE UNDERWORLD OF DIMENSION K'VORE.
ELEVEN LIGHT-YEARS AND FIFTEEN PARA-DIMENSIONS FROM EARTH.
THE
DUST
DAUGHTERS
WILL
REIGN
FOREVER!
MORE LIKE THE NEXT TEN MINUTES.
I'M IN KIND OF A HURRY, KIDS.
OL' BLUE EYES. YOU MUST BE THE QUEEN.

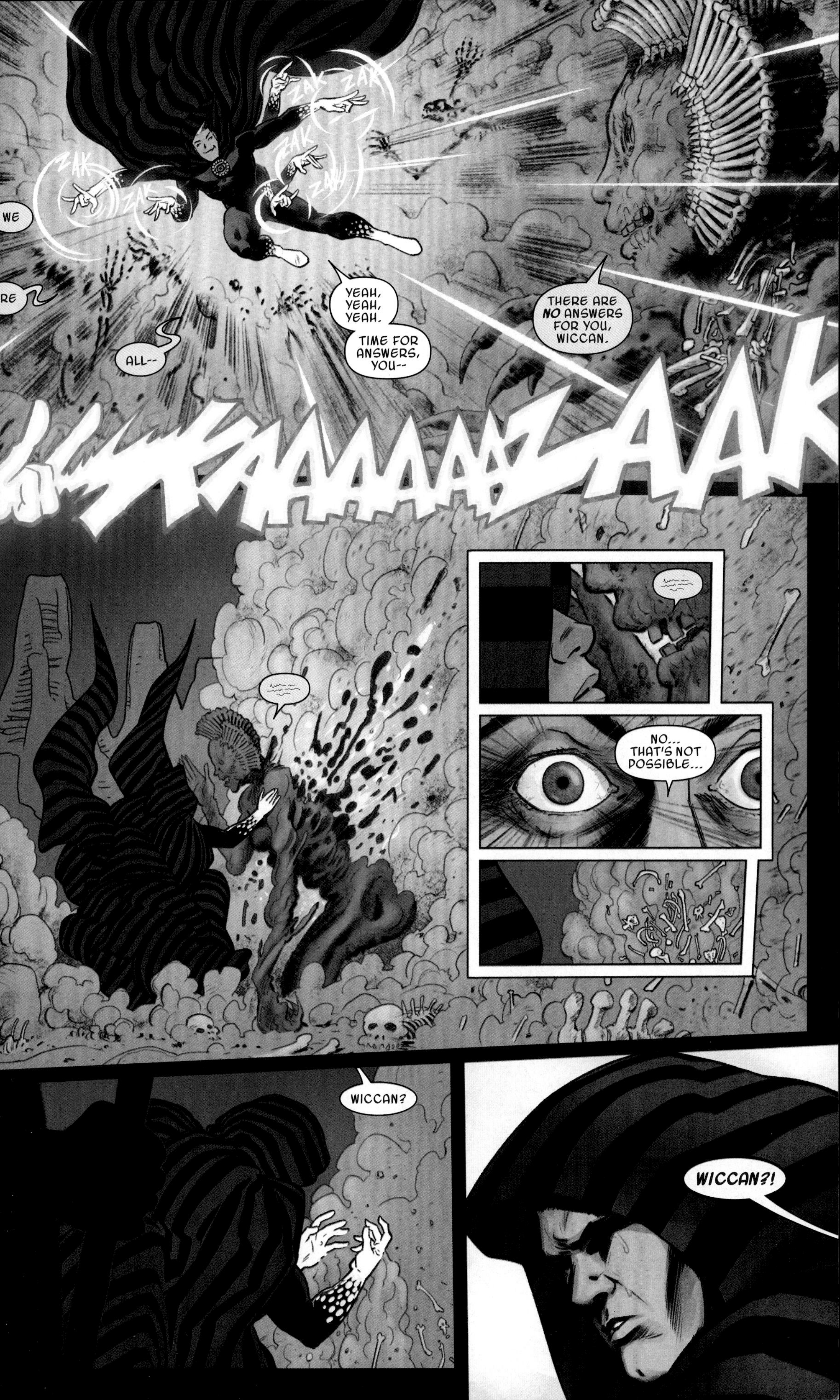

WE
RE
ALL--
ZAK
ZAK
ZAK
ZAK
ZAK
ZAK
YEAH, YEAH, YEAH.
TIME FOR ANSWERS, YOU--
THERE ARE NO ANSWERS FOR YOU, WICCAN.
KAAAAAZAAK
NO... THAT'S NOT POSSIBLE...
WICCAN?
WICCAN?!

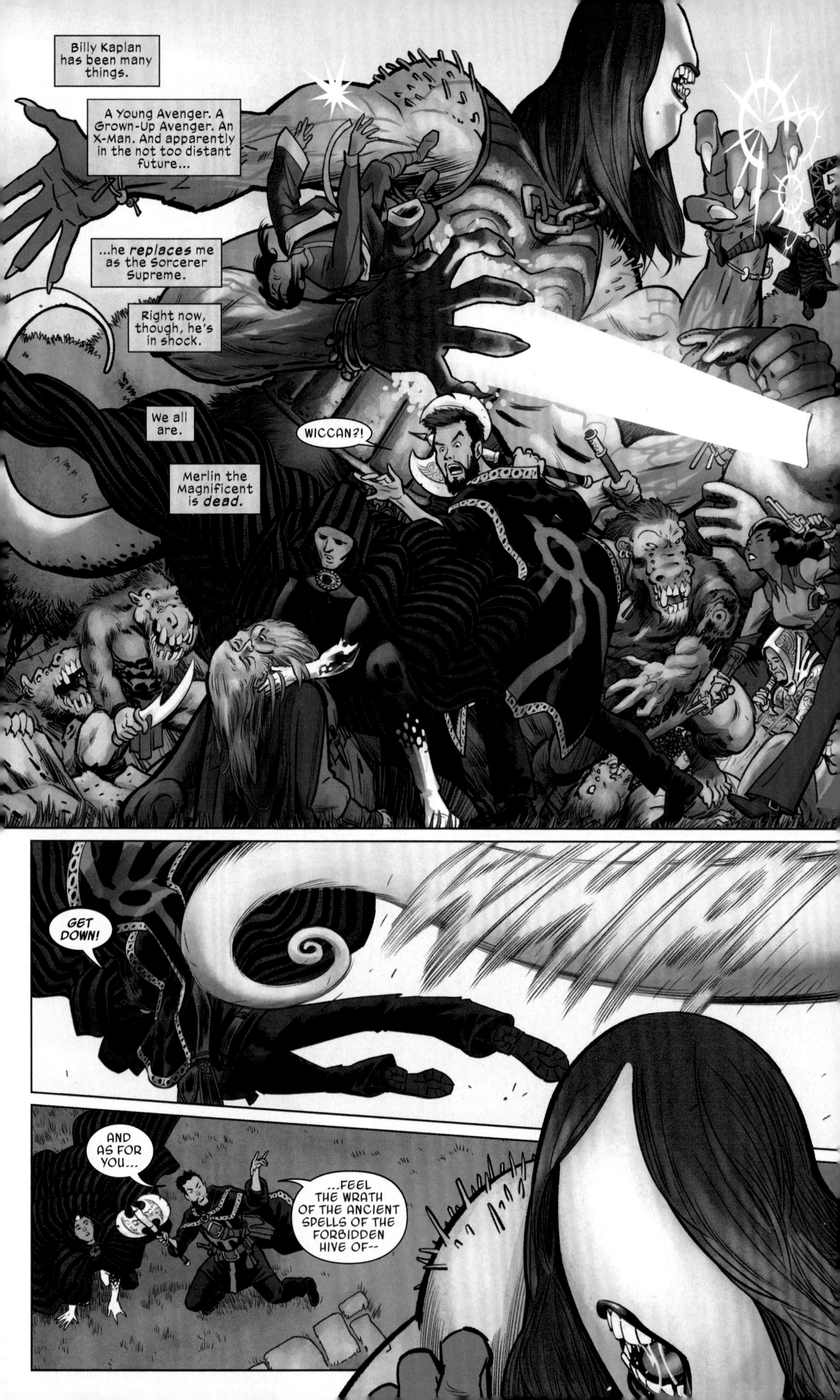

Billy Kaplan has been many things.
A Young Avenger. A Grown-Up Avenger. An X-Man. And apparently in the not too distant future...
...he *replaces* me as the Sorcerer Supreme.
Right now, though, he's in shock.
We all are.
WICCAN?!
Merlin the Magnificent is *dead.*
GET DOWN!
AND AS FOR YOU...
...FEEL THE WRATH OF THE ANCIENT SPELLS OF THE FORBIDDEN HIVE OF--

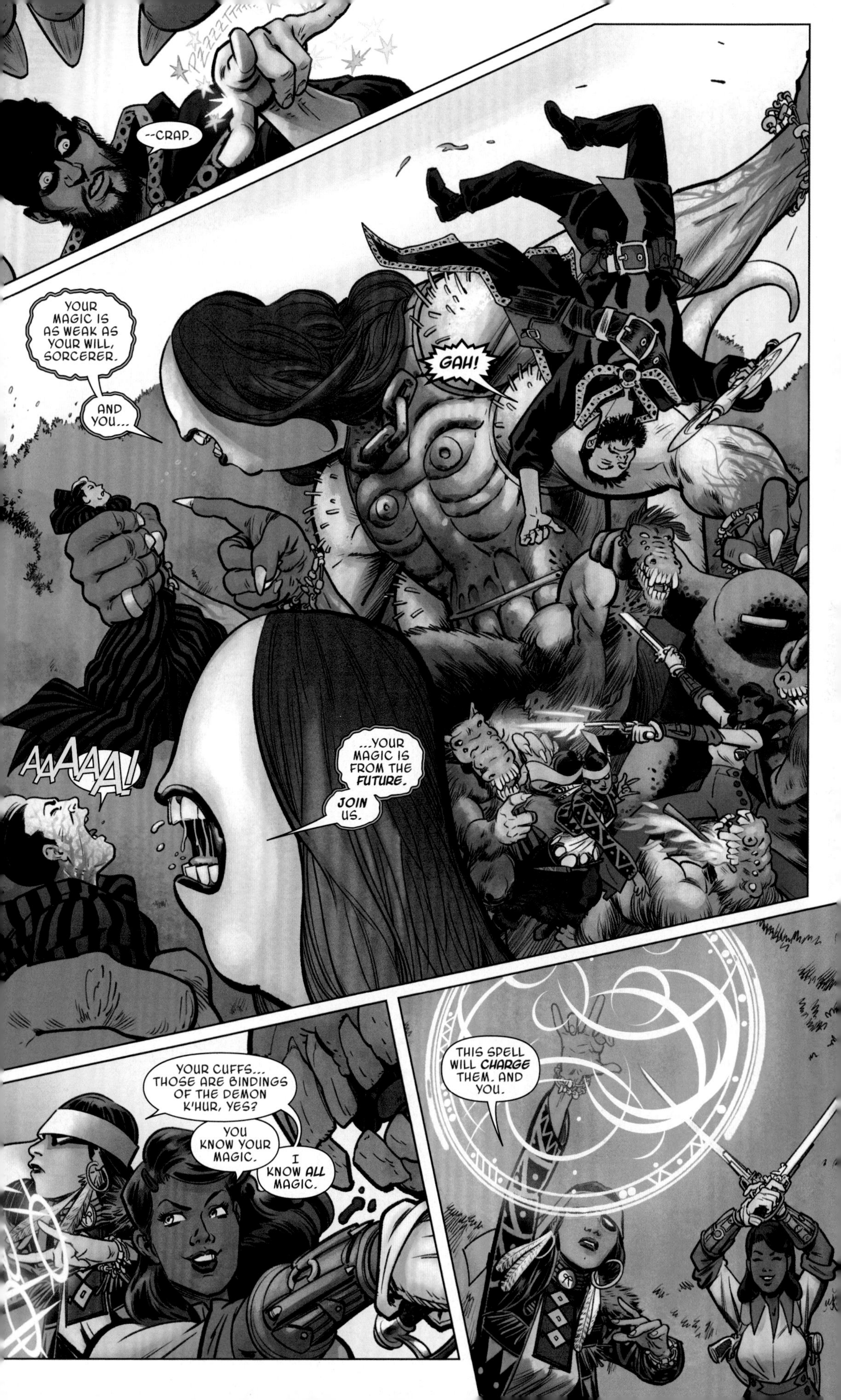
PZZZZTT
--CRAP.
YOUR MAGIC IS AS WEAK AS YOUR WILL, SORCERER.
AND YOU...
GAH!
AAAAAAI!
...YOUR MAGIC IS FROM THE FUTURE.
JOIN US.
YOUR CUFFS... THOSE ARE BINDINGS OF THE DEMON K'HUR, YES?
YOU KNOW YOUR MAGIC.
I KNOW ALL MAGIC.
THIS SPELL WILL CHARGE THEM. AND YOU.

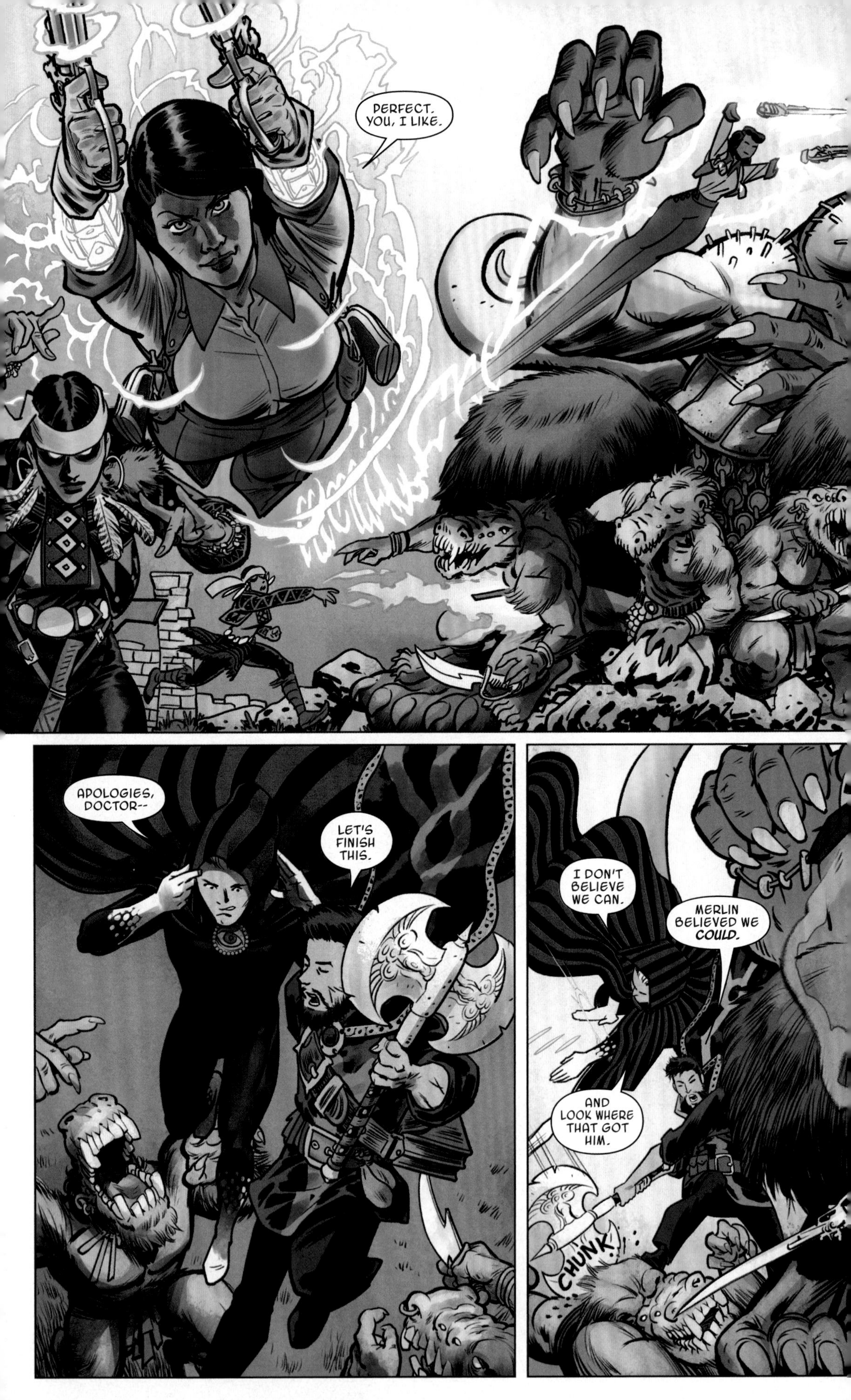
PERFECT. YOU, I LIKE.
APOLOGIES, DOCTOR--
LET'S FINISH THIS.
I DON'T BELIEVE WE CAN.
MERLIN BELIEVED WE COULD.
AND LOOK WHERE THAT GOT HIM.
CHUNK!

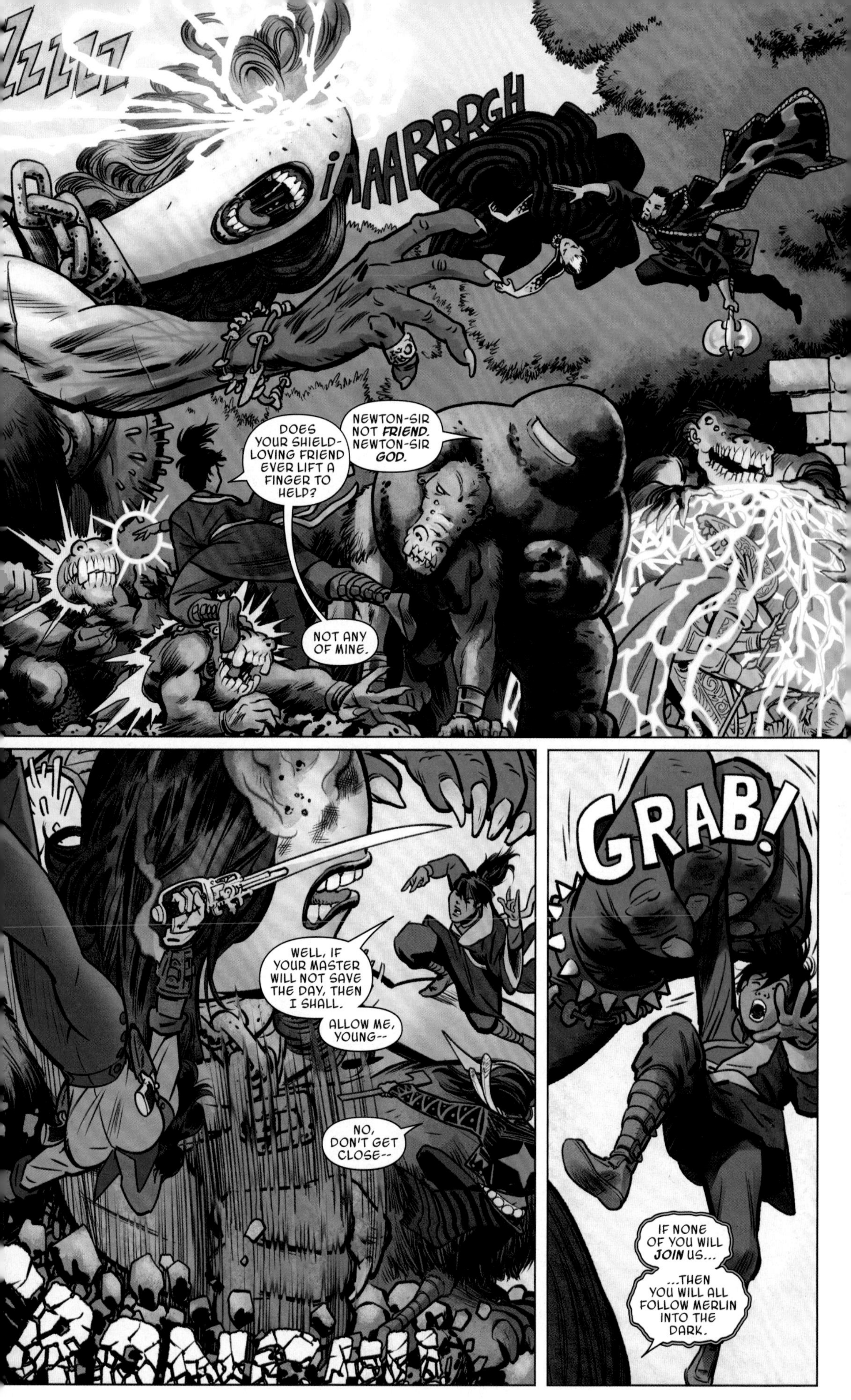
ZZZZZ
¡AAARRRGH
DOES YOUR SHIELD-LOVING FRIEND EVER LIFT A FINGER TO HELP?
NEWTON-SIR NOT FRIEND. NEWTON-SIR GOD.
NOT ANY OF MINE.
WELL, IF YOUR MASTER WILL NOT SAVE THE DAY, THEN I SHALL.
ALLOW ME, YOUNG--
NO, DON'T GET CLOSE--
GRAB!
IF NONE OF YOU WILL JOIN US...
...THEN YOU WILL ALL FOLLOW MERLIN INTO THE DARK.

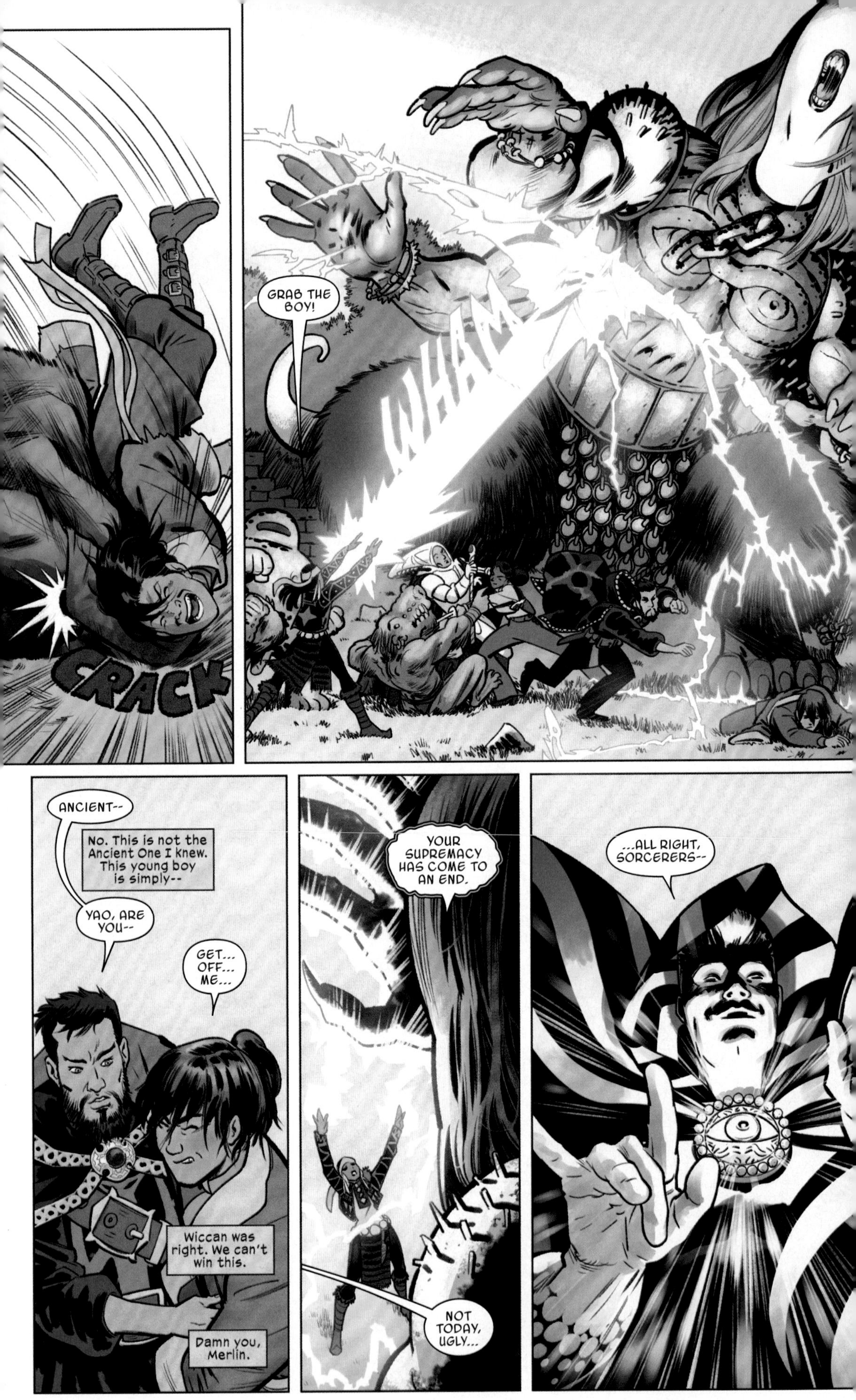
CRACK
GRAB THE BOY!
WHAM
ANCIENT--
No. This is not the Ancient One I knew. This young boy is simply--
YAO, ARE YOU--
GET... OFF... ME...
Wiccan was right. We can't win this.
Damn you, Merlin.
YOUR SUPREMACY HAS COME TO AN END.
NOT TODAY, UGLY...
...ALL RIGHT, SORCERERS--

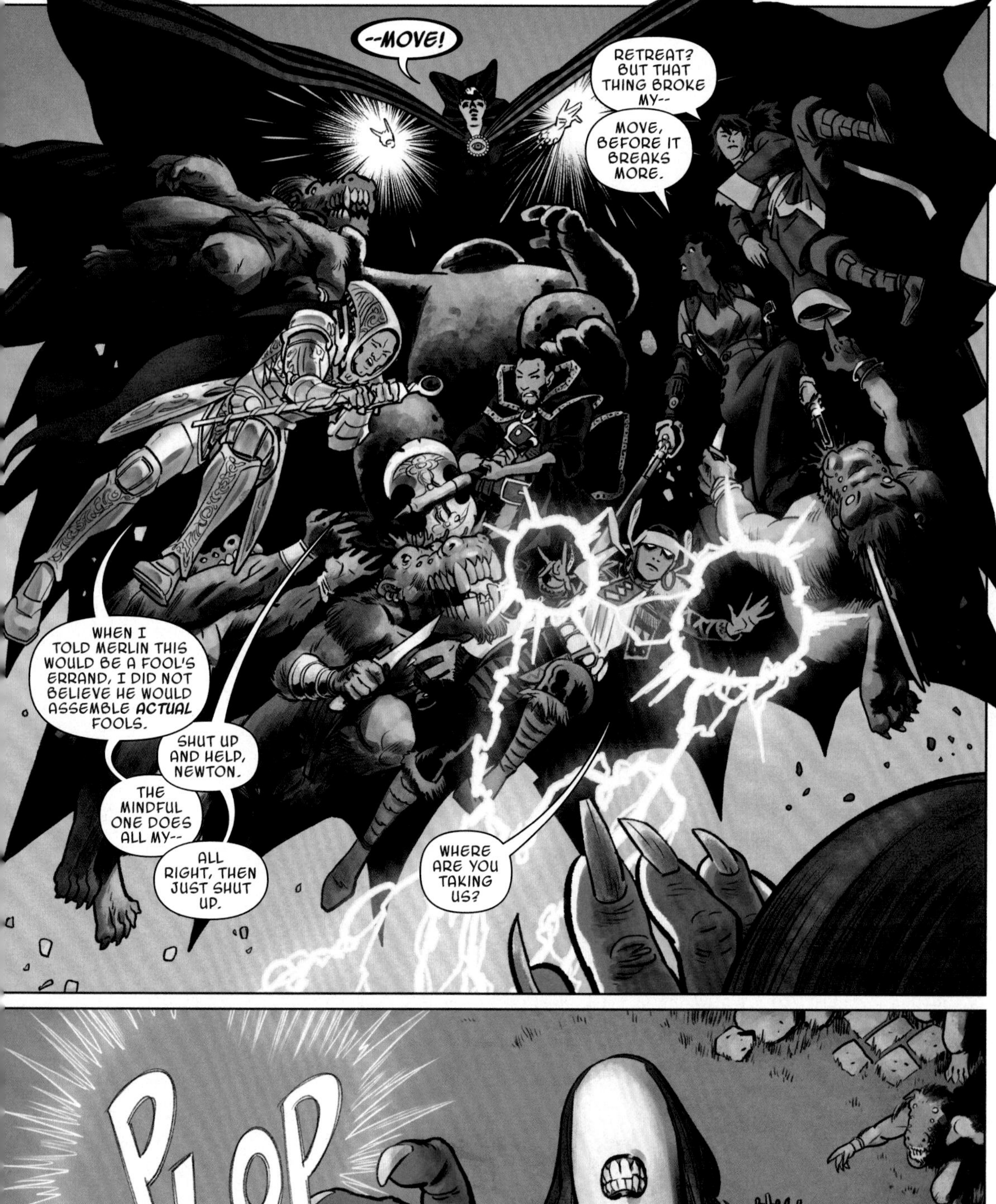
--MOVE!
RETREAT? BUT THAT THING BROKE MY--
MOVE, BEFORE IT BREAKS MORE.
WHEN I TOLD MERLIN THIS WOULD BE A FOOL'S ERRAND, I DID NOT BELIEVE HE WOULD ASSEMBLE ACTUAL FOOLS.
SHUT UP AND HELP, NEWTON.
THE MINDFUL ONE DOES ALL MY--
ALL RIGHT, THEN JUST SHUT UP.
WHERE ARE YOU TAKING US?

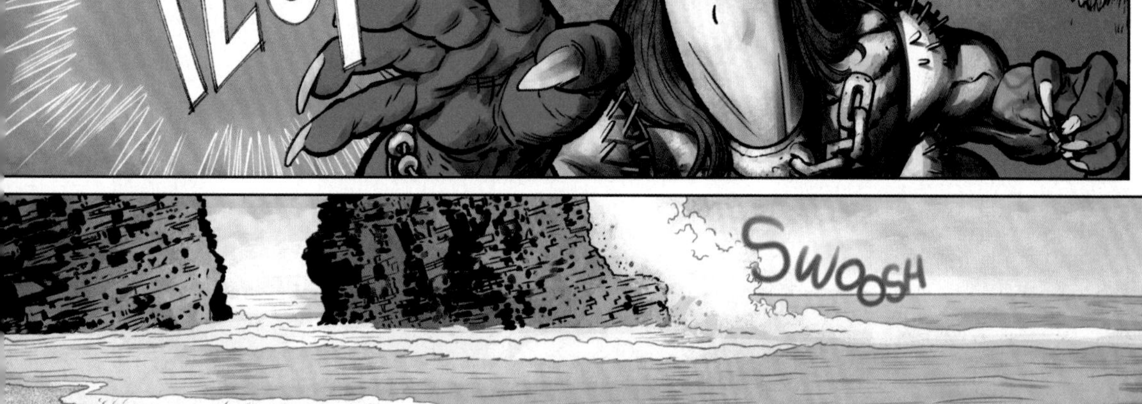
PLOP

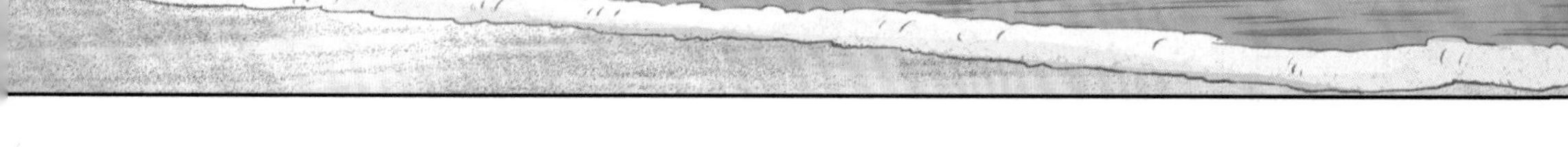
SWOOSH

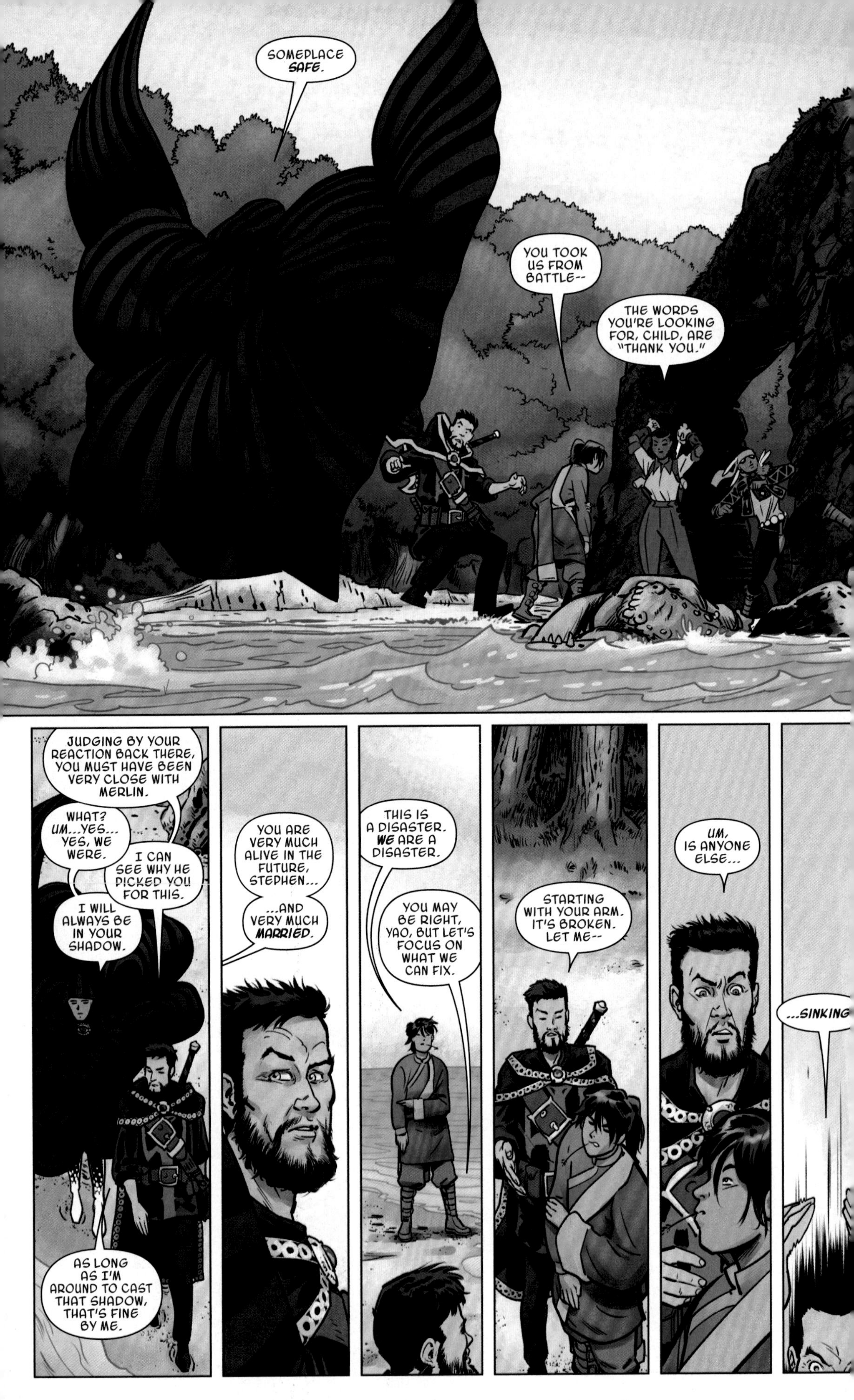
SOMEPLACE SAFE.
YOU TOOK US FROM BATTLE--
THE WORDS YOU'RE LOOKING FOR, CHILD, ARE "THANK YOU."
JUDGING BY YOUR REACTION BACK THERE, YOU MUST HAVE BEEN VERY CLOSE WITH MERLIN.
WHAT? UM...YES... YES, WE WERE.
I CAN SEE WHY HE PICKED YOU FOR THIS.
I WILL ALWAYS BE IN YOUR SHADOW.
AS LONG AS I'M AROUND TO CAST THAT SHADOW, THAT'S FINE BY ME.
YOU ARE VERY MUCH ALIVE IN THE FUTURE, STEPHEN...
...AND VERY MUCH MARRIED.
THIS IS A DISASTER. WE ARE A DISASTER.
YOU MAY BE RIGHT, YAO, BUT LET'S FOCUS ON WHAT WE CAN FIX.
STARTING WITH YOUR ARM. IT'S BROKEN. LET ME--
UM, IS ANYONE ELSE...
...SINKING

WATER SOFT.

I THOUGHT YOU TOOK US SOMEPLACE SAFE!

I TOOK US TO MERLIN'S HOME. I FIGURED WE WOULD FIND SAFE HAVEN--

YES, WELL...

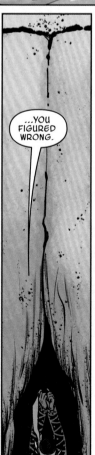

...YOU FIGURED WRONG.

ALONE. SAD.

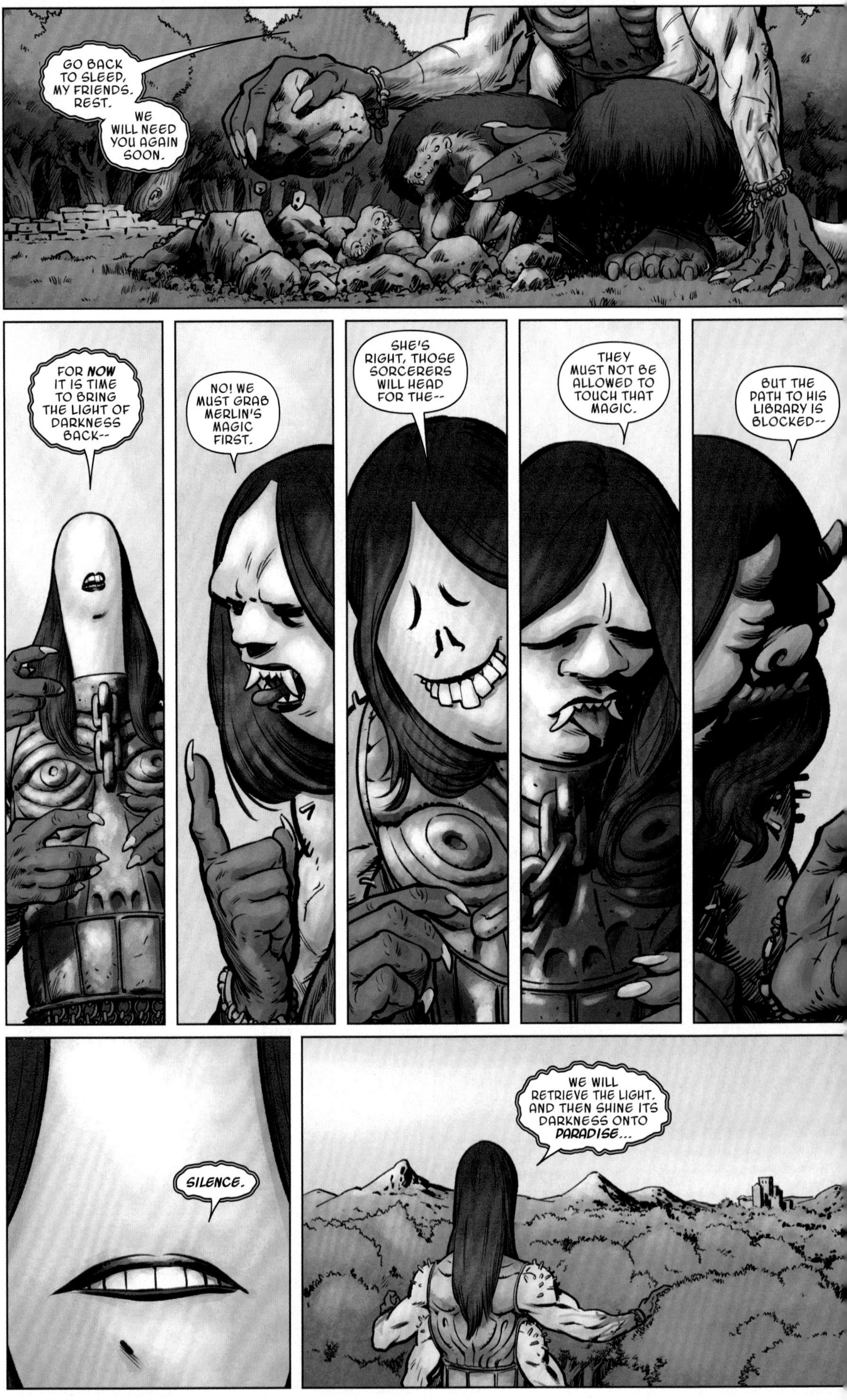
GO BACK TO SLEEP, MY FRIENDS. REST.
WE WILL NEED YOU AGAIN SOON.
FOR NOW IT IS TIME TO BRING THE LIGHT OF DARKNESS BACK--
NO! WE MUST GRAB MERLIN'S MAGIC FIRST.
SHE'S RIGHT, THOSE SORCERERS WILL HEAD FOR THE--
THEY MUST NOT BE ALLOWED TO TOUCH THAT MAGIC.
BUT THE PATH TO HIS LIBRARY IS BLOCKED--
SILENCE.
WE WILL RETRIEVE THE LIGHT. AND THEN SHINE ITS DARKNESS ONTO PARADISE...

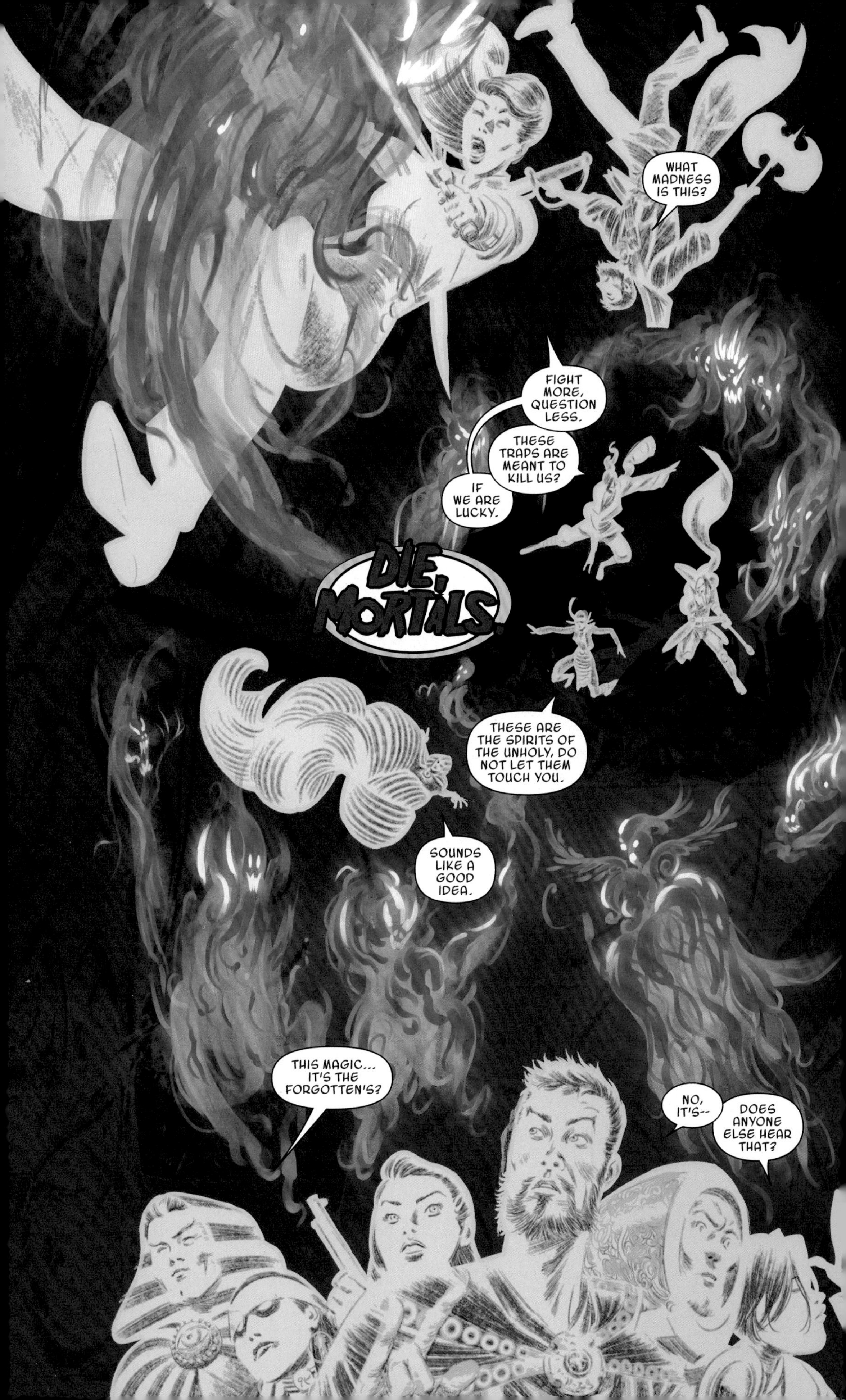
WHAT MADNESS IS THIS?
FIGHT MORE, QUESTION LESS.
THESE TRAPS ARE MEANT TO KILL US?
IF WE ARE LUCKY.
DIE, MORTALS.
THESE ARE THE SPIRITS OF THE UNHOLY, DO NOT LET THEM TOUCH YOU.
SOUNDS LIKE A GOOD IDEA.
THIS MAGIC... IT'S THE FORGOTTEN'S?
NO, IT'S--
DOES ANYONE ELSE HEAR THAT?

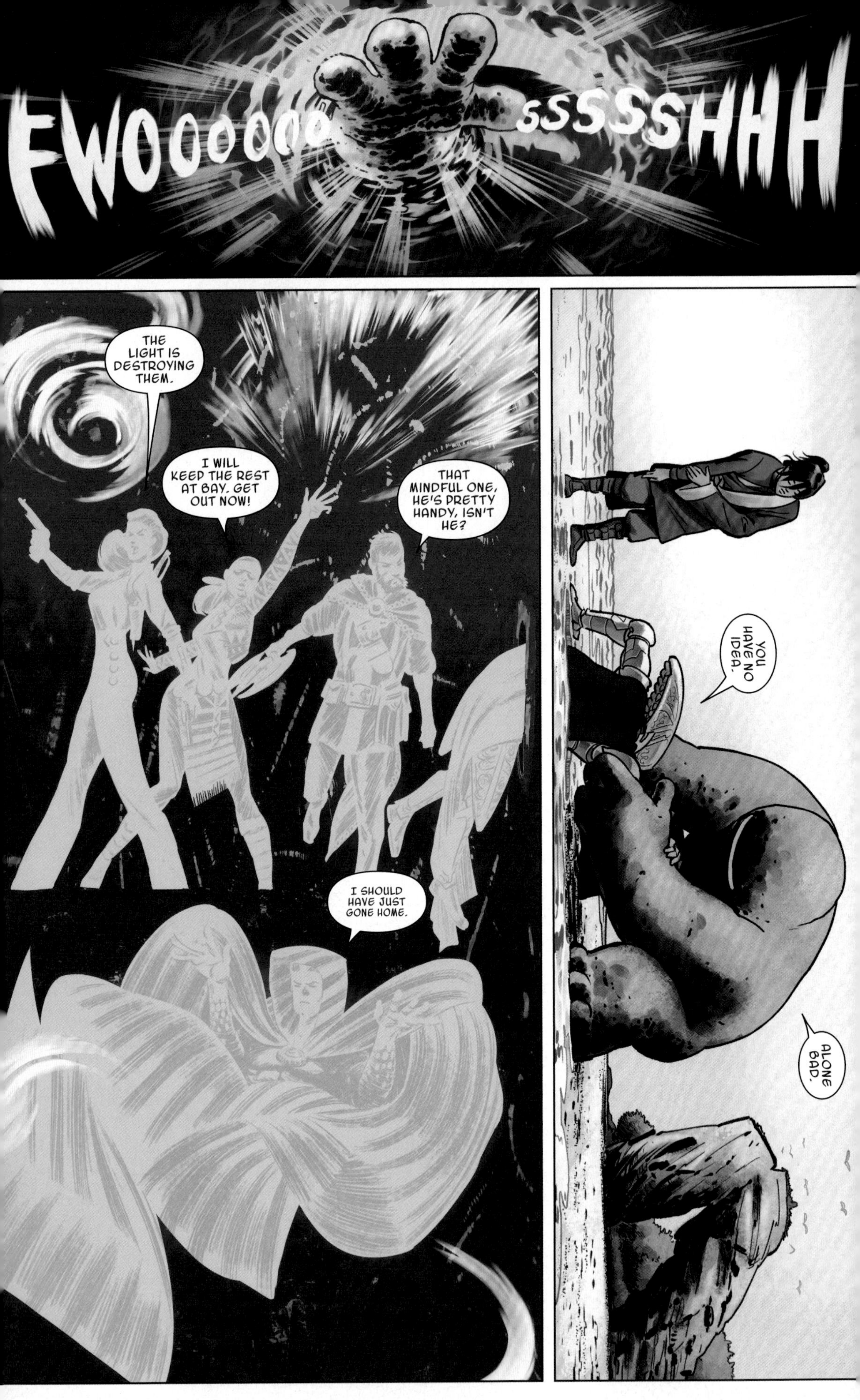
FWOOOOOO SSSSSHHH
THE LIGHT IS DESTROYING THEM.
I WILL KEEP THE REST AT BAY. GET OUT NOW!
THAT MINDFUL ONE, HE'S PRETTY HANDY, ISN'T HE?
I SHOULD HAVE JUST GONE HOME.
YOU HAVE NO IDEA.
ALONE BAD.

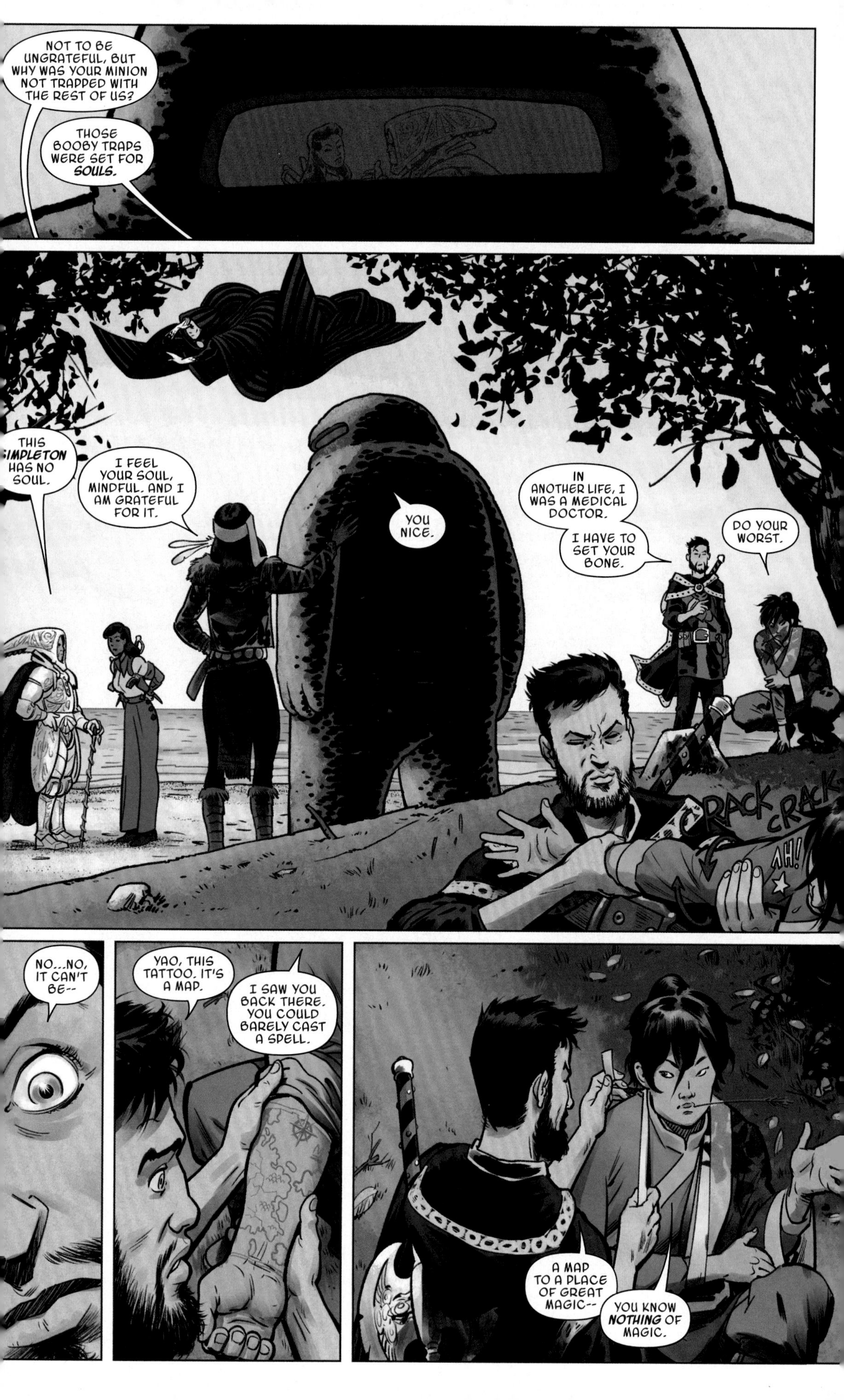
NOT TO BE UNGRATEFUL, BUT WHY WAS YOUR MINION NOT TRAPPED WITH THE REST OF US?
THOSE BOOBY TRAPS WERE SET FOR *SOULS.*
THIS *SIMPLETON* HAS NO SOUL.
I FEEL YOUR SOUL, MINDFUL. AND I AM GRATEFUL FOR IT.
YOU NICE.
IN ANOTHER LIFE, I WAS A MEDICAL DOCTOR.
I HAVE TO SET YOUR BONE.
DO YOUR WORST.
CRACK
CRACK
AH!
NO...NO, IT CAN'T BE--
YAO, THIS TATTOO. IT'S A MAP.
I SAW YOU BACK THERE. YOU COULD BARELY CAST A SPELL.
A MAP TO A PLACE OF GREAT MAGIC--
YOU KNOW ***NOTHING*** OF MAGIC.

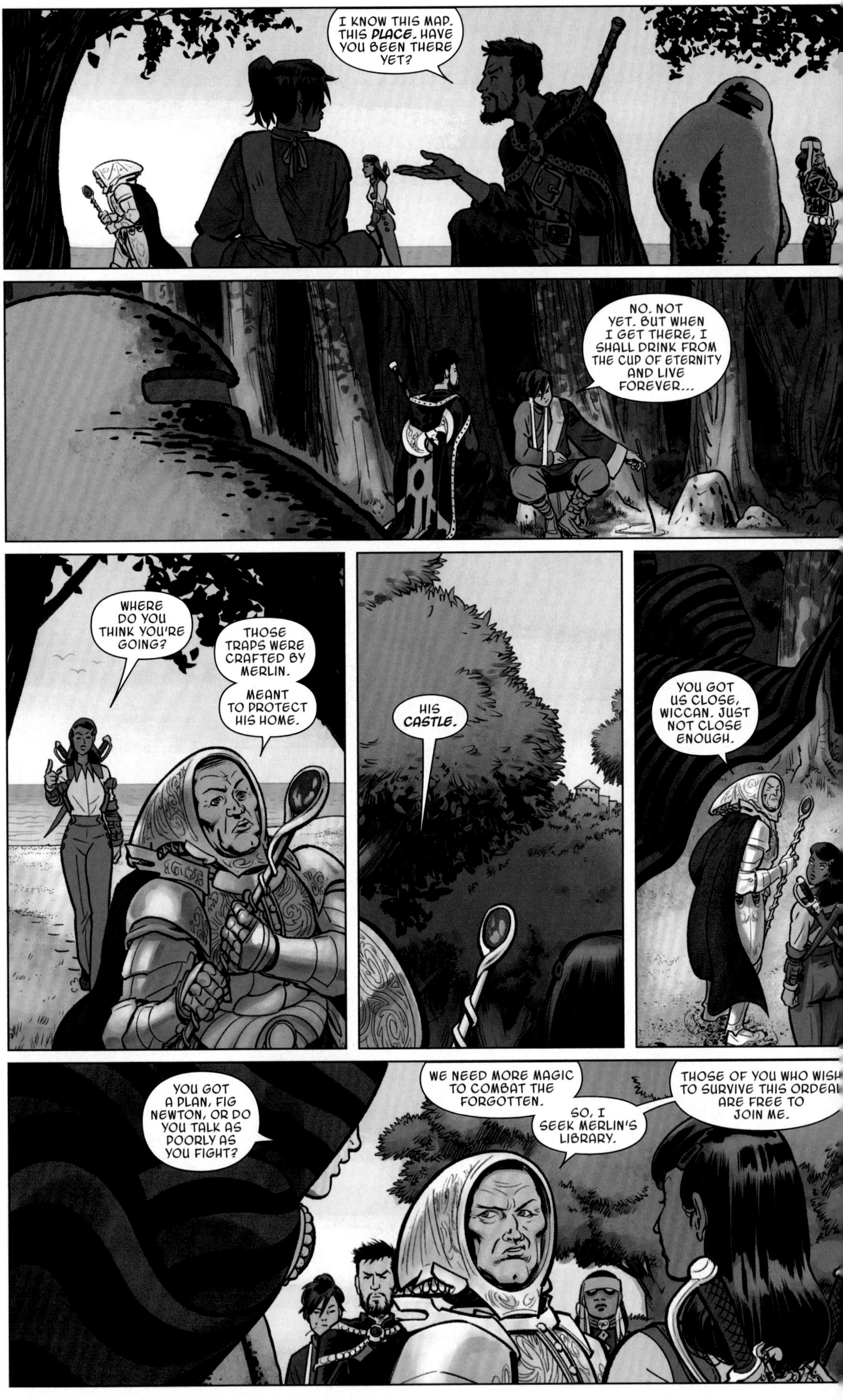
I KNOW THIS MAP. THIS PLACE. HAVE YOU BEEN THERE YET?
NO. NOT YET. BUT WHEN I GET THERE, I SHALL DRINK FROM THE CUP OF ETERNITY AND LIVE FOREVER...
WHERE DO YOU THINK YOU'RE GOING?
THOSE TRAPS WERE CRAFTED BY MERLIN.
MEANT TO PROTECT HIS HOME.
HIS CASTLE.
YOU GOT US CLOSE, WICCAN. JUST NOT CLOSE ENOUGH.
YOU GOT A PLAN, FIG NEWTON, OR DO YOU TALK AS POORLY AS YOU FIGHT?
WE NEED MORE MAGIC TO COMBAT THE FORGOTTEN.
SO, I SEEK MERLIN'S LIBRARY.
THOSE OF YOU WHO WISH TO SURVIVE THIS ORDEAL ARE FREE TO JOIN ME.

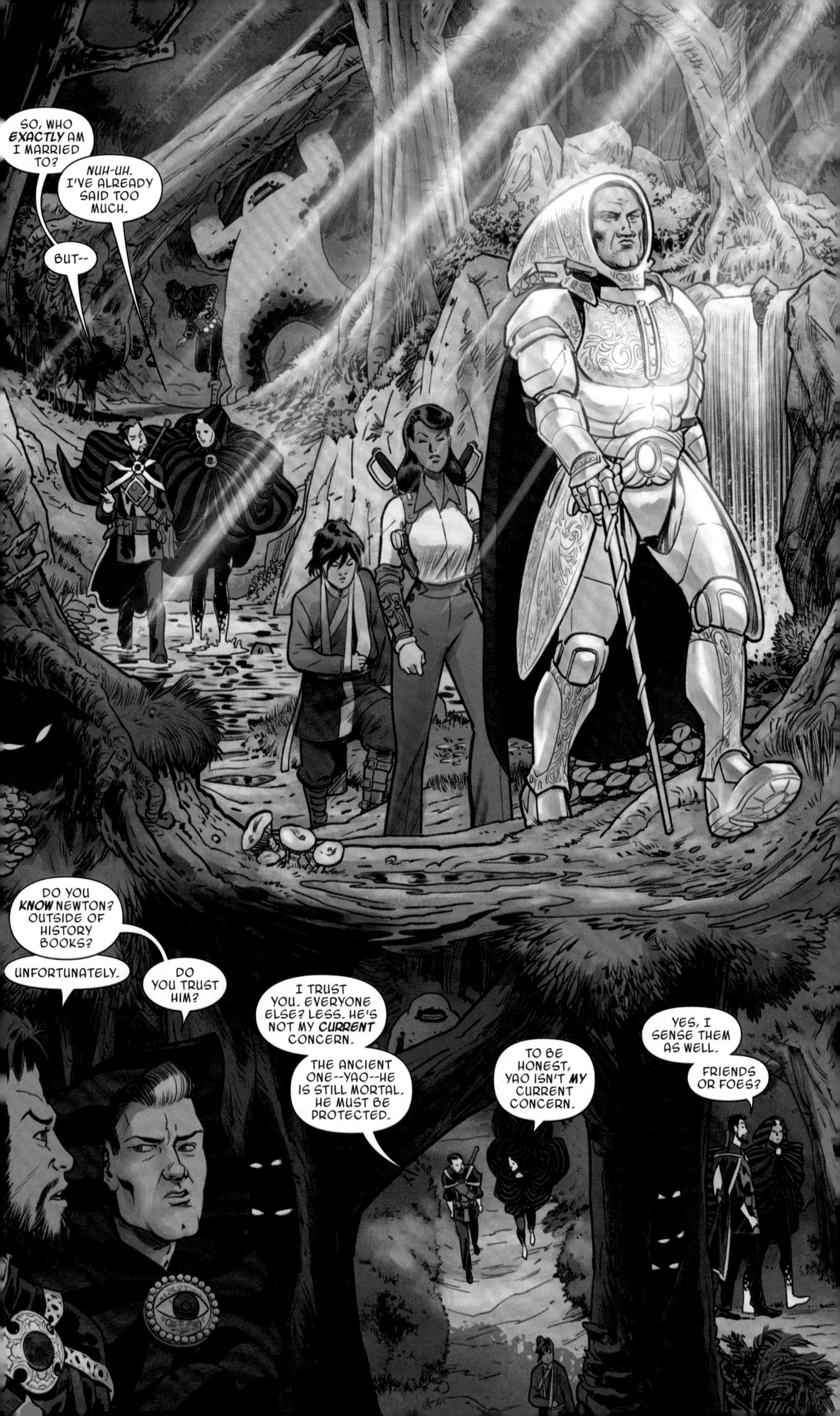
SO, WHO EXACTLY AM I MARRIED TO?
NUH-UH. I'VE ALREADY SAID TOO MUCH.
BUT--
DO YOU KNOW NEWTON? OUTSIDE OF HISTORY BOOKS?
UNFORTUNATELY.
DO YOU TRUST HIM?
I TRUST YOU. EVERYONE ELSE? LESS. HE'S NOT MY CURRENT CONCERN.
THE ANCIENT ONE--YAO--HE IS STILL MORTAL. HE MUST BE PROTECTED.
TO BE HONEST, YAO ISN'T MY CURRENT CONCERN.
YES, I SENSE THEM AS WELL.
FRIENDS OR FOES?

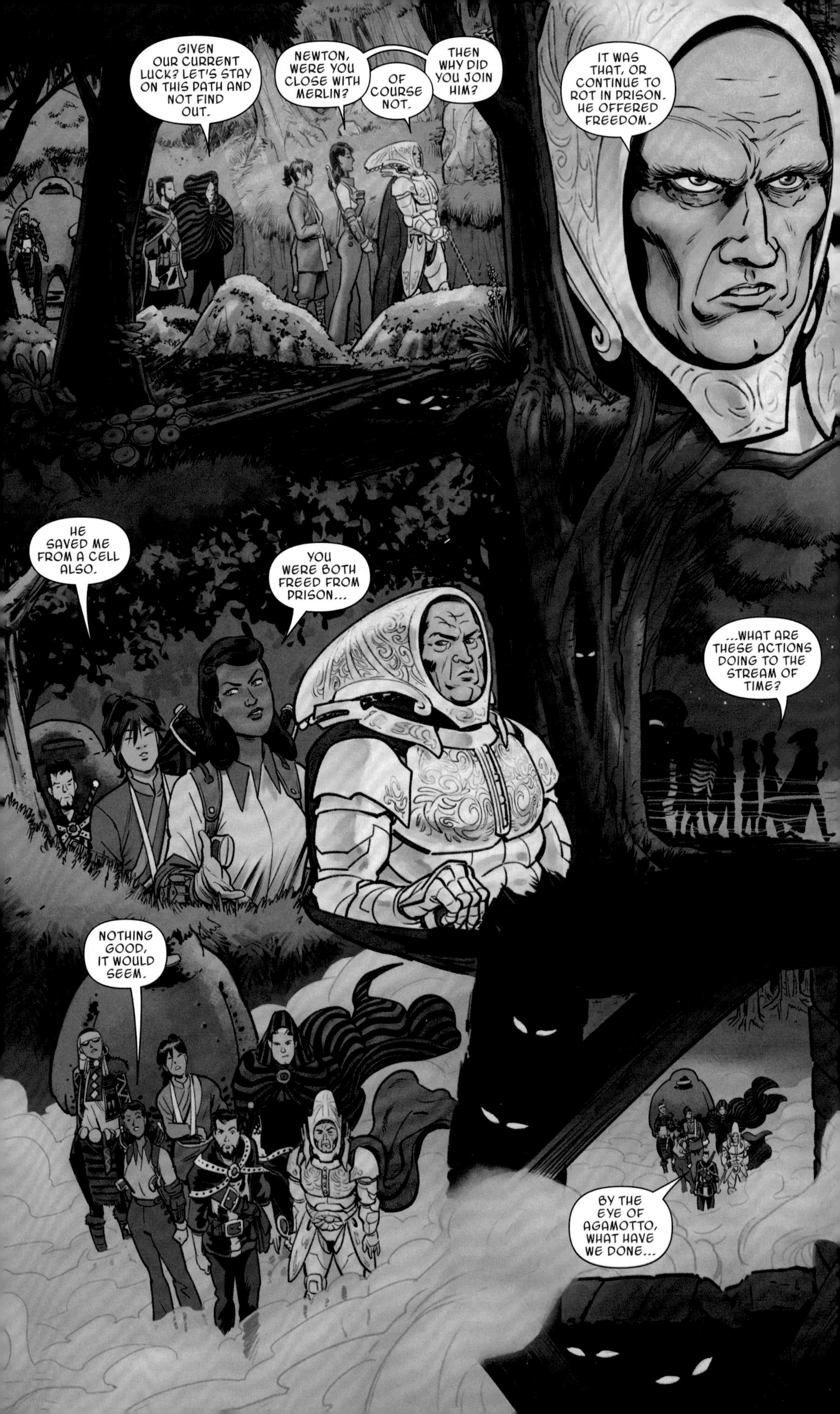
GIVEN OUR CURRENT LUCK? LET'S STAY ON THIS PATH AND NOT FIND OUT.
NEWTON, WERE YOU CLOSE WITH MERLIN?
OF COURSE NOT.
THEN WHY DID YOU JOIN HIM?
IT WAS THAT, OR CONTINUE TO ROT IN PRISON. HE OFFERED FREEDOM.
HE SAVED ME FROM A CELL ALSO.
YOU WERE BOTH FREED FROM PRISON...
...WHAT ARE THESE ACTIONS DOING TO THE STREAM OF TIME?
NOTHING GOOD, IT WOULD SEEM.
BY THE EYE OF AGAMOTTO, WHAT HAVE WE DONE...

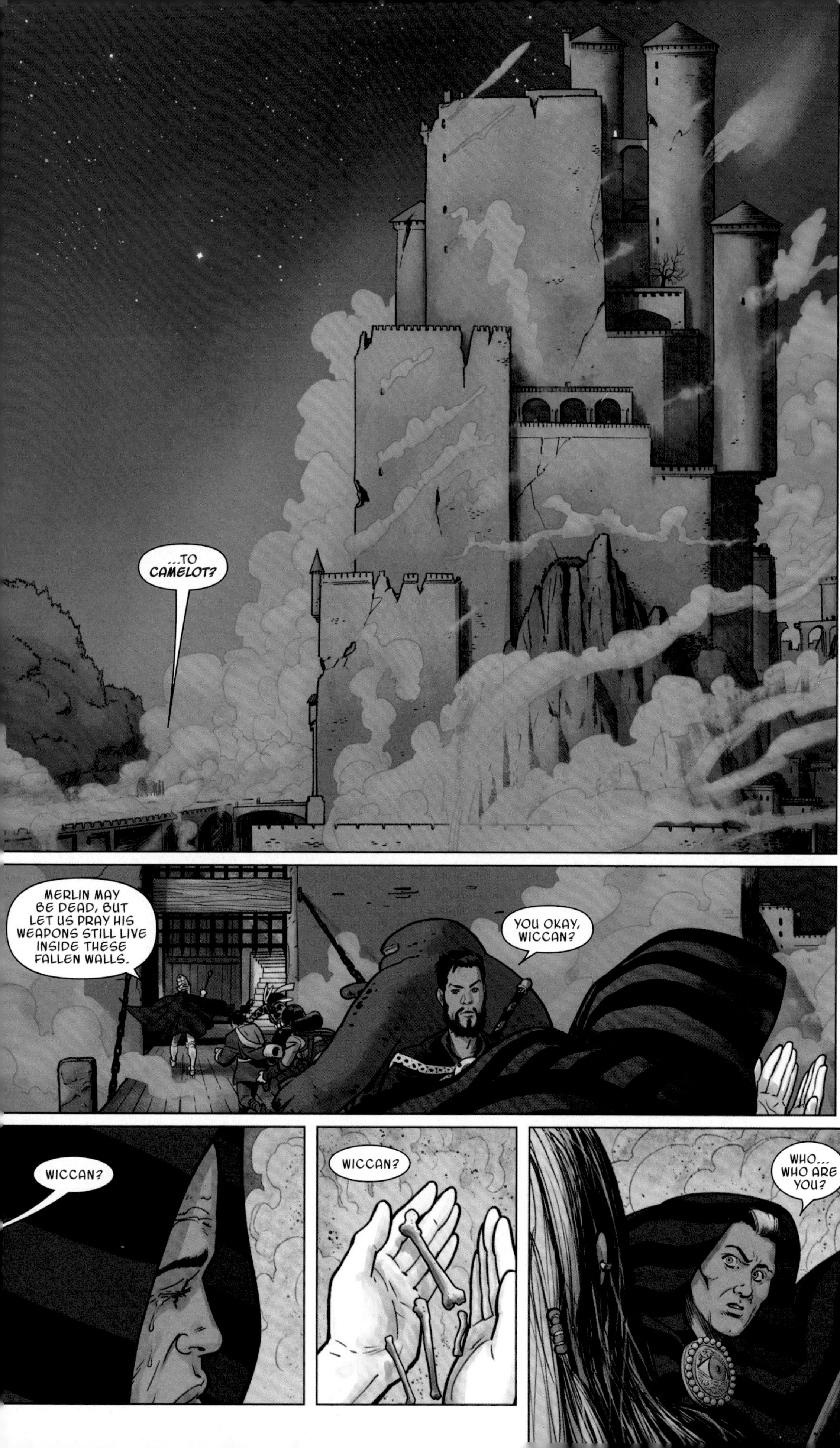
...TO CAMELOT?
MERLIN MAY BE DEAD, BUT LET US PRAY HIS WEAPONS STILL LIVE INSIDE THESE FALLEN WALLS.
YOU OKAY, WICCAN?
WICCAN?
WICCAN?
WHO... WHO ARE YOU?

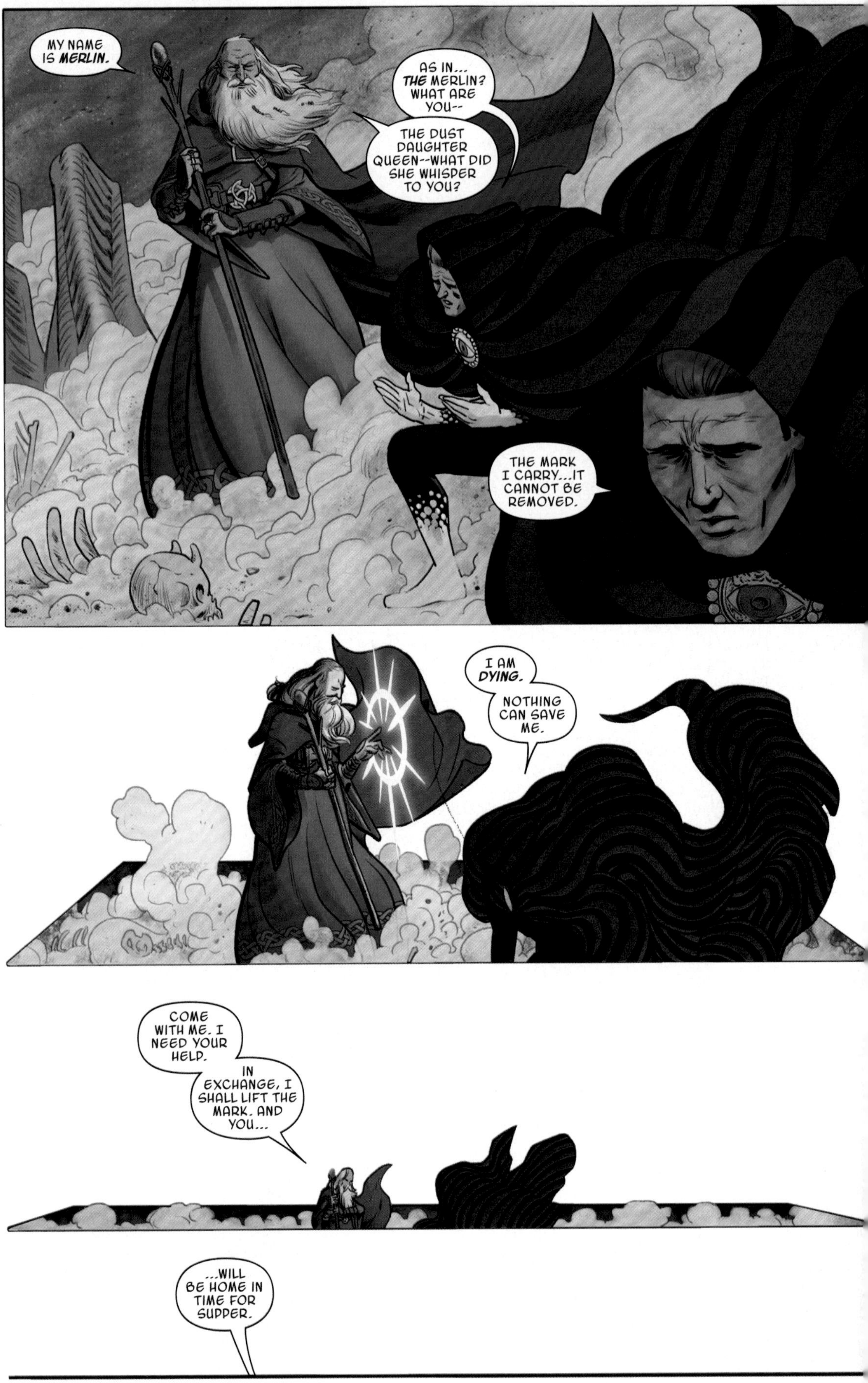
MY NAME IS ***MERLIN.***
AS IN... ***THE*** MERLIN? WHAT ARE YOU--
THE DUST DAUGHTER QUEEN--WHAT DID SHE WHISPER TO YOU?
THE MARK I CARRY...IT CANNOT BE REMOVED.
I AM ***DYING.***
NOTHING CAN SAVE ME.
COME WITH ME. I NEED YOUR HELP.
IN EXCHANGE, I SHALL LIFT THE MARK. AND YOU...
...WILL BE HOME IN TIME FOR SUPPER.

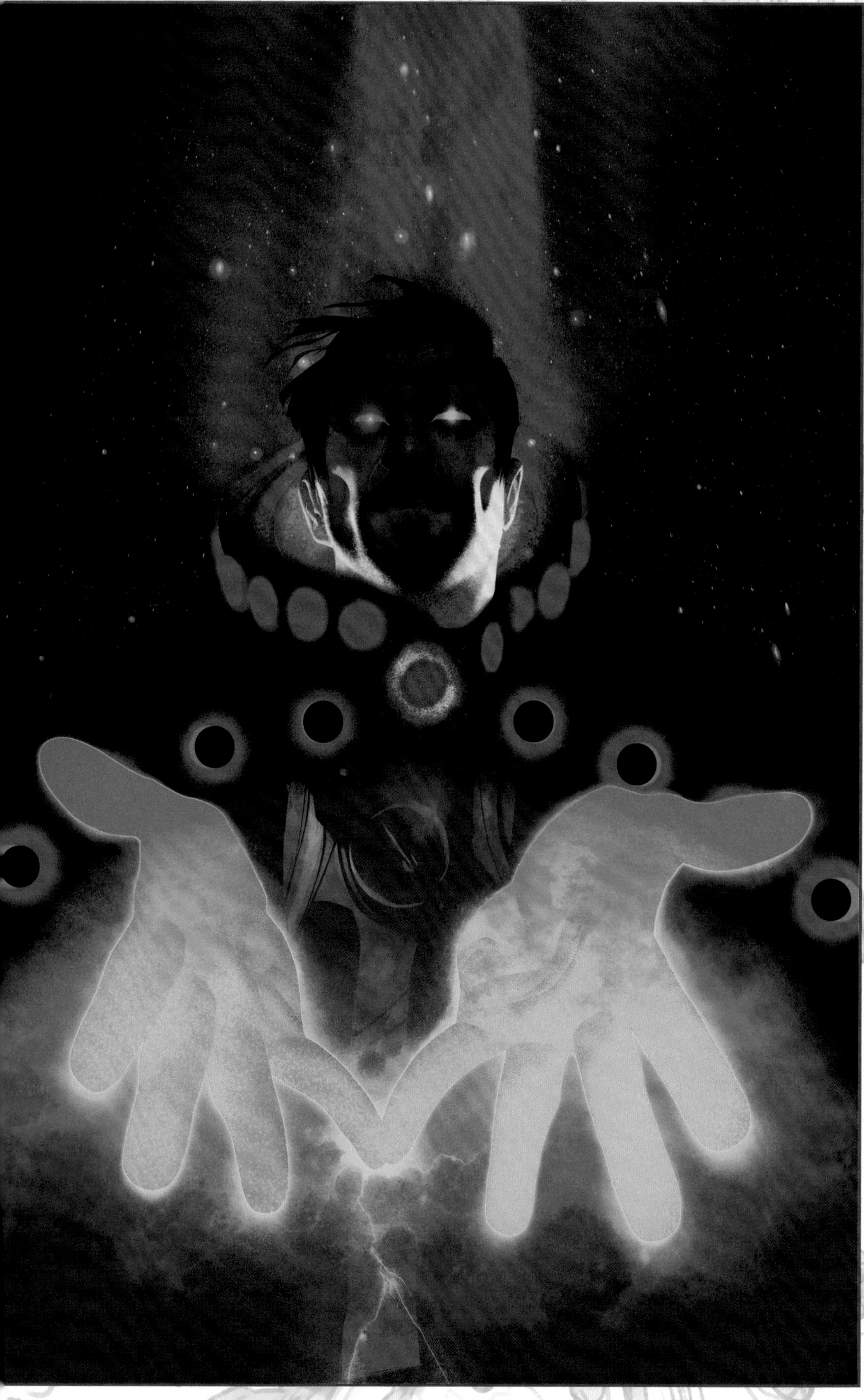

NO. 2 VARIANT BY **FRAZER IRVING**

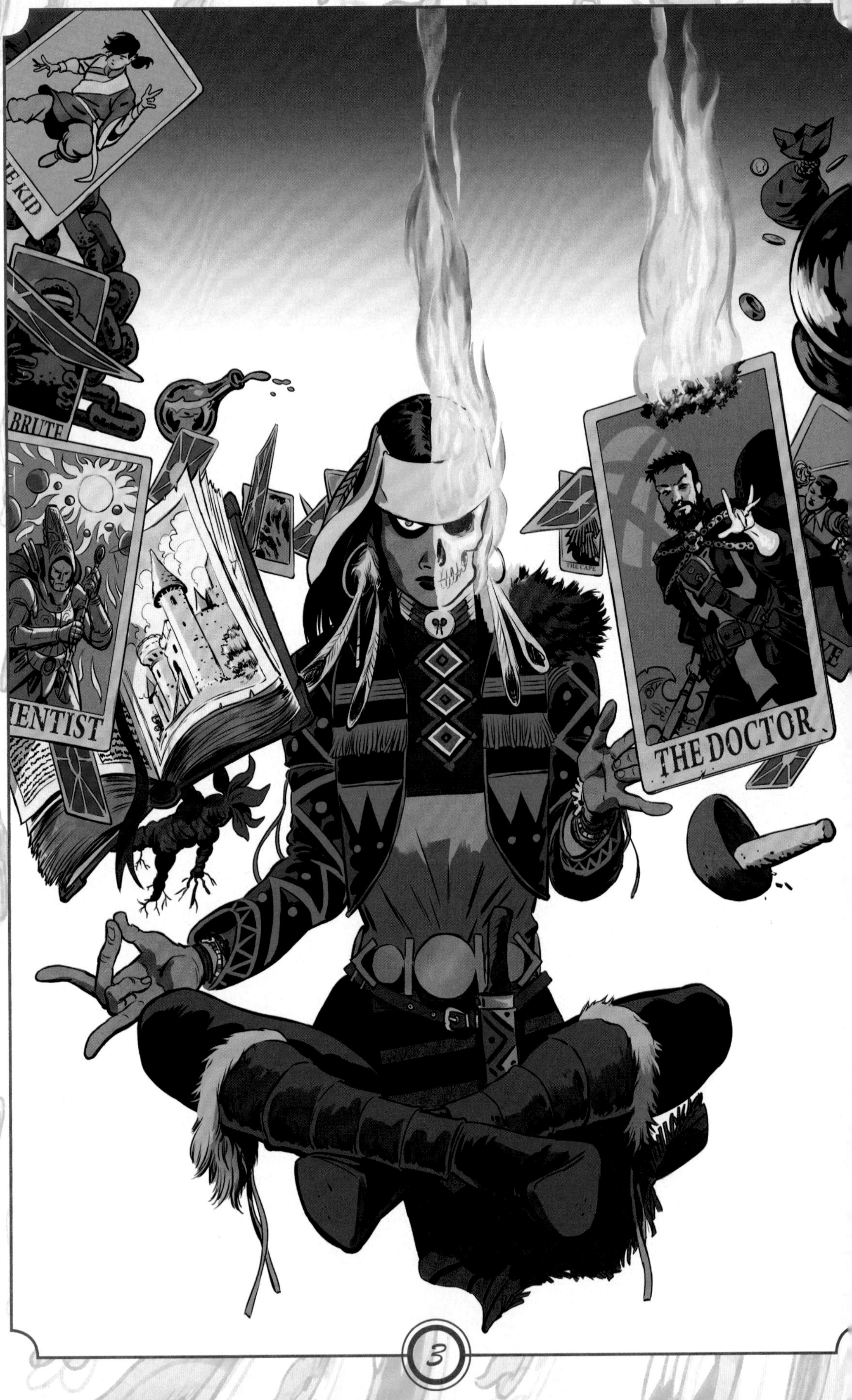

THE KID
BRUTE
IENTIST
THE CAPE
THE DOCTOR

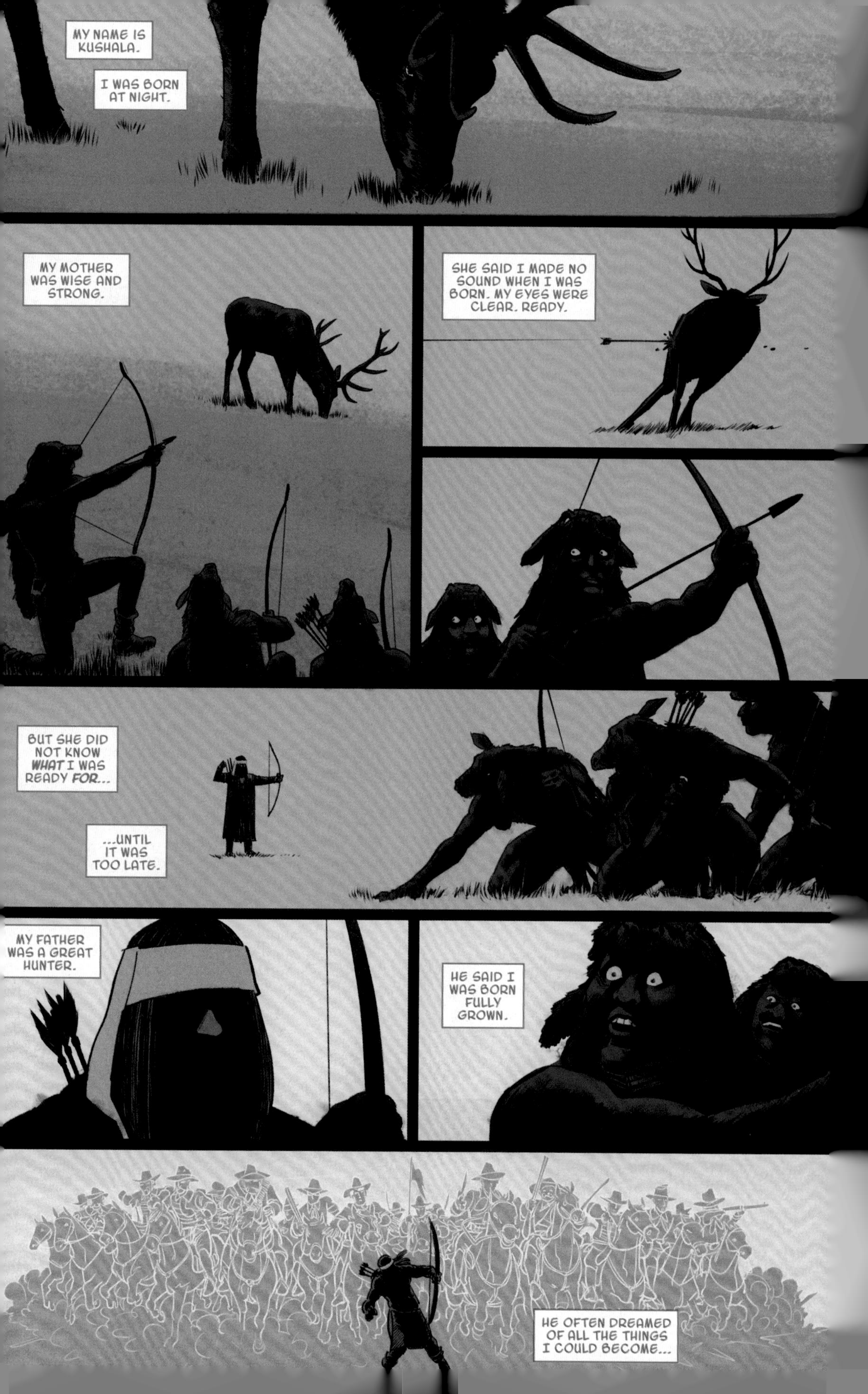

MY NAME IS KUSHALA.
I WAS BORN AT NIGHT.
MY MOTHER WAS WISE AND STRONG.
SHE SAID I MADE NO SOUND WHEN I WAS BORN. MY EYES WERE CLEAR. READY.
BUT SHE DID NOT KNOW *WHAT* I WAS READY *FOR*...
...UNTIL IT WAS TOO LATE.
MY FATHER WAS A GREAT HUNTER.
HE SAID I WAS BORN FULLY GROWN.
HE OFTEN DREAMED OF ALL THE THINGS I COULD BECOME...

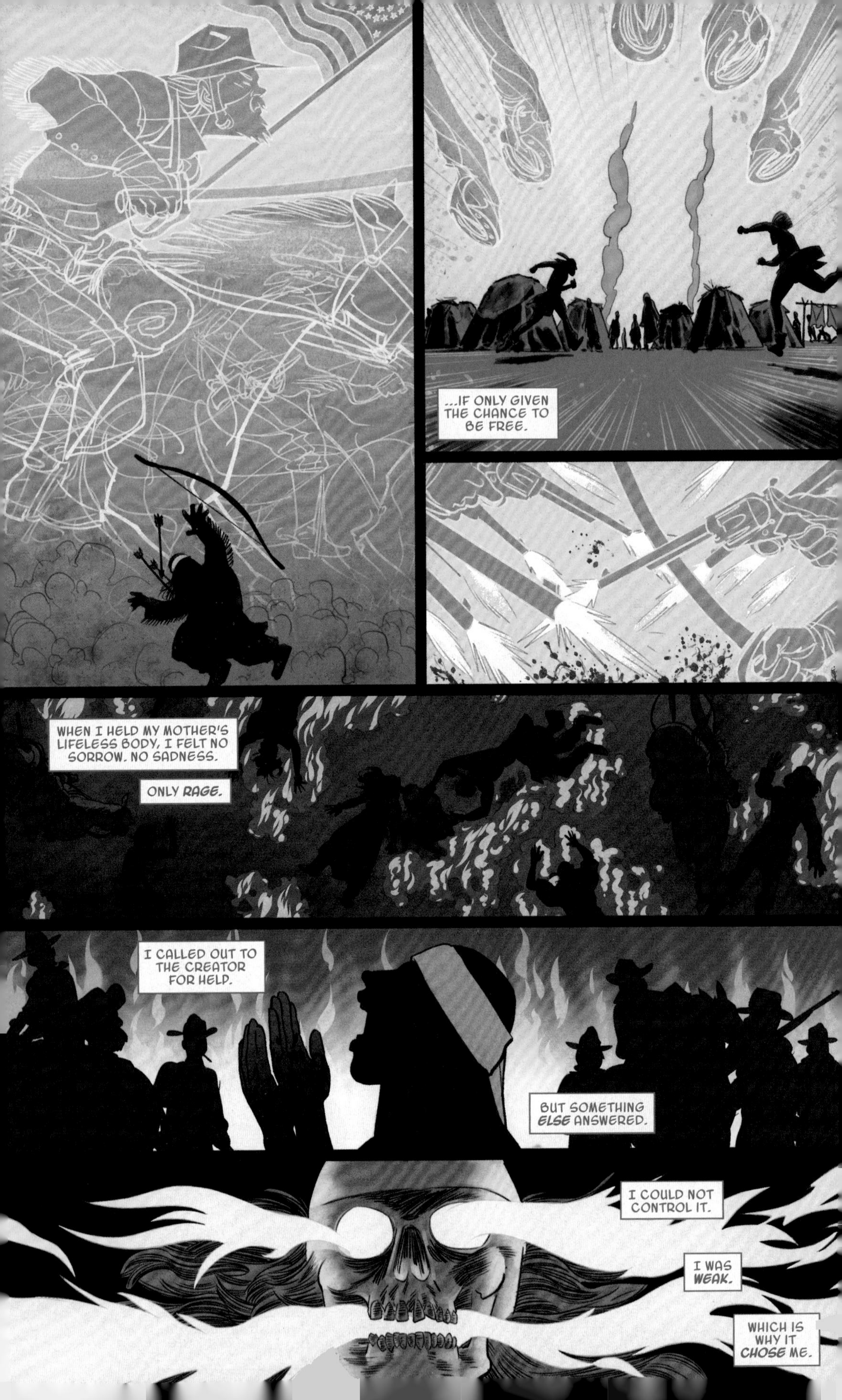
...IF ONLY GIVEN THE CHANCE TO BE FREE.
WHEN I HELD MY MOTHER'S LIFELESS BODY, I FELT NO SORROW. NO SADNESS.
ONLY *RAGE*.
I CALLED OUT TO THE CREATOR FOR HELP.
BUT SOMETHING *ELSE* ANSWERED.
I COULD NOT CONTROL IT.
I WAS *WEAK*.
WHICH IS WHY IT *CHOSE* ME.

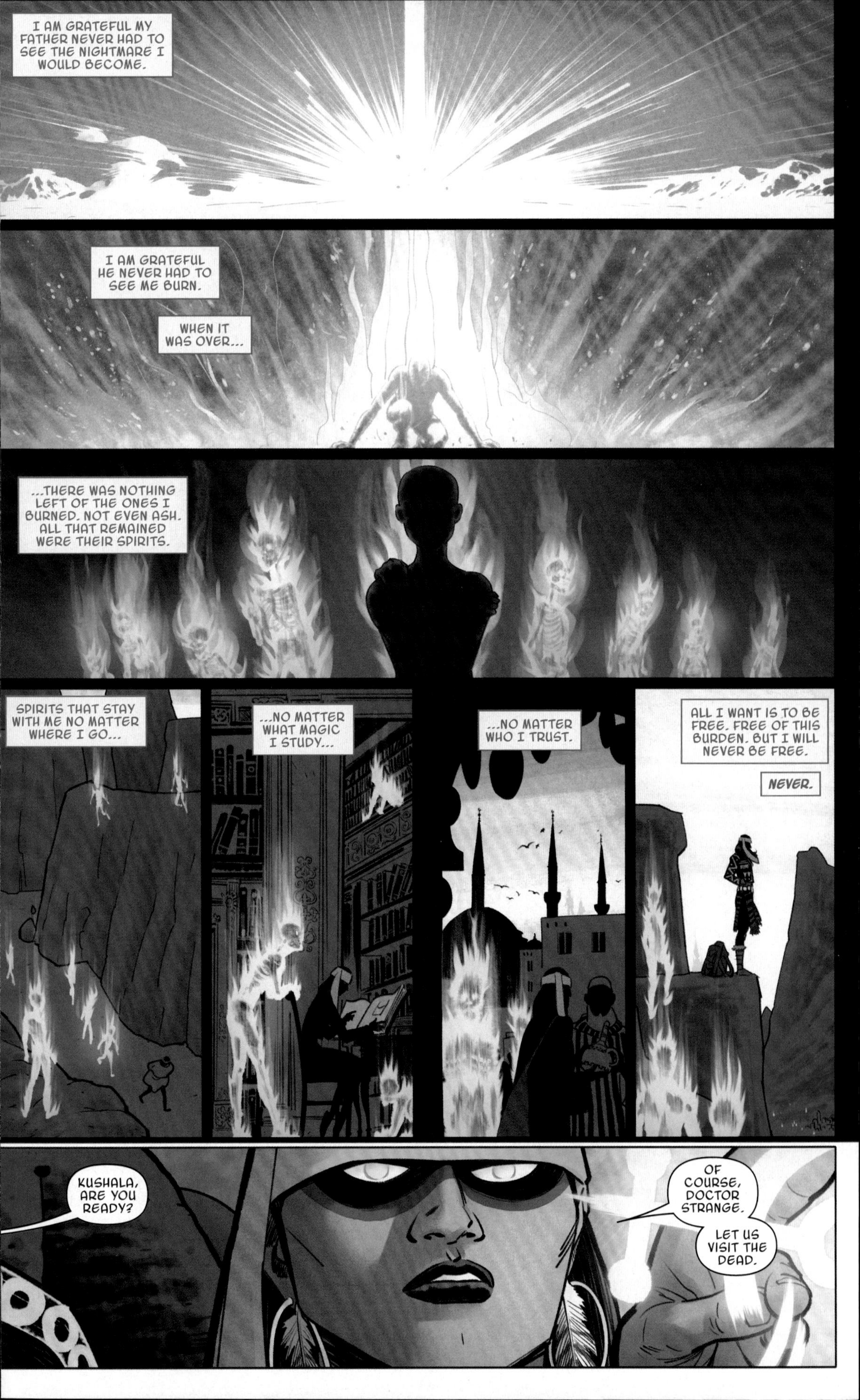

I AM GRATEFUL MY FATHER NEVER HAD TO SEE THE NIGHTMARE I WOULD BECOME.
I AM GRATEFUL HE NEVER HAD TO SEE ME BURN.
WHEN IT WAS OVER...
...THERE WAS NOTHING LEFT OF THE ONES I BURNED. NOT EVEN ASH. ALL THAT REMAINED WERE THEIR SPIRITS.
SPIRITS THAT STAY WITH ME NO MATTER WHERE I GO...
...NO MATTER WHAT MAGIC I STUDY...
...NO MATTER WHO I TRUST.
ALL I WANT IS TO BE FREE. FREE OF THIS BURDEN. BUT I WILL NEVER BE FREE.
NEVER.
KUSHALA, ARE YOU READY?
OF COURSE, DOCTOR STRANGE.
LET US VISIT THE DEAD.

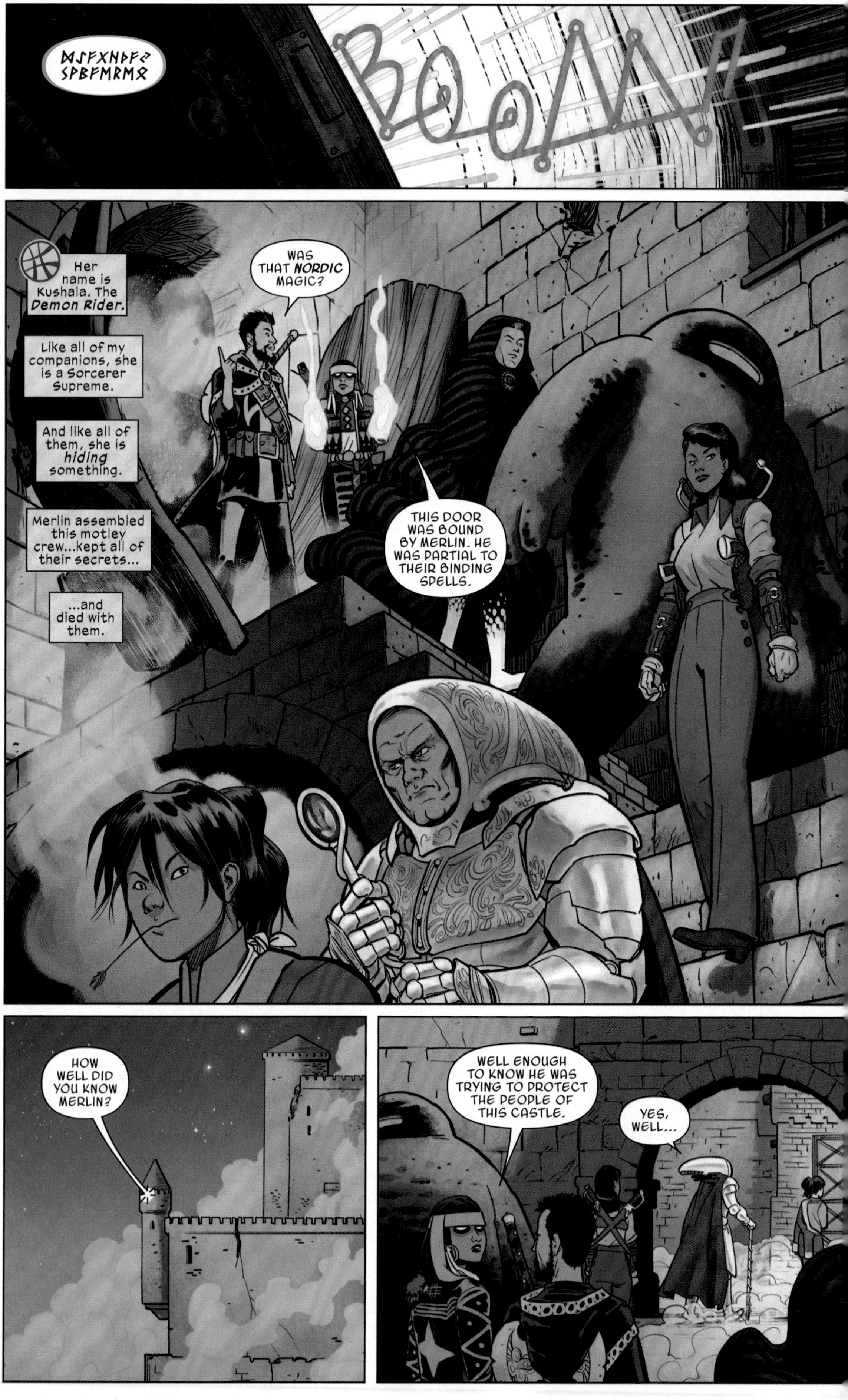

Her name is Kushala. The *Demon Rider*.
WAS THAT **NORDIC** MAGIC?
Like all of my companions, she is a Sorcerer Supreme.
And like all of them, she is *hiding* something.
Merlin assembled this motley crew...kept all of their secrets...
...and died with them.
THIS DOOR WAS BOUND BY MERLIN. HE WAS PARTIAL TO THEIR BINDING SPELLS.
HOW WELL DID YOU KNOW MERLIN?
WELL ENOUGH TO KNOW HE WAS TRYING TO PROTECT THE PEOPLE OF THIS CASTLE.
YES, WELL...

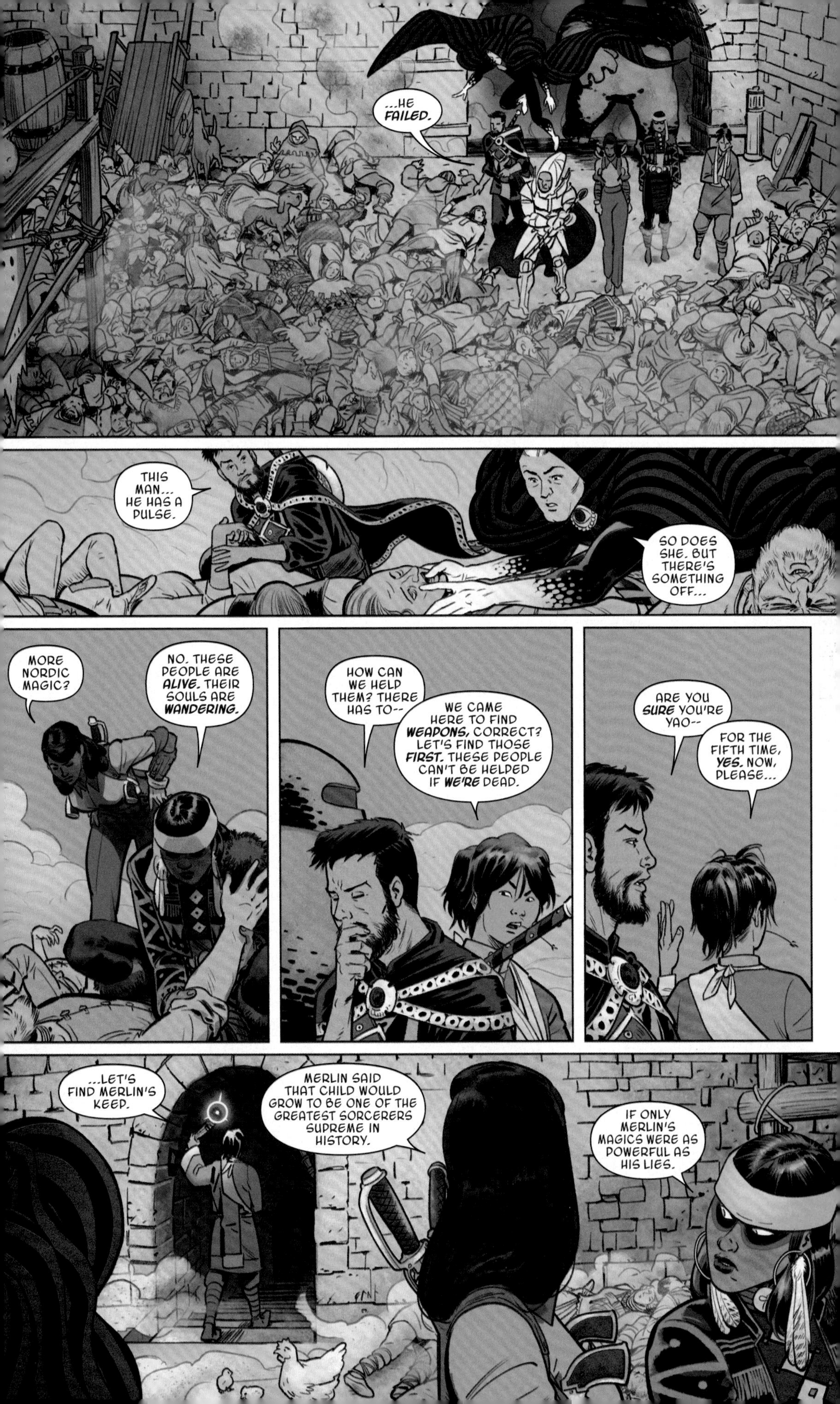

...HE FAILED.
THIS MAN... HE HAS A PULSE.
SO DOES SHE. BUT THERE'S SOMETHING OFF...
MORE NORDIC MAGIC?
NO. THESE PEOPLE ARE ALIVE. THEIR SOULS ARE WANDERING.
HOW CAN WE HELP THEM? THERE HAS TO--
WE CAME HERE TO FIND WEAPONS, CORRECT? LET'S FIND THOSE FIRST. THESE PEOPLE CAN'T BE HELPED IF WE'RE DEAD.
ARE YOU SURE YOU'RE YAO--
FOR THE FIFTH TIME, YES. NOW, PLEASE...
...LET'S FIND MERLIN'S KEEP.
MERLIN SAID THAT CHILD WOULD GROW TO BE ONE OF THE GREATEST SORCERERS SUPREME IN HISTORY.
IF ONLY MERLIN'S MAGICS WERE AS POWERFUL AS HIS LIES.

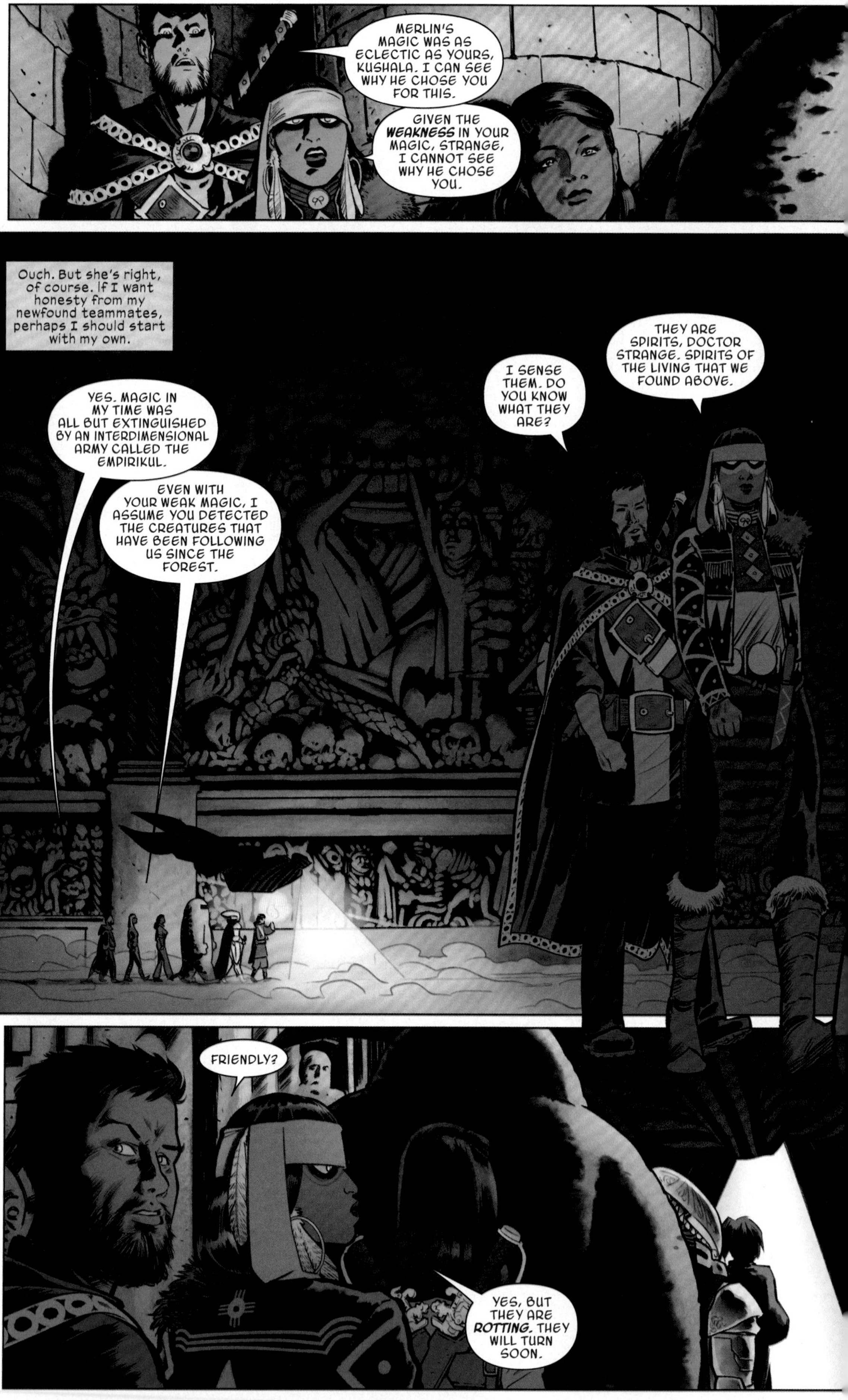
MERLIN'S MAGIC WAS AS ECLECTIC AS YOURS, KUSHALA. I CAN SEE WHY HE CHOSE YOU FOR THIS.
GIVEN THE WEAKNESS IN YOUR MAGIC, STRANGE, I CANNOT SEE WHY HE CHOSE YOU.
Ouch. But she's right, of course. If I want honesty from my newfound teammates, perhaps I should start with my own.
YES. MAGIC IN MY TIME WAS ALL BUT EXTINGUISHED BY AN INTERDIMENSIONAL ARMY CALLED THE EMPIRIKUL.
EVEN WITH YOUR WEAK MAGIC, I ASSUME YOU DETECTED THE CREATURES THAT HAVE BEEN FOLLOWING US SINCE THE FOREST.
I SENSE THEM. DO YOU KNOW WHAT THEY ARE?
THEY ARE SPIRITS, DOCTOR STRANGE. SPIRITS OF THE LIVING THAT WE FOUND ABOVE.
FRIENDLY?
YES, BUT THEY ARE ROTTING. THEY WILL TURN SOON.

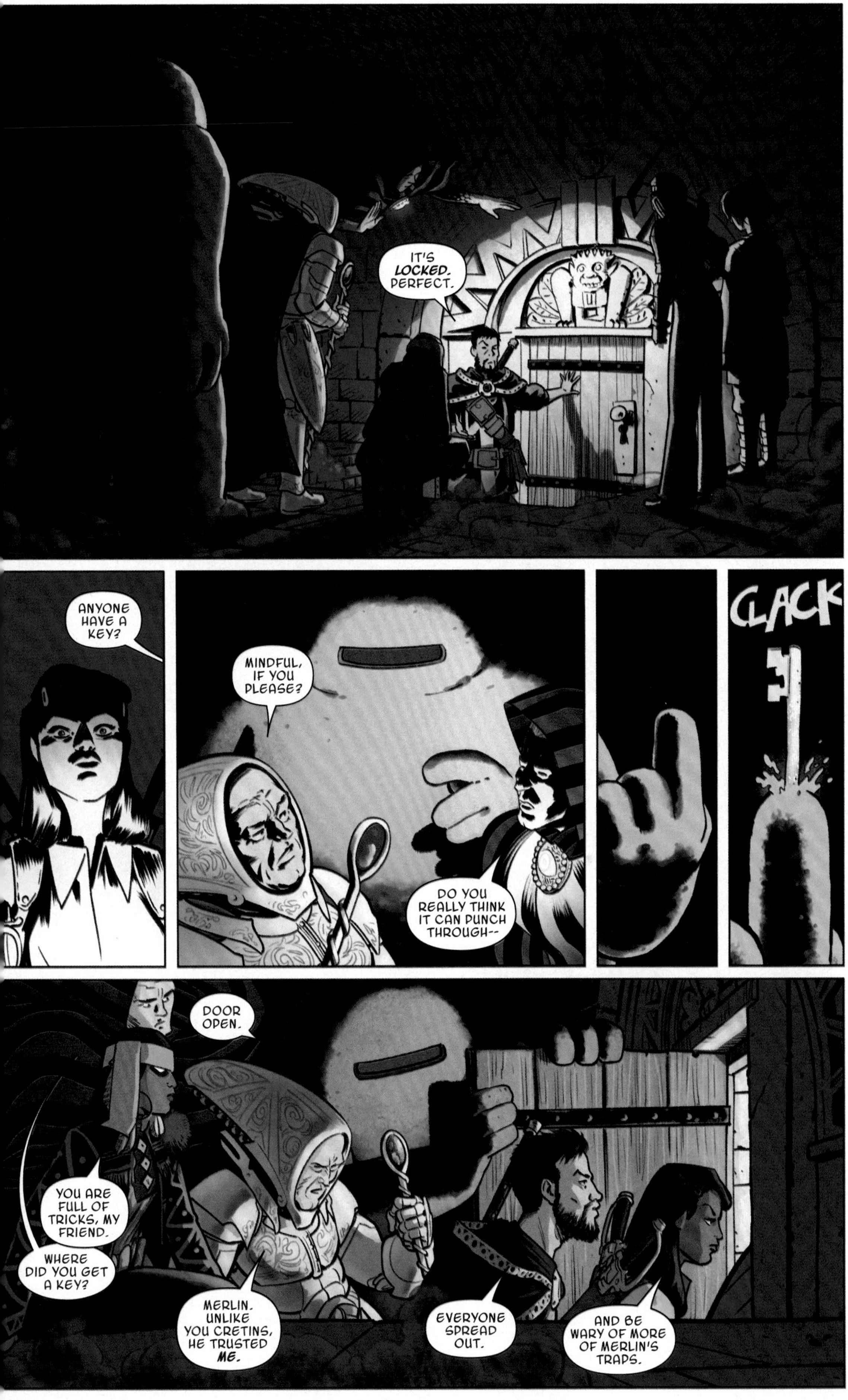
IT'S LOCKED. PERFECT.
ANYONE HAVE A KEY?
MINDFUL, IF YOU PLEASE?
DO YOU REALLY THINK IT CAN PUNCH THROUGH--
CLACK
DOOR OPEN.
YOU ARE FULL OF TRICKS, MY FRIEND.
WHERE DID YOU GET A KEY?
MERLIN. UNLIKE YOU CRETINS, HE TRUSTED ME.
EVERYONE SPREAD OUT.
AND BE WARY OF MORE OF MERLIN'S TRAPS.

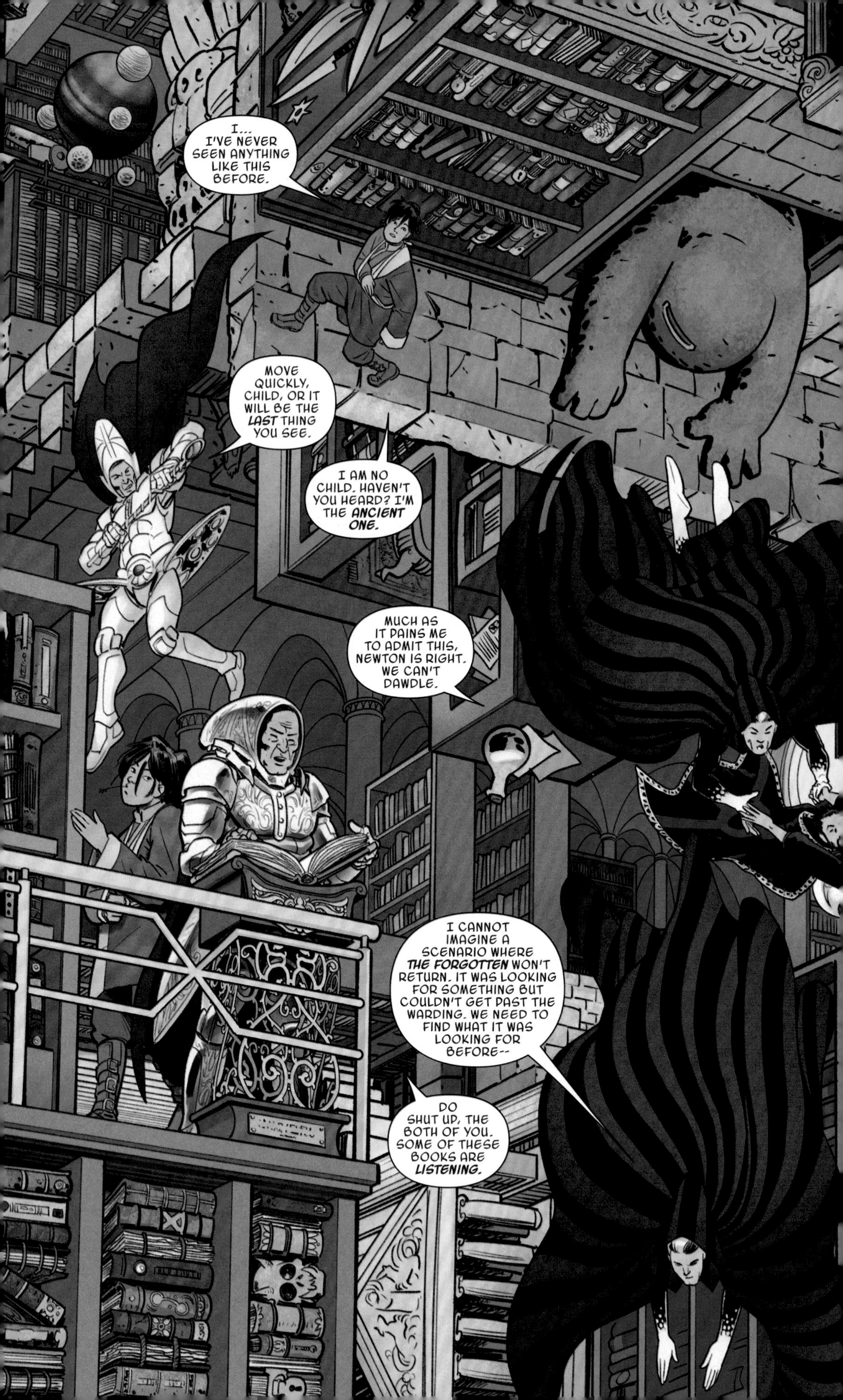

I... I'VE NEVER SEEN ANYTHING LIKE THIS BEFORE.
MOVE QUICKLY, CHILD, OR IT WILL BE THE LAST THING YOU SEE.
I AM NO CHILD. HAVEN'T YOU HEARD? I'M THE ANCIENT ONE.
MUCH AS IT PAINS ME TO ADMIT THIS, NEWTON IS RIGHT. WE CAN'T DAWDLE.
I CANNOT IMAGINE A SCENARIO WHERE THE FORGOTTEN WON'T RETURN. IT WAS LOOKING FOR SOMETHING BUT COULDN'T GET PAST THE WARDING. WE NEED TO FIND WHAT IT WAS LOOKING FOR BEFORE--
DO SHUT UP, THE BOTH OF YOU. SOME OF THESE BOOKS ARE LISTENING.

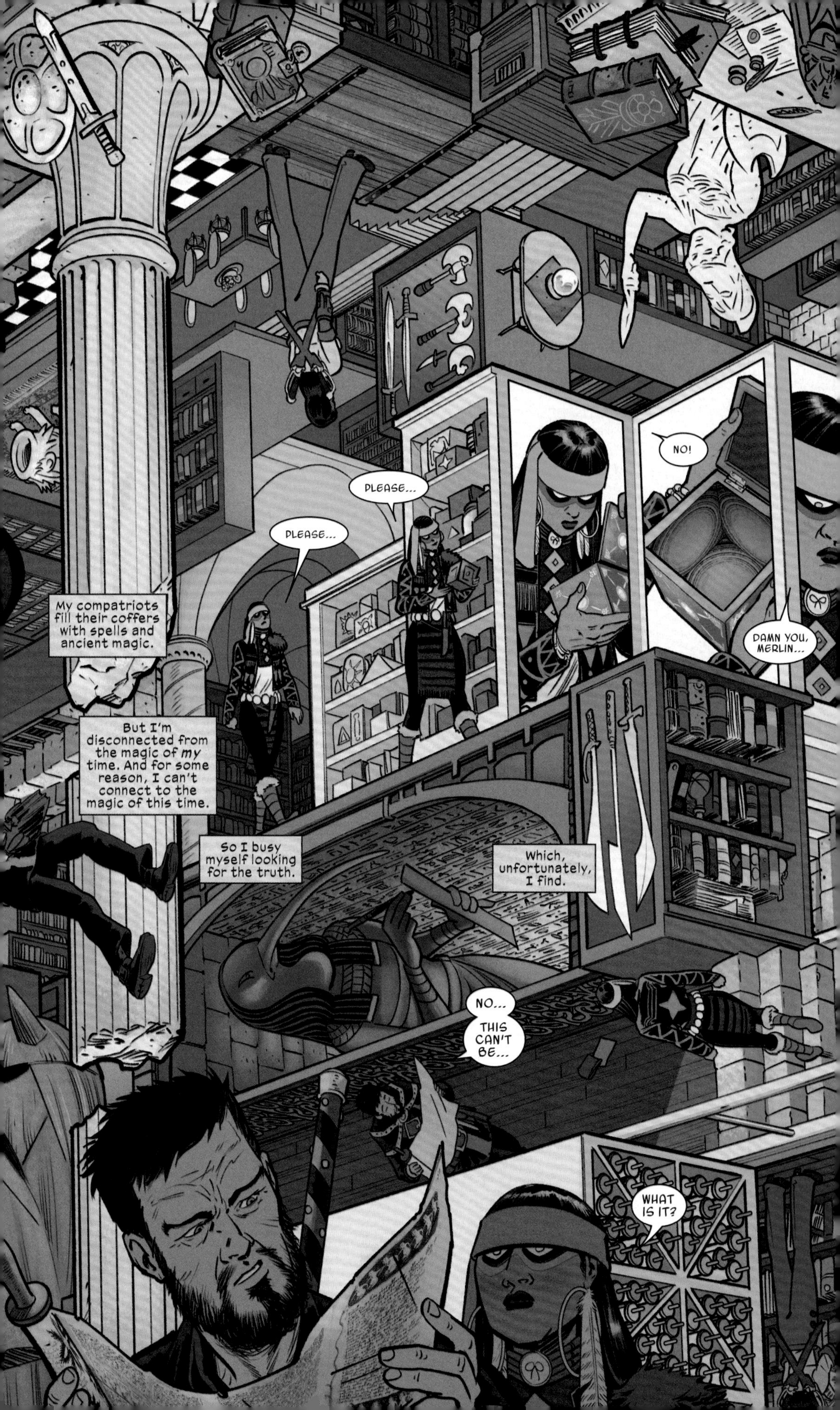
NO!
PLEASE...
PLEASE...
My compatriots fill their coffers with spells and ancient magic.
DAMN YOU, MERLIN...
But I'm disconnected from the magic of *my* time. And for some reason, I can't connect to the magic of this time.
So I busy myself looking for the truth.
Which, unfortunately, I find.
NO...
THIS CAN'T BE...
WHAT IS IT?

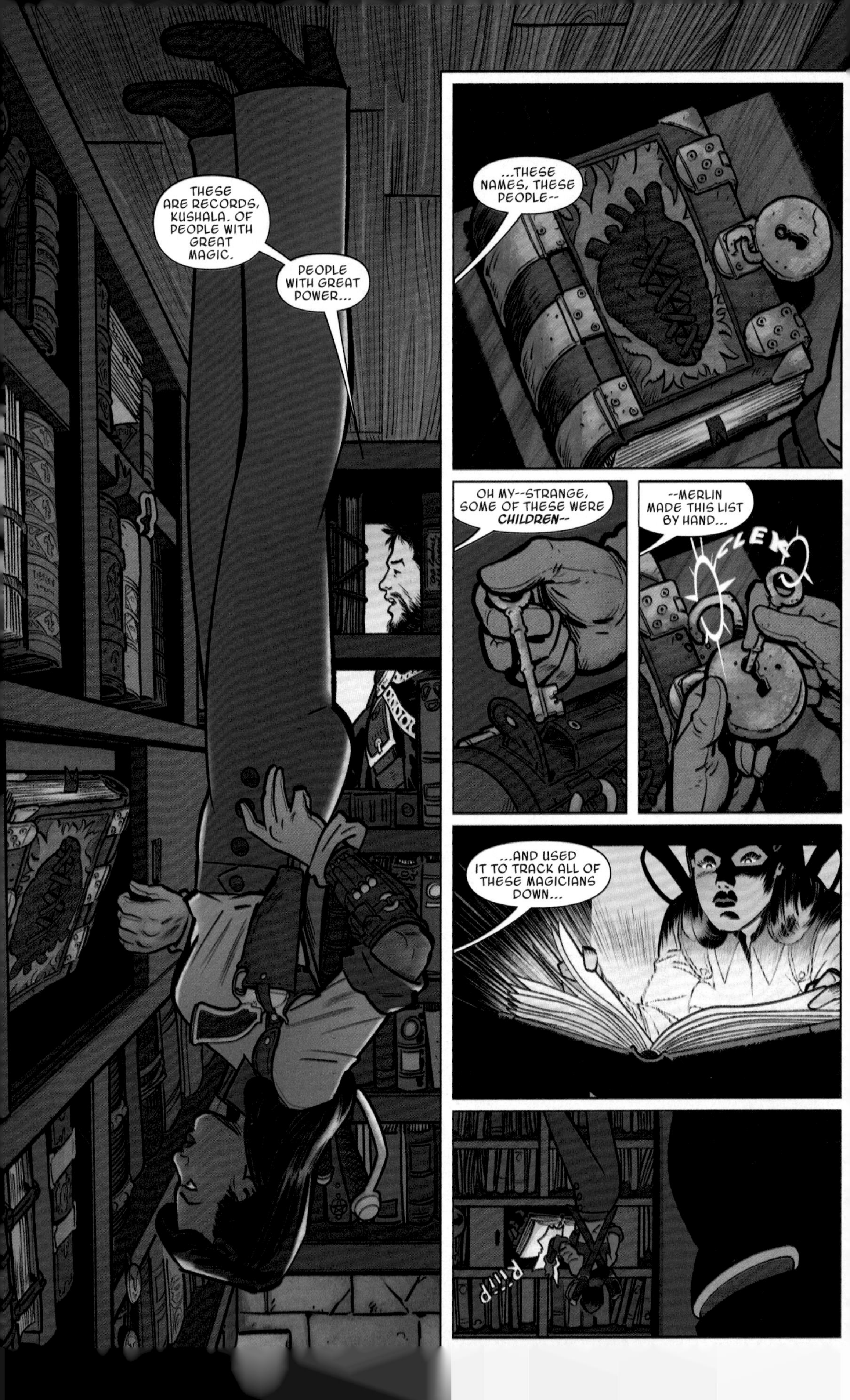
THESE ARE RECORDS, KUSHALA. OF PEOPLE WITH GREAT MAGIC.
PEOPLE WITH GREAT POWER...
...THESE NAMES, THESE PEOPLE--
OH MY--STRANGE, SOME OF THESE WERE **CHILDREN--**
--MERLIN MADE THIS LIST BY HAND...
CLEK
...AND USED IT TO TRACK ALL OF THESE MAGICIANS DOWN...

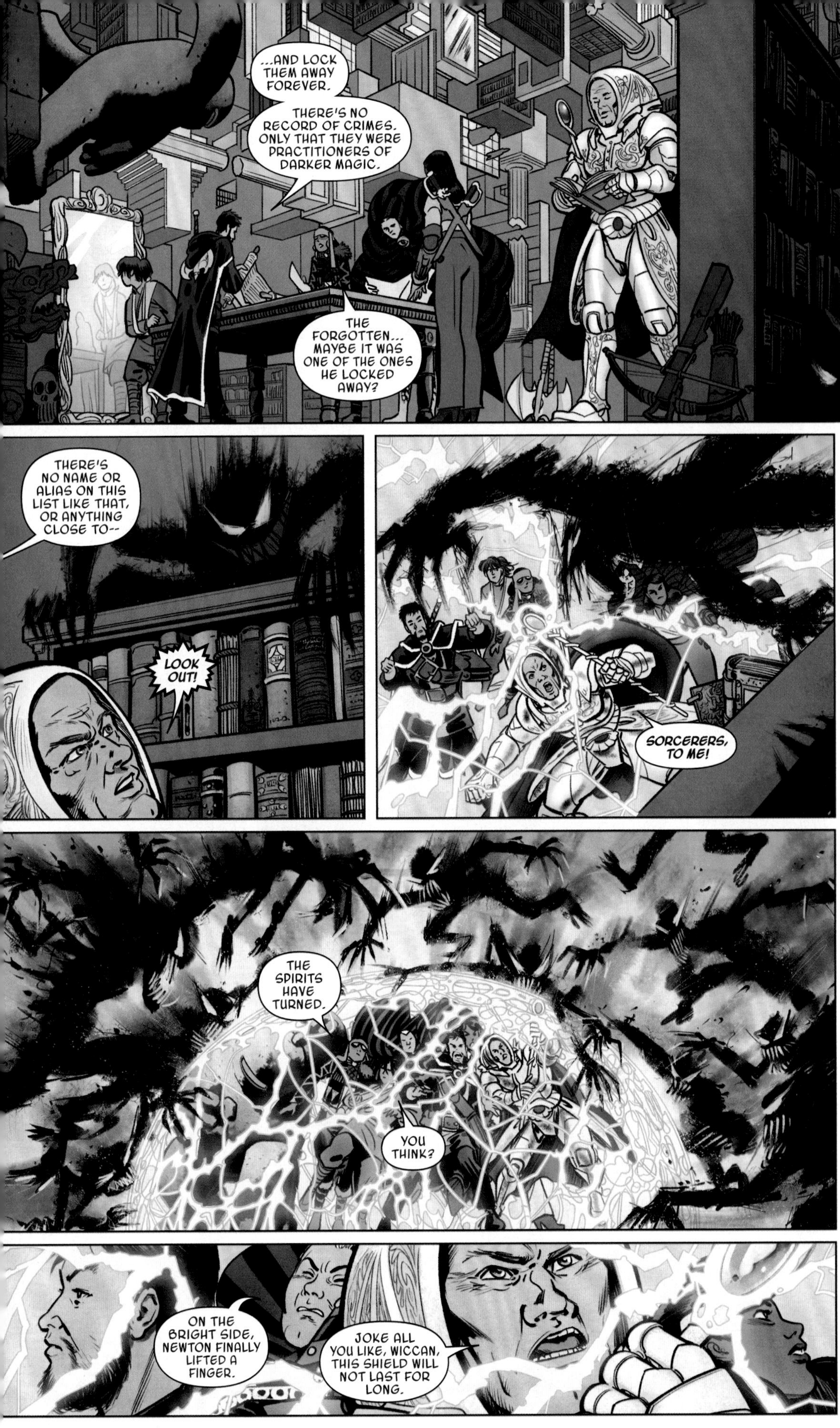
...AND LOCK THEM AWAY FOREVER.
THERE'S NO RECORD OF CRIMES. ONLY THAT THEY WERE PRACTITIONERS OF DARKER MAGIC.
THE FORGOTTEN... MAYBE IT WAS ONE OF THE ONES HE LOCKED AWAY?
THERE'S NO NAME OR ALIAS ON THIS LIST LIKE THAT, OR ANYTHING CLOSE TO--
LOOK OUT!
SORCERERS, TO ME!
THE SPIRITS HAVE TURNED.
YOU THINK?
ON THE BRIGHT SIDE, NEWTON FINALLY LIFTED A FINGER.
JOKE ALL YOU LIKE, WICCAN, THIS SHIELD WILL NOT LAST FOR LONG.

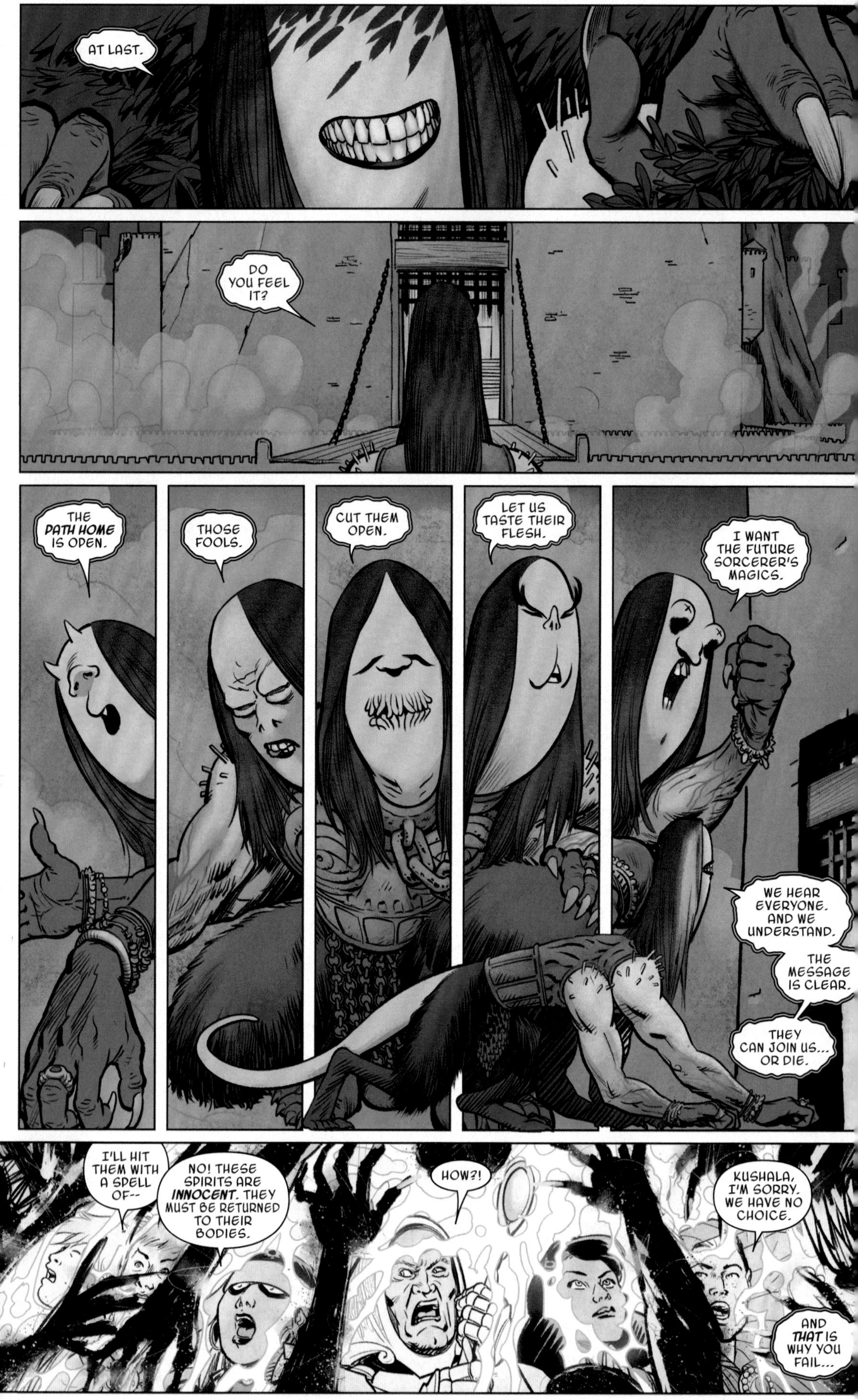
AT LAST.
DO YOU FEEL IT?
THE *PATH HOME* IS OPEN.
THOSE FOOLS.
CUT THEM OPEN.
LET US TASTE THEIR FLESH.
I WANT THE FUTURE SORCERER'S MAGICS.
WE HEAR EVERYONE. AND WE UNDERSTAND.
THE MESSAGE IS CLEAR.
THEY CAN JOIN US... OR DIE.
I'LL HIT THEM WITH A SPELL OF--
NO! THESE SPIRITS ARE *INNOCENT*. THEY MUST BE RETURNED TO THEIR BODIES.
HOW?!
KUSHALA, I'M SORRY. WE HAVE NO CHOICE.
AND *THAT* IS WHY YOU FAIL...

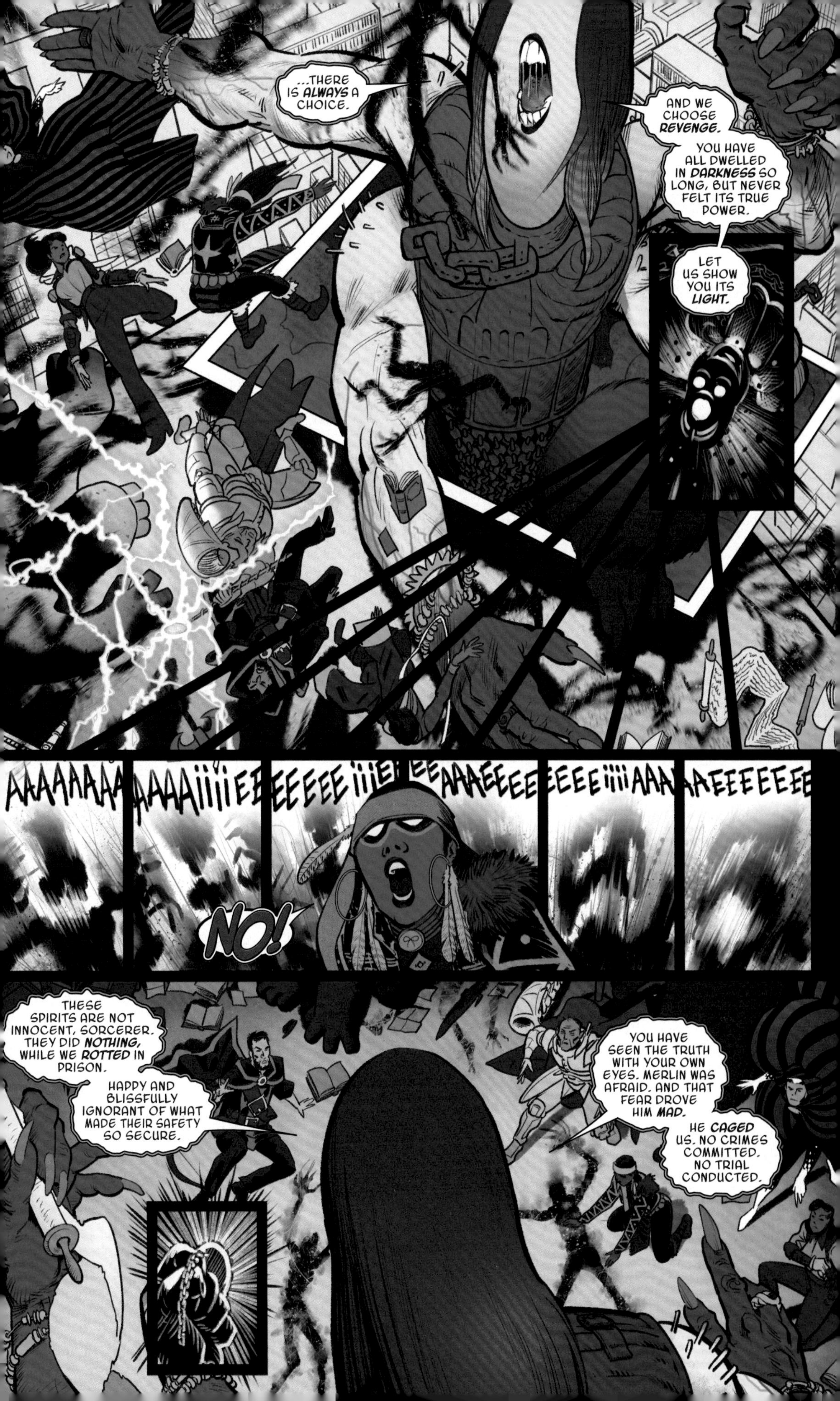

...THERE IS ALWAYS A CHOICE.
AND WE CHOOSE REVENGE.
YOU HAVE ALL DWELLED IN DARKNESS SO LONG, BUT NEVER FELT ITS TRUE POWER.
LET US SHOW YOU ITS LIGHT.
AAAAAAAAAAAiiiiEEEEEEiiiEEEAAAEEEEEEEiiiiAAAAEEEEEEE
NO!
THESE SPIRITS ARE NOT INNOCENT, SORCERER. THEY DID NOTHING, WHILE WE ROTTED IN PRISON.
HAPPY AND BLISSFULLY IGNORANT OF WHAT MADE THEIR SAFETY SO SECURE.
YOU HAVE SEEN THE TRUTH WITH YOUR OWN EYES. MERLIN WAS AFRAID. AND THAT FEAR DROVE HIM MAD.
HE CAGED US. NO CRIMES COMMITTED. NO TRIAL CONDUCTED.

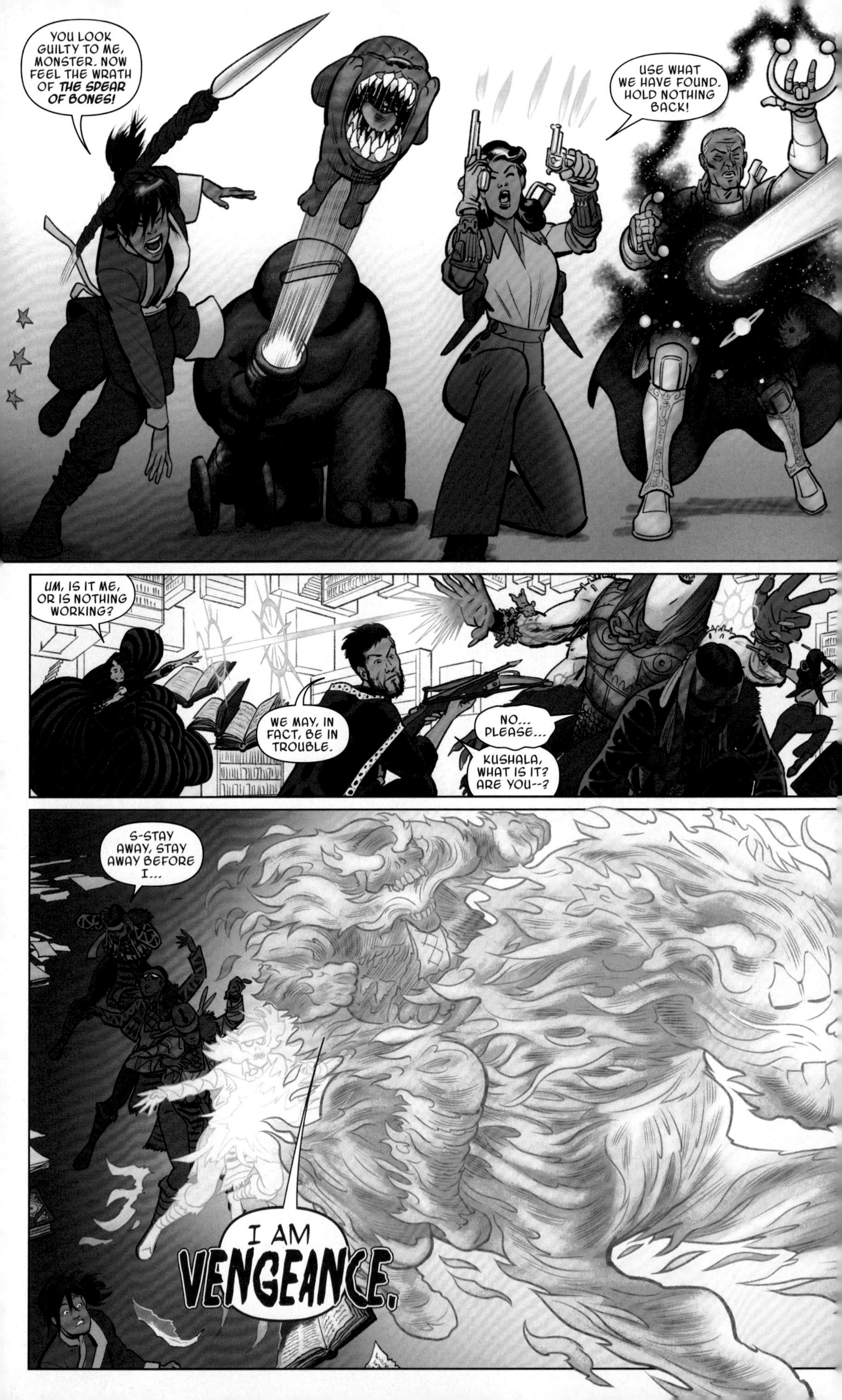

YOU LOOK GUILTY TO ME, MONSTER. NOW FEEL THE WRATH OF THE SPEAR OF BONES!
USE WHAT WE HAVE FOUND. HOLD NOTHING BACK!
UM, IS IT ME, OR IS NOTHING WORKING?
WE MAY, IN FACT, BE IN TROUBLE.
NO... PLEASE...
KUSHALA, WHAT IS IT? ARE YOU--?
S-STAY AWAY, STAY AWAY BEFORE I...
I AM VENGEANCE.

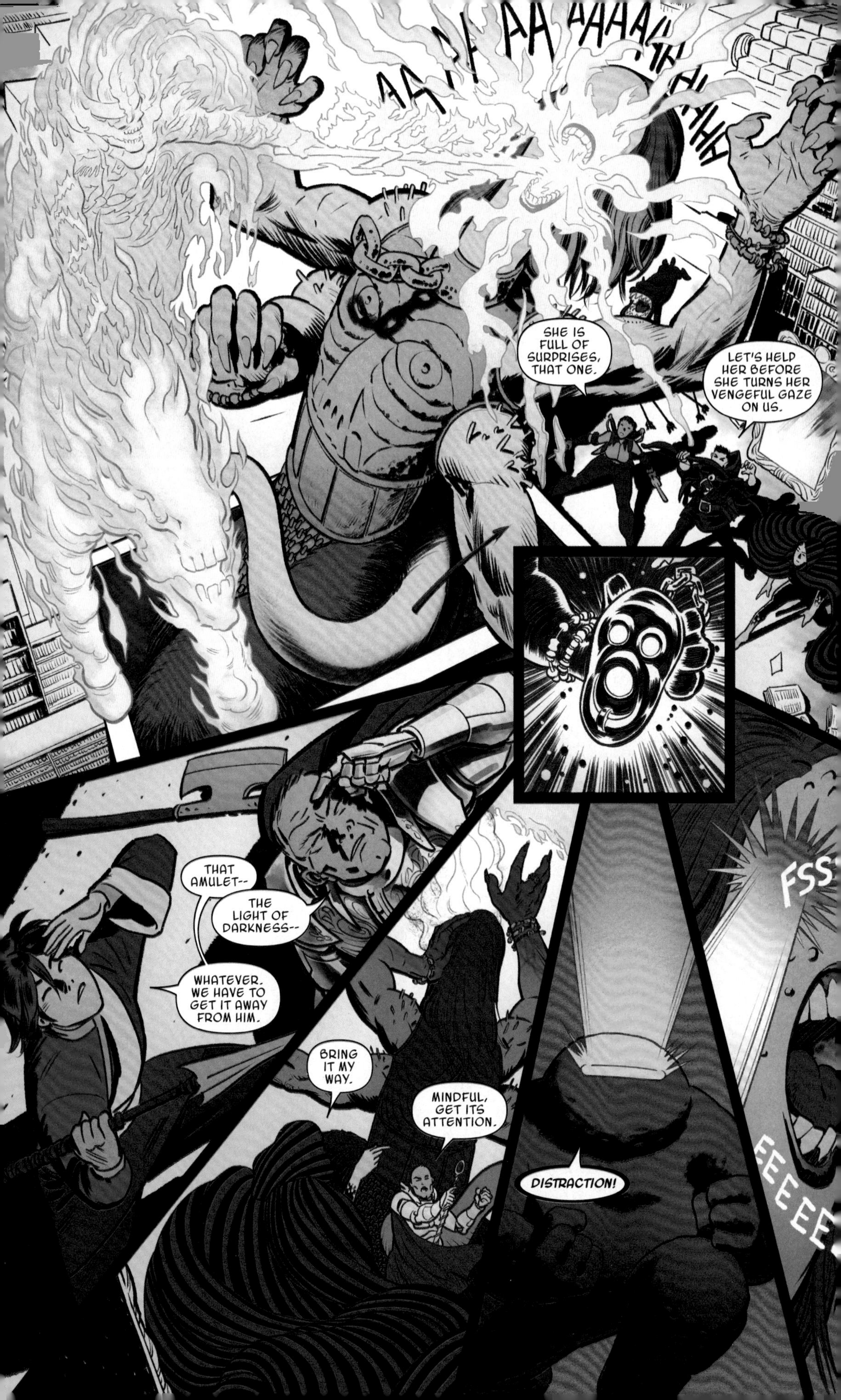
AAAAAAAAAAAHHHH
SHE IS FULL OF SURPRISES, THAT ONE.
LET'S HELP HER BEFORE SHE TURNS HER VENGEFUL GAZE ON US.
THAT AMULET--
THE LIGHT OF DARKNESS--
WHATEVER. WE HAVE TO GET IT AWAY FROM HIM.
BRING IT MY WAY.
MINDFUL, GET ITS ATTENTION.
DISTRACTION!
FSS
EEEEE

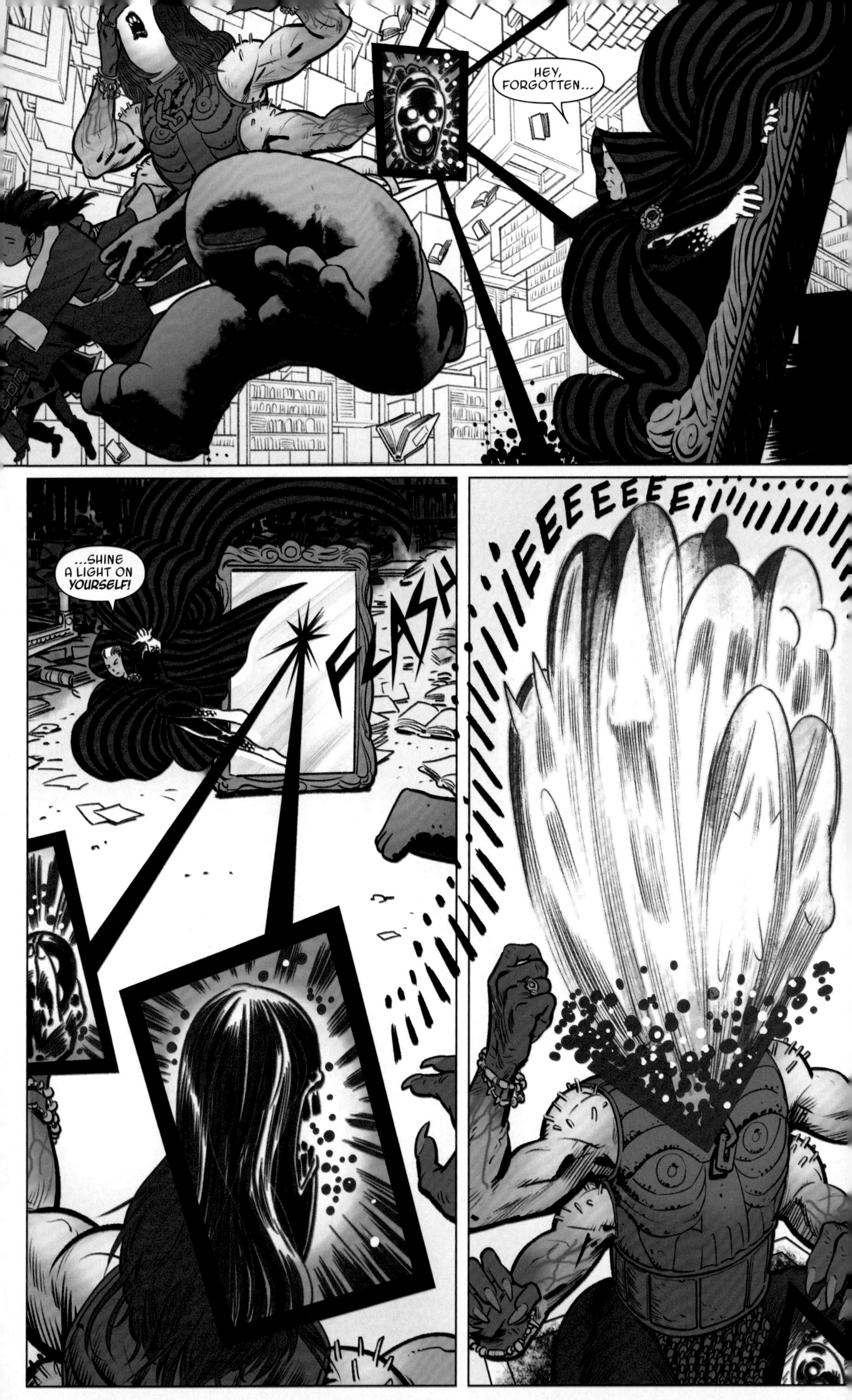
HEY, FORGOTTEN...
...SHINE A LIGHT ON YOURSELF!
FLASH
¡¡¡¡¡¡¡¡¡¡¡¡¡EEEEEEE¡¡¡¡¡¡¡¡¡

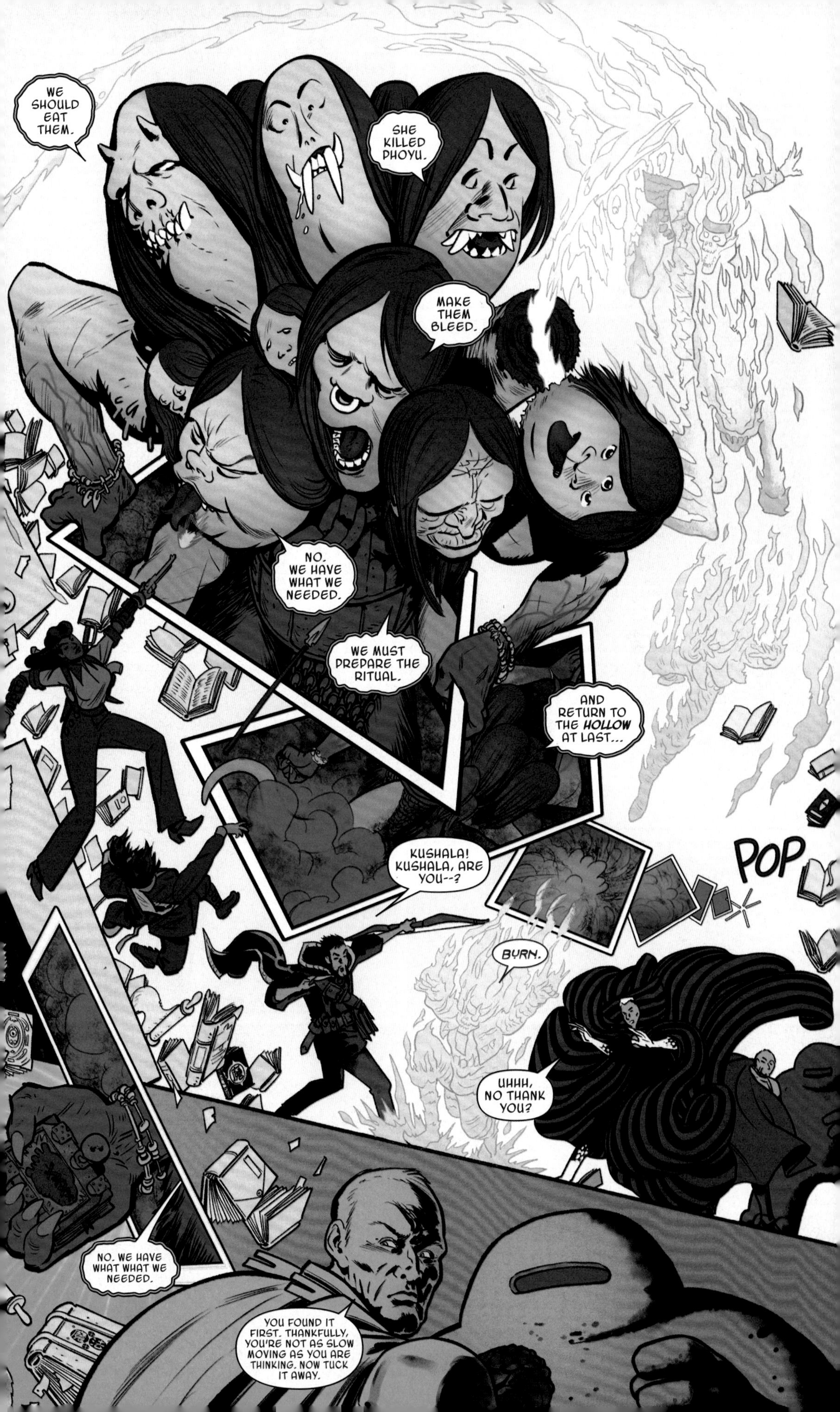
WE SHOULD EAT THEM.
SHE KILLED PHOYU.
MAKE THEM BLEED.
NO. WE HAVE WHAT WE NEEDED.
WE MUST PREPARE THE RITUAL.
AND RETURN TO THE HOLLOW AT LAST...
KUSHALA! KUSHALA, ARE YOU--?
POP
BURN.
UHHH, NO THANK YOU?
NO. WE HAVE WHAT WHAT WE NEEDED.
YOU FOUND IT FIRST. THANKFULLY, YOU'RE NOT AS SLOW MOVING AS YOU ARE THINKING. NOW TUCK IT AWAY.

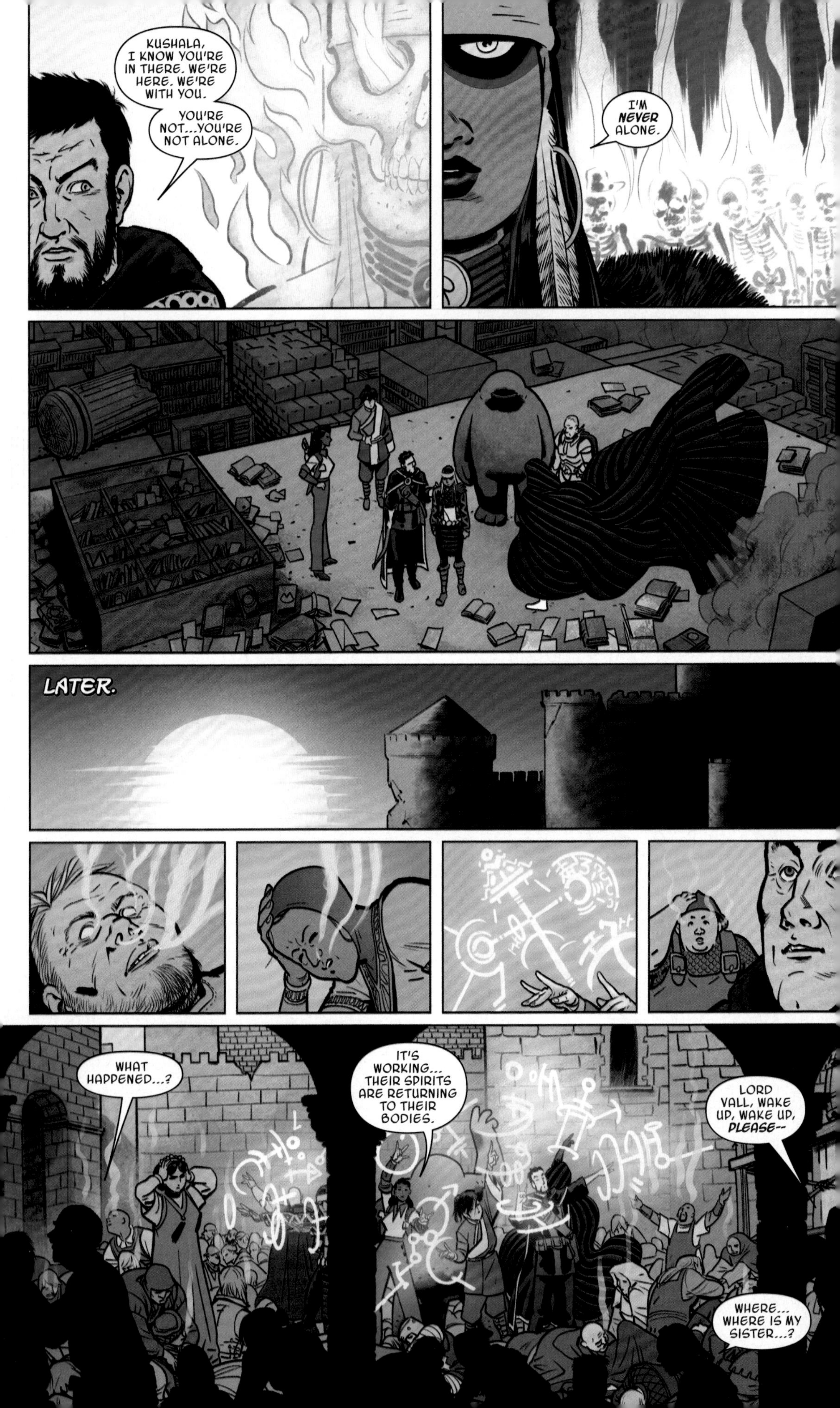
KUSHALA, I KNOW YOU'RE IN THERE. WE'RE HERE. WE'RE WITH YOU.
YOU'RE NOT...YOU'RE NOT ALONE.
I'M NEVER ALONE.
LATER.
WHAT HAPPENED...?
IT'S WORKING... THEIR SPIRITS ARE RETURNING TO THEIR BODIES.
LORD VALL, WAKE UP, WAKE UP, PLEASE--
WHERE... WHERE IS MY SISTER...?

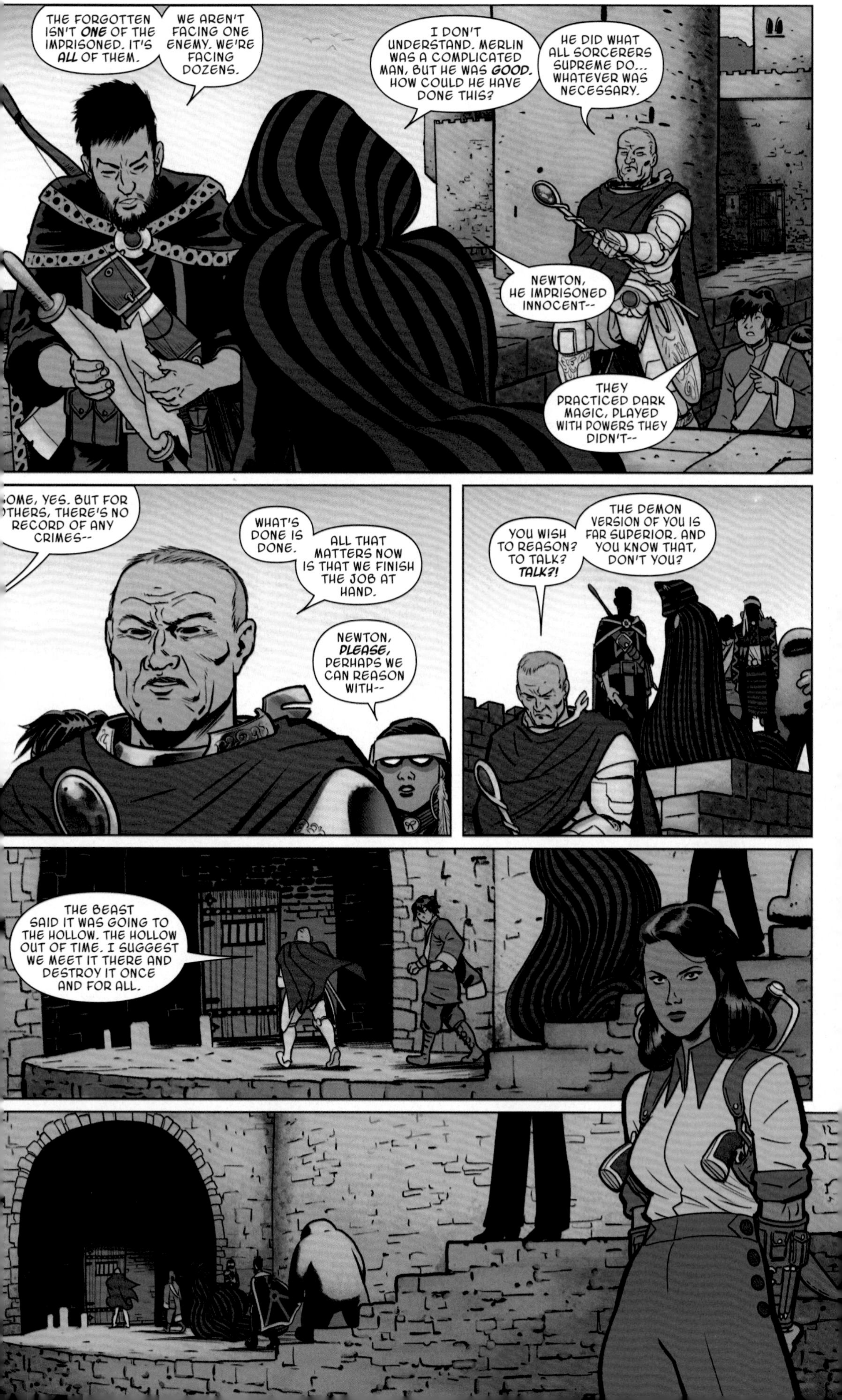
THE FORGOTTEN ISN'T ONE OF THE IMPRISONED. IT'S ALL OF THEM.
WE AREN'T FACING ONE ENEMY. WE'RE FACING DOZENS.
I DON'T UNDERSTAND. MERLIN WAS A COMPLICATED MAN, BUT HE WAS GOOD. HOW COULD HE HAVE DONE THIS?
HE DID WHAT ALL SORCERERS SUPREME DO... WHATEVER WAS NECESSARY.
NEWTON, HE IMPRISONED INNOCENT--
THEY PRACTICED DARK MAGIC, PLAYED WITH POWERS THEY DIDN'T--
SOME, YES. BUT FOR OTHERS, THERE'S NO RECORD OF ANY CRIMES--
WHAT'S DONE IS DONE.
ALL THAT MATTERS NOW IS THAT WE FINISH THE JOB AT HAND.
NEWTON, PLEASE, PERHAPS WE CAN REASON WITH--
YOU WISH TO REASON? TO TALK? TALK?!
THE DEMON VERSION OF YOU IS FAR SUPERIOR. AND YOU KNOW THAT, DON'T YOU?
THE BEAST SAID IT WAS GOING TO THE HOLLOW. THE HOLLOW OUT OF TIME. I SUGGEST WE MEET IT THERE AND DESTROY IT ONCE AND FOR ALL.

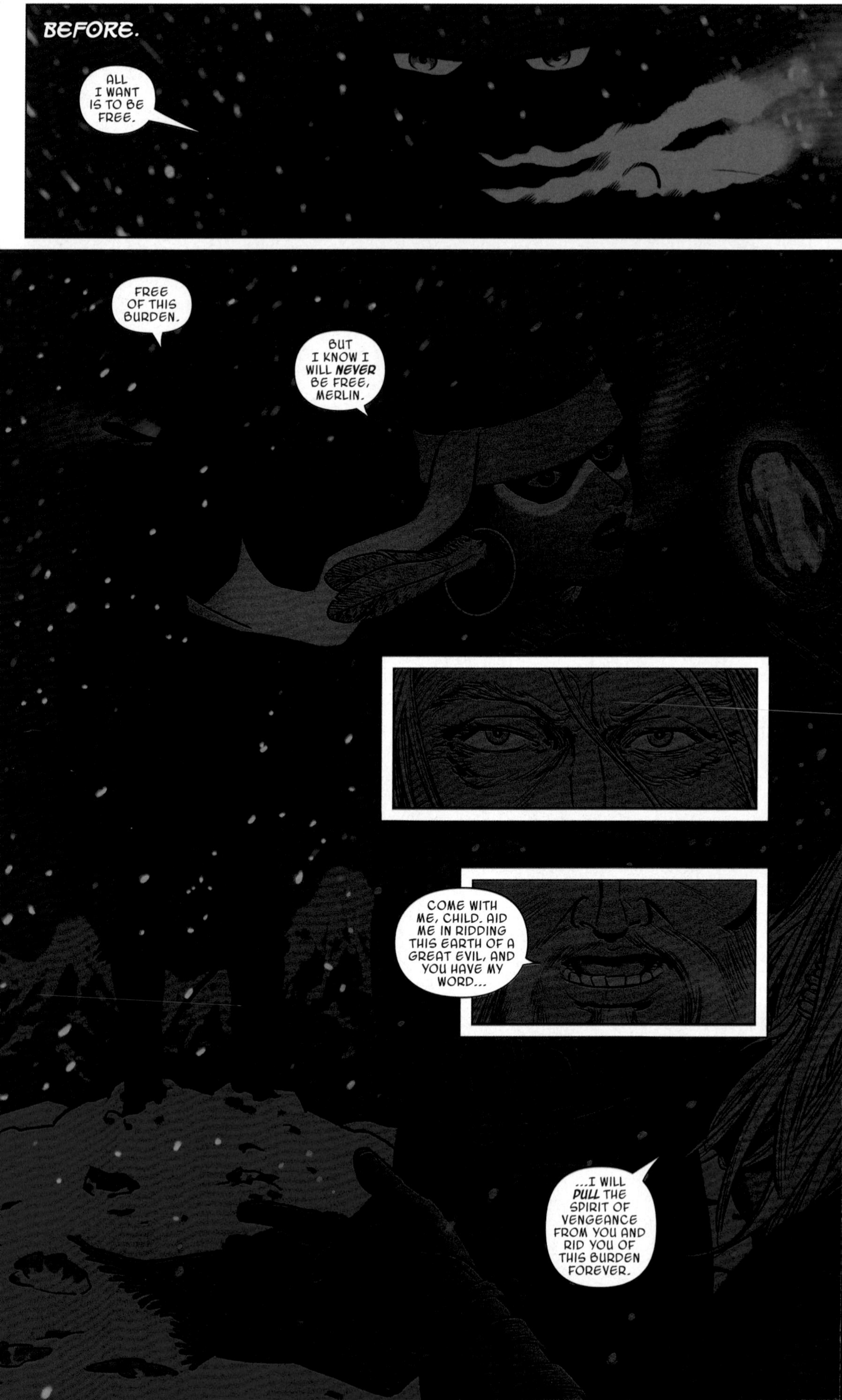
BEFORE.
ALL I WANT IS TO BE FREE.
FREE OF THIS BURDEN.
BUT I KNOW I WILL NEVER BE FREE, MERLIN.
COME WITH ME, CHILD. AID ME IN RIDDING THIS EARTH OF A GREAT EVIL, AND YOU HAVE MY WORD...
...I WILL PULL THE SPIRIT OF VENGEANCE FROM YOU AND RID YOU OF THIS BURDEN FOREVER.

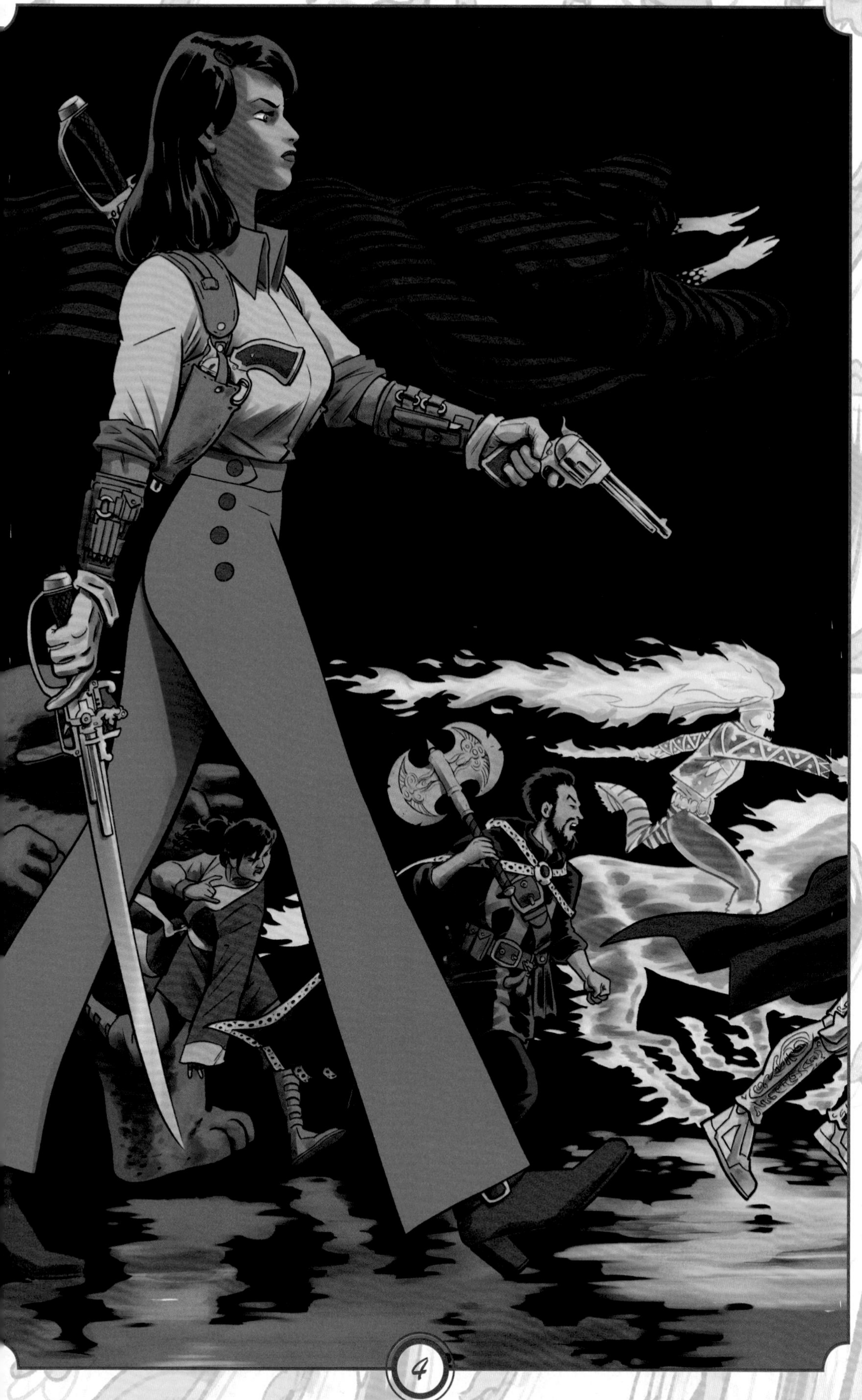

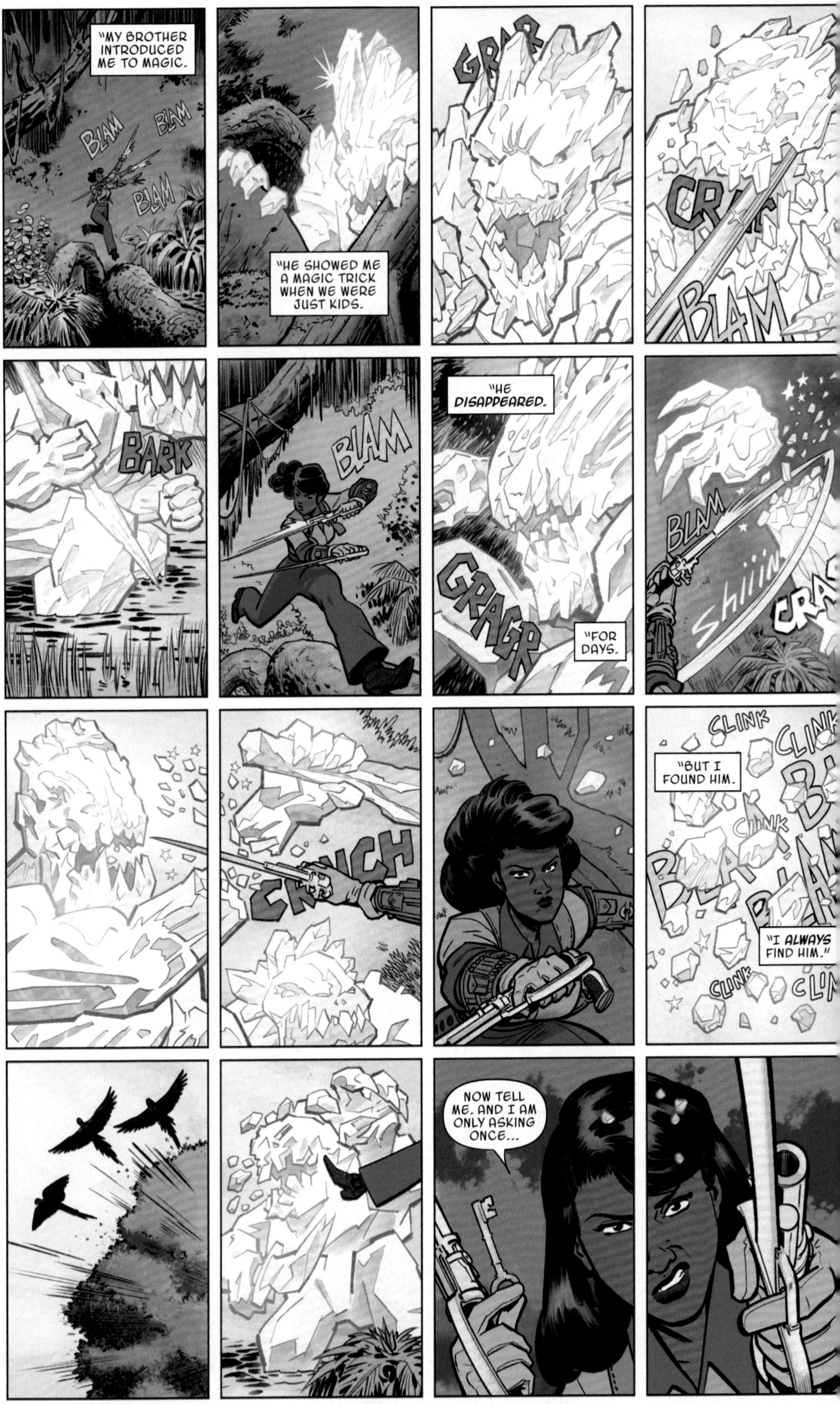
"MY BROTHER INTRODUCED ME TO MAGIC.
BLAM
BLAM
BLAM
"HE SHOWED ME A MAGIC TRICK WHEN WE WERE JUST KIDS.
GRAR
BLAM
BARK
BLAM
"HE DISAPPEARED.
GRAGR
"FOR DAYS.
BLAM
Shiiiin
CRUNCH
CLINK
"BUT I FOUND HIM.
CLINK
"I ALWAYS FIND HIM."
CLINK
NOW TELL ME. AND I AM ONLY ASKING ONCE...

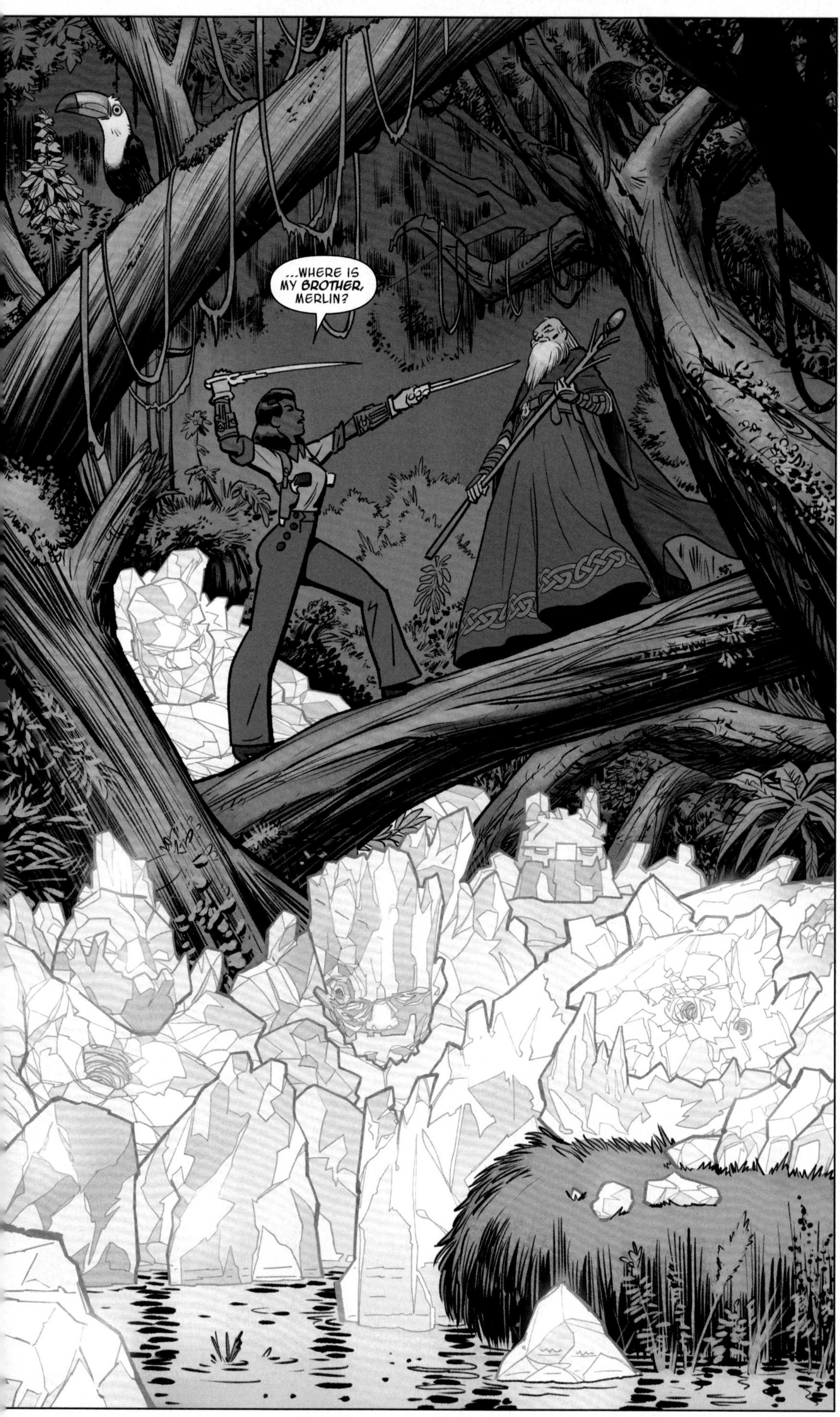
...WHERE IS MY BROTHER, MERLIN?

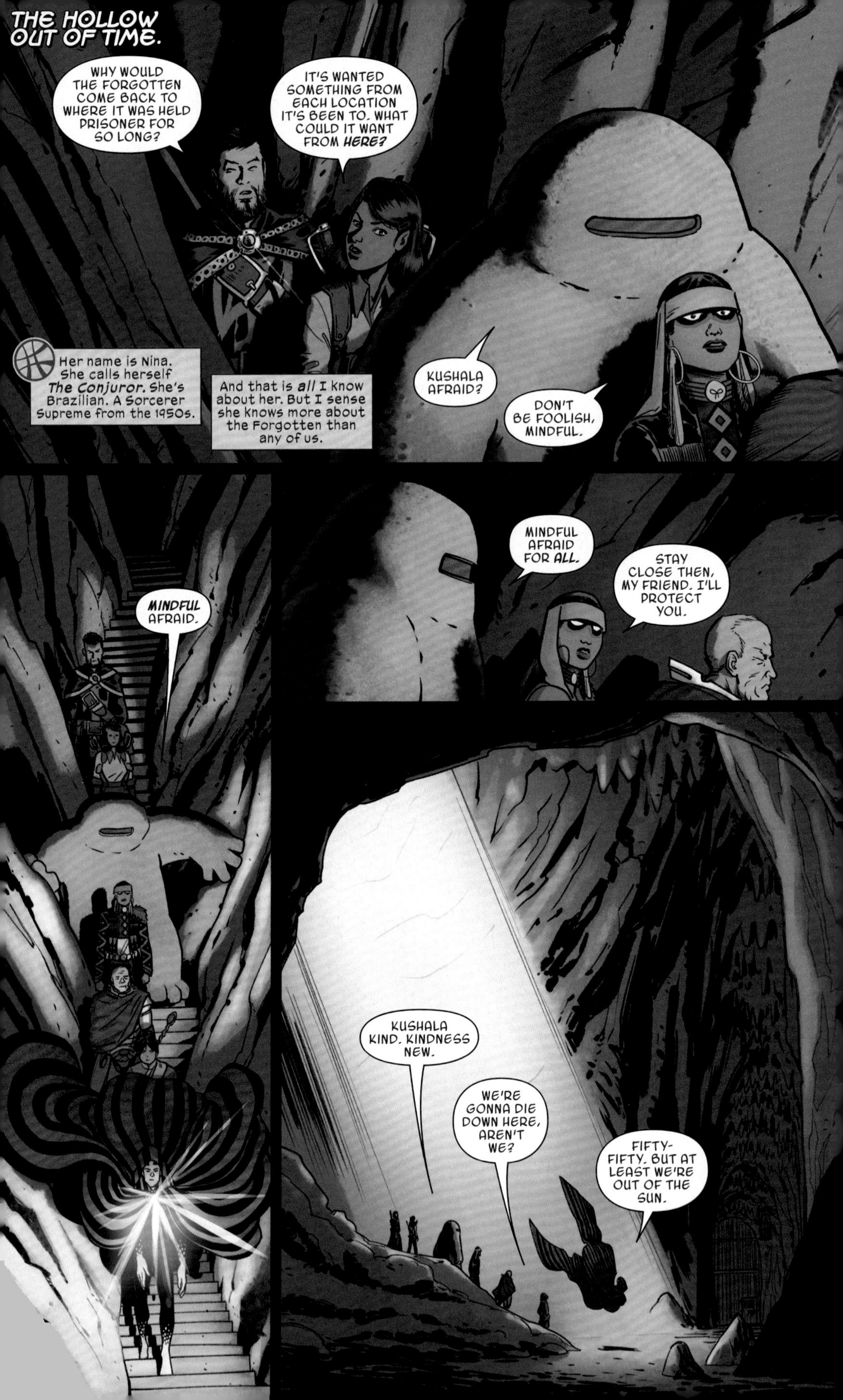
THE HOLLOW OUT OF TIME.
WHY WOULD THE FORGOTTEN COME BACK TO WHERE IT WAS HELD PRISONER FOR SO LONG?
IT'S WANTED SOMETHING FROM EACH LOCATION IT'S BEEN TO. WHAT COULD IT WANT FROM *HERE?*
Her name is Nina. She calls herself *The Conjuror.* She's Brazilian. A Sorcerer Supreme from the 1950s.
And that is *all* I know about her. But I sense she knows more about the Forgotten than any of us.
KUSHALA AFRAID?
DON'T BE FOOLISH, MINDFUL.
MINDFUL AFRAID.
MINDFUL AFRAID FOR *ALL.*
STAY CLOSE THEN, MY FRIEND. I'LL PROTECT YOU.
KUSHALA KIND. KINDNESS NEW.
WE'RE GONNA DIE DOWN HERE, AREN'T WE?
FIFTY-FIFTY. BUT AT LEAST WE'RE OUT OF THE SUN.

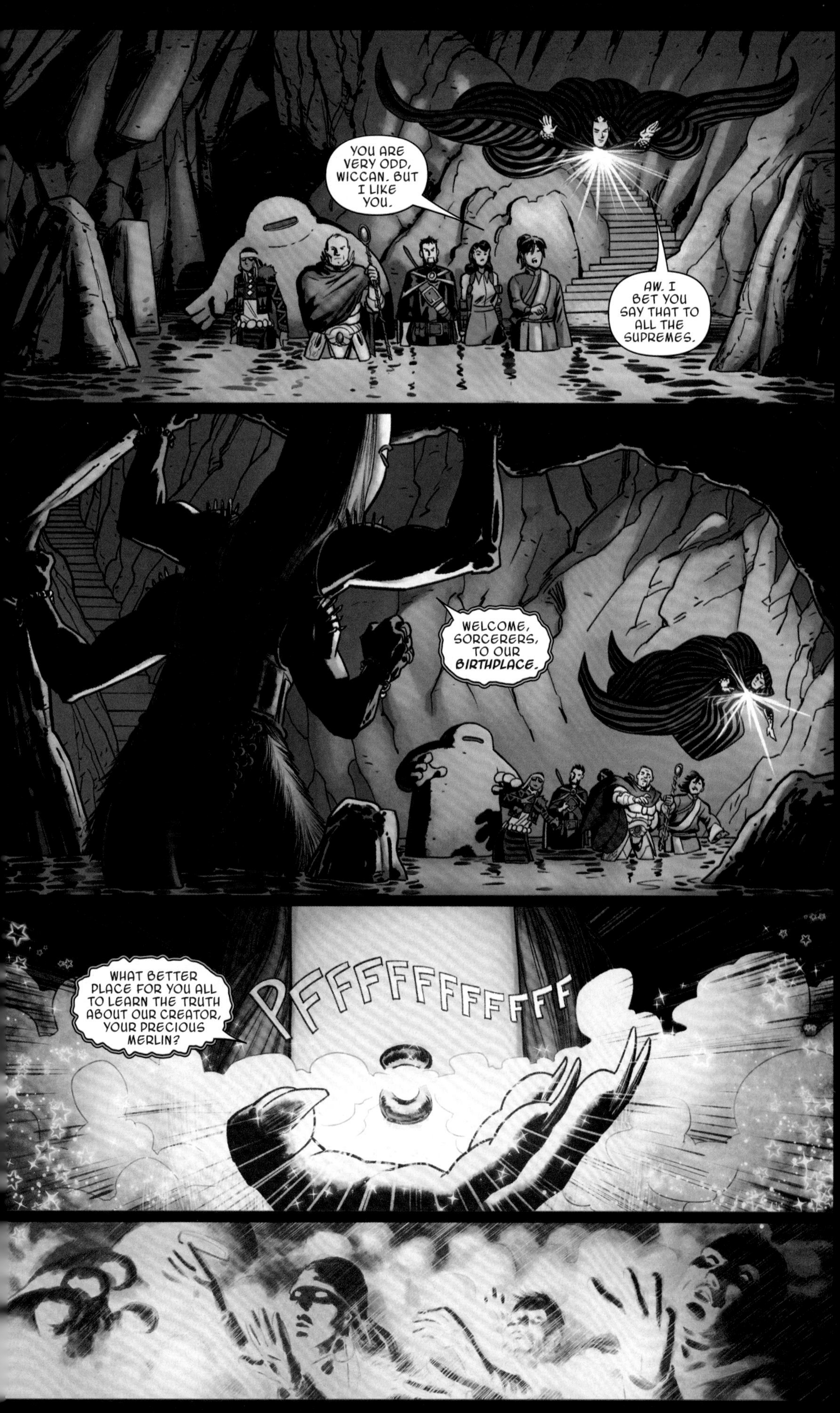
YOU ARE VERY ODD, WICCAN. BUT I LIKE YOU.
AW. I BET YOU SAY THAT TO ALL THE SUPREMES.
WELCOME, SORCERERS, TO OUR BIRTHPLACE.
WHAT BETTER PLACE FOR YOU ALL TO LEARN THE TRUTH ABOUT OUR CREATOR, YOUR PRECIOUS MERLIN?
PFFFFFFFFFFFF

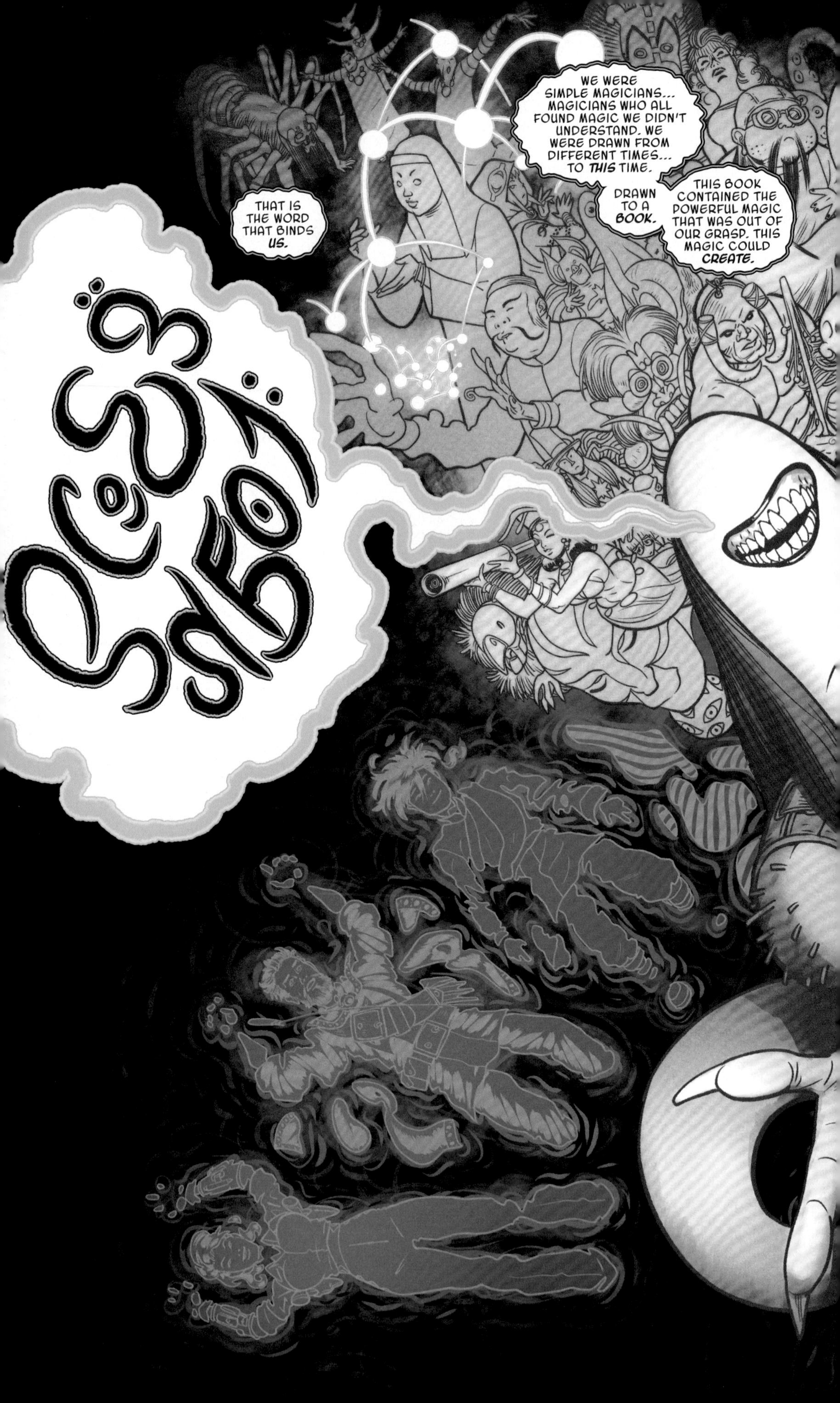
WE WERE SIMPLE MAGICIANS... MAGICIANS WHO ALL FOUND MAGIC WE DIDN'T UNDERSTAND. WE WERE DRAWN FROM DIFFERENT TIMES... TO THIS TIME.
DRAWN TO A BOOK.
THIS BOOK CONTAINED THE POWERFUL MAGIC THAT WAS OUT OF OUR GRASP. THIS MAGIC COULD CREATE.
THAT IS THE WORD THAT BINDS US.

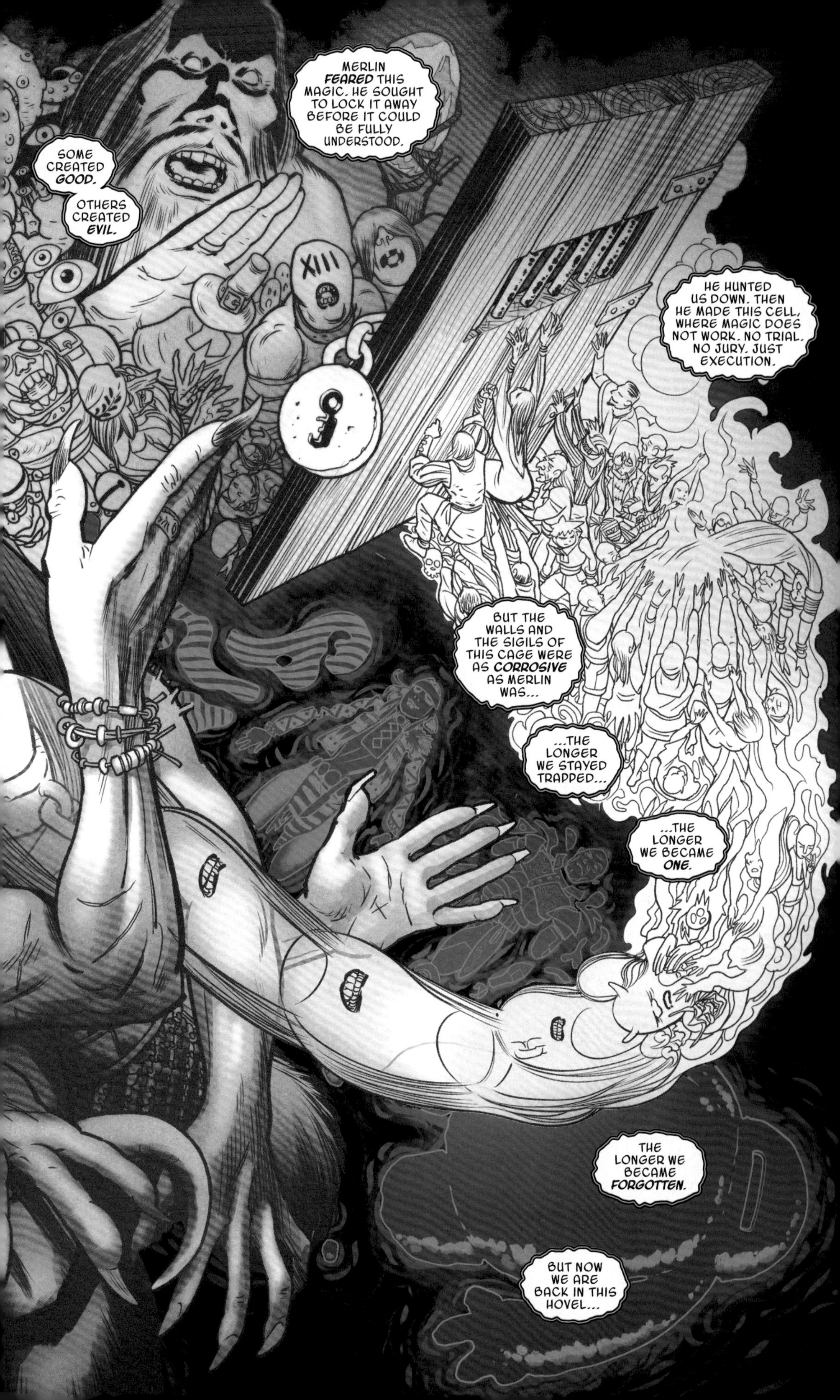

SOME CREATED GOOD.
OTHERS CREATED EVIL.
MERLIN FEARED THIS MAGIC. HE SOUGHT TO LOCK IT AWAY BEFORE IT COULD BE FULLY UNDERSTOOD.
XIII
HE HUNTED US DOWN. THEN HE MADE THIS CELL, WHERE MAGIC DOES NOT WORK. NO TRIAL. NO JURY. JUST EXECUTION.
BUT THE WALLS AND THE SIGILS OF THIS CAGE WERE AS CORROSIVE AS MERLIN WAS...
...THE LONGER WE STAYED TRAPPED...
...THE LONGER WE BECAME ONE.
THE LONGER WE BECAME FORGOTTEN.
BUT NOW WE ARE BACK IN THIS HOVEL...

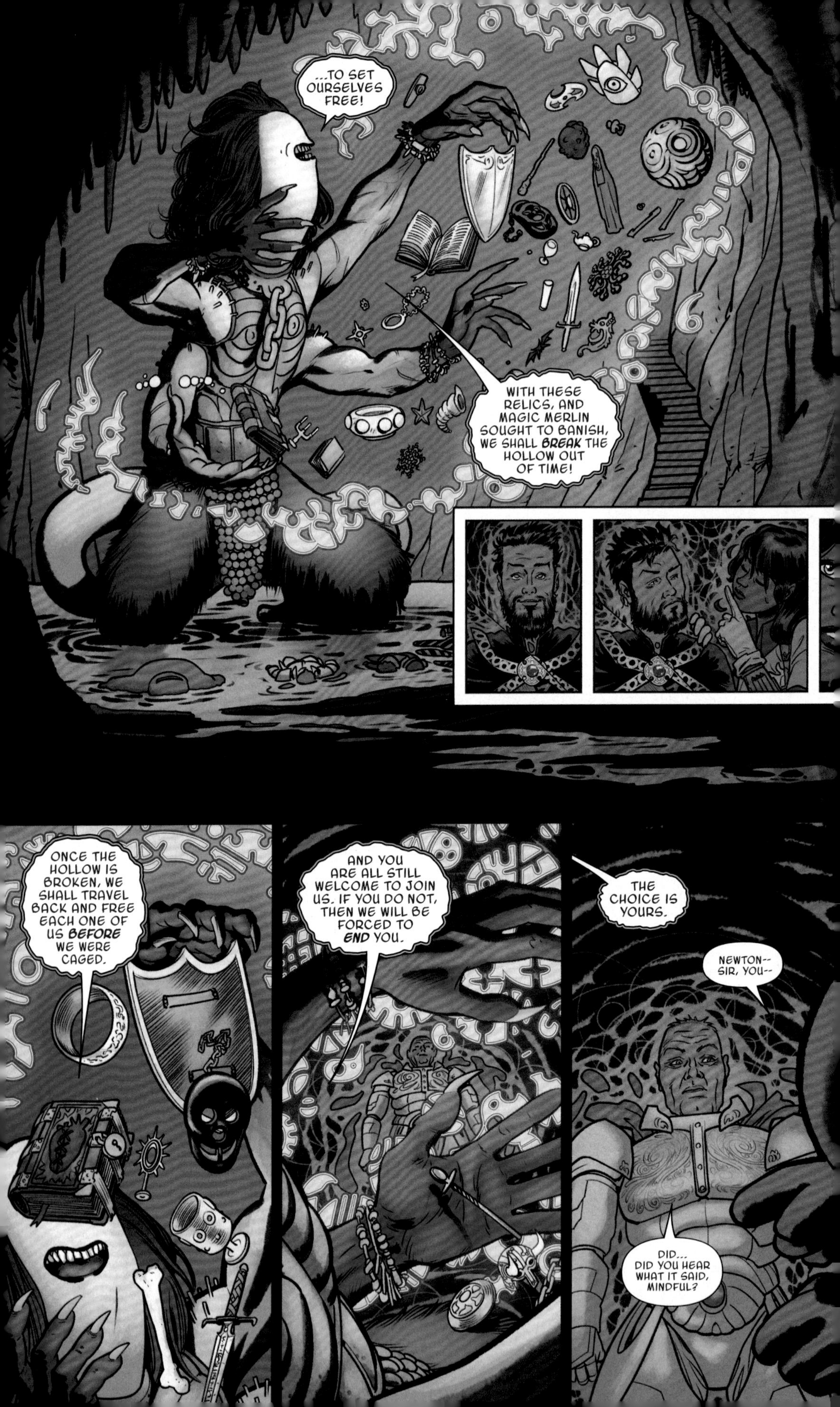
...TO SET OURSELVES FREE!
WITH THESE RELICS, AND MAGIC MERLIN SOUGHT TO BANISH, WE SHALL BREAK THE HOLLOW OUT OF TIME!
ONCE THE HOLLOW IS BROKEN, WE SHALL TRAVEL BACK AND FREE EACH ONE OF US BEFORE WE WERE CAGED.
AND YOU ARE ALL STILL WELCOME TO JOIN US. IF YOU DO NOT, THEN WE WILL BE FORCED TO END YOU.
THE CHOICE IS YOURS.
NEWTON-- SIR, YOU--
DID... DID YOU HEAR WHAT IT SAID, MINDFUL?

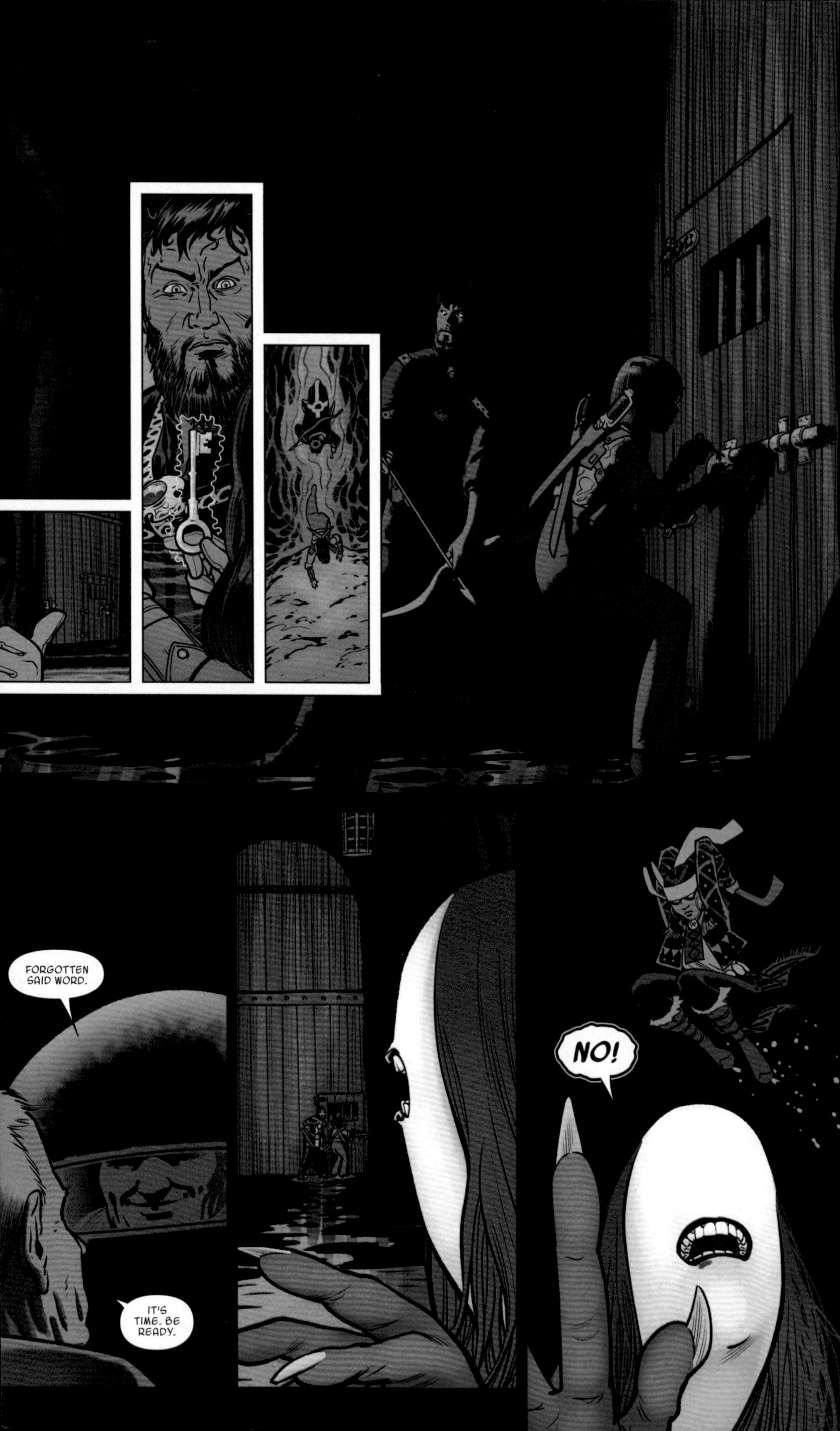
FORGOTTEN SAID WORD.
IT'S TIME. BE READY.
NO!

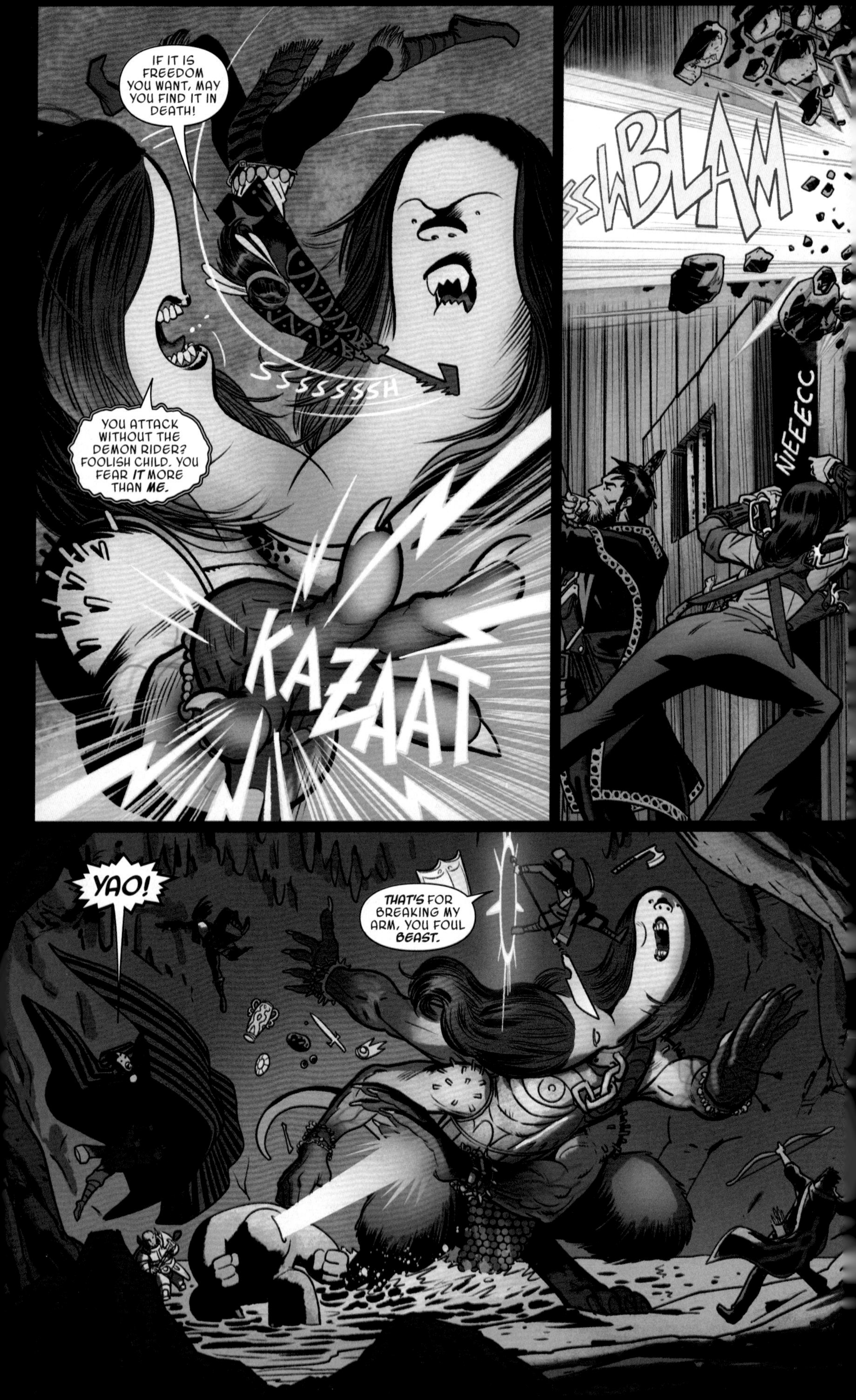
IF IT IS FREEDOM YOU WANT, MAY YOU FIND IT IN DEATH!
SSSSSSSH
YOU ATTACK WITHOUT THE DEMON RIDER? FOOLISH CHILD. YOU FEAR IT MORE THAN ME.
KAZAAT
SSWBLAM
NIEEECC
YAO!
THAT'S FOR BREAKING MY ARM, YOU FOUL BEAST.

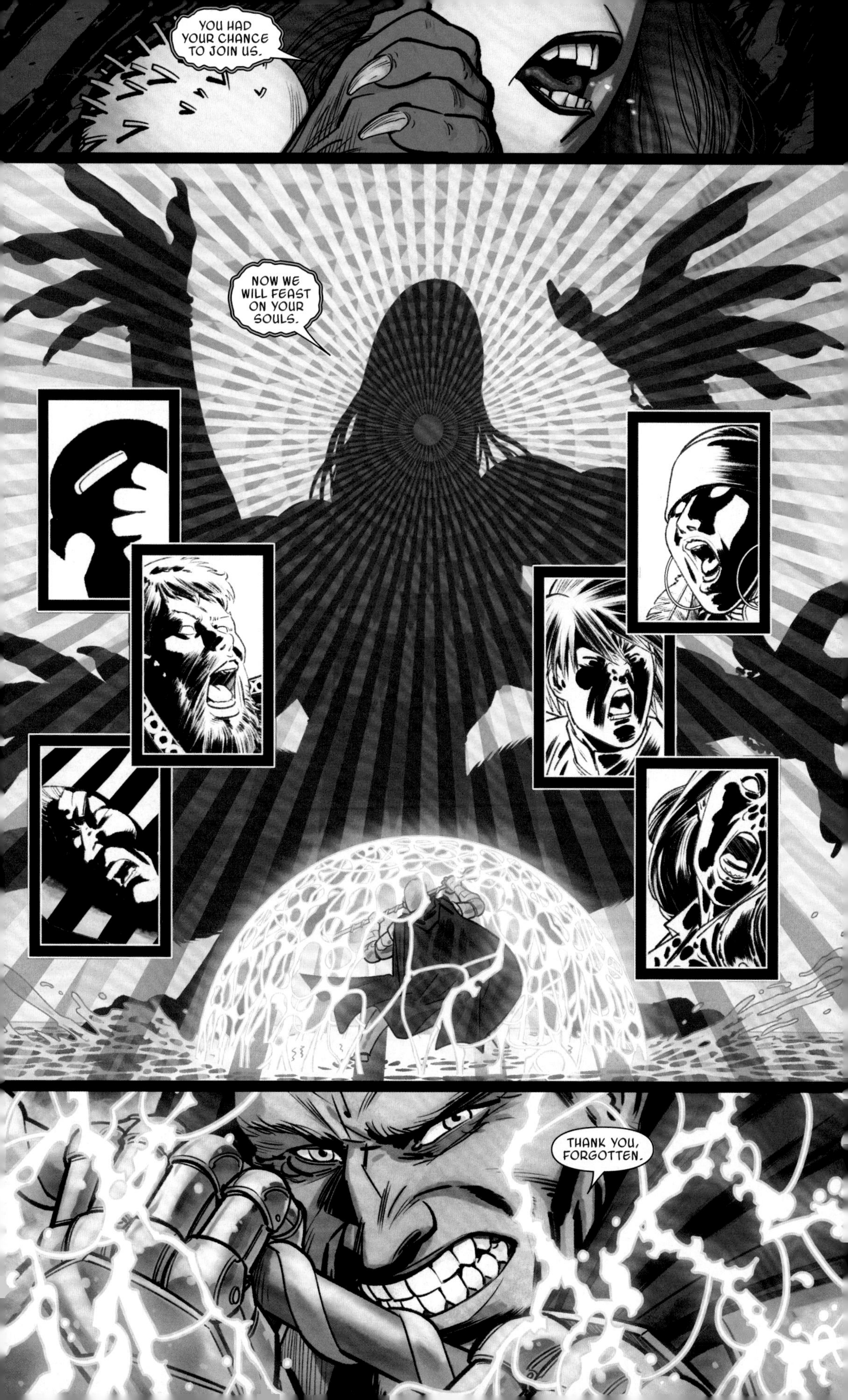
YOU HAD YOUR CHANCE TO JOIN US.
NOW WE WILL FEAST ON YOUR SOULS.
THANK YOU, FORGOTTEN.

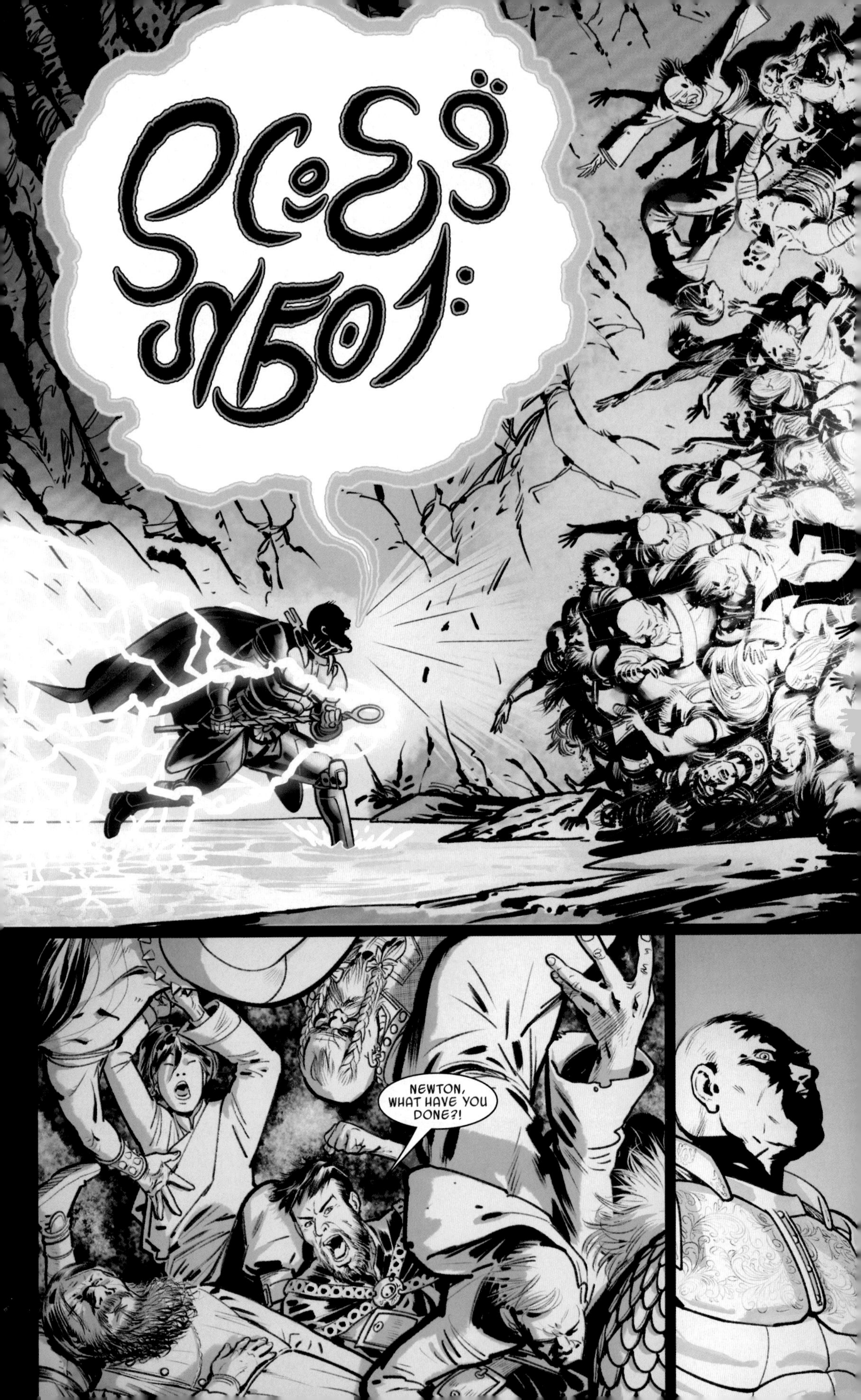
NEWTON, WHAT HAVE YOU DONE?!

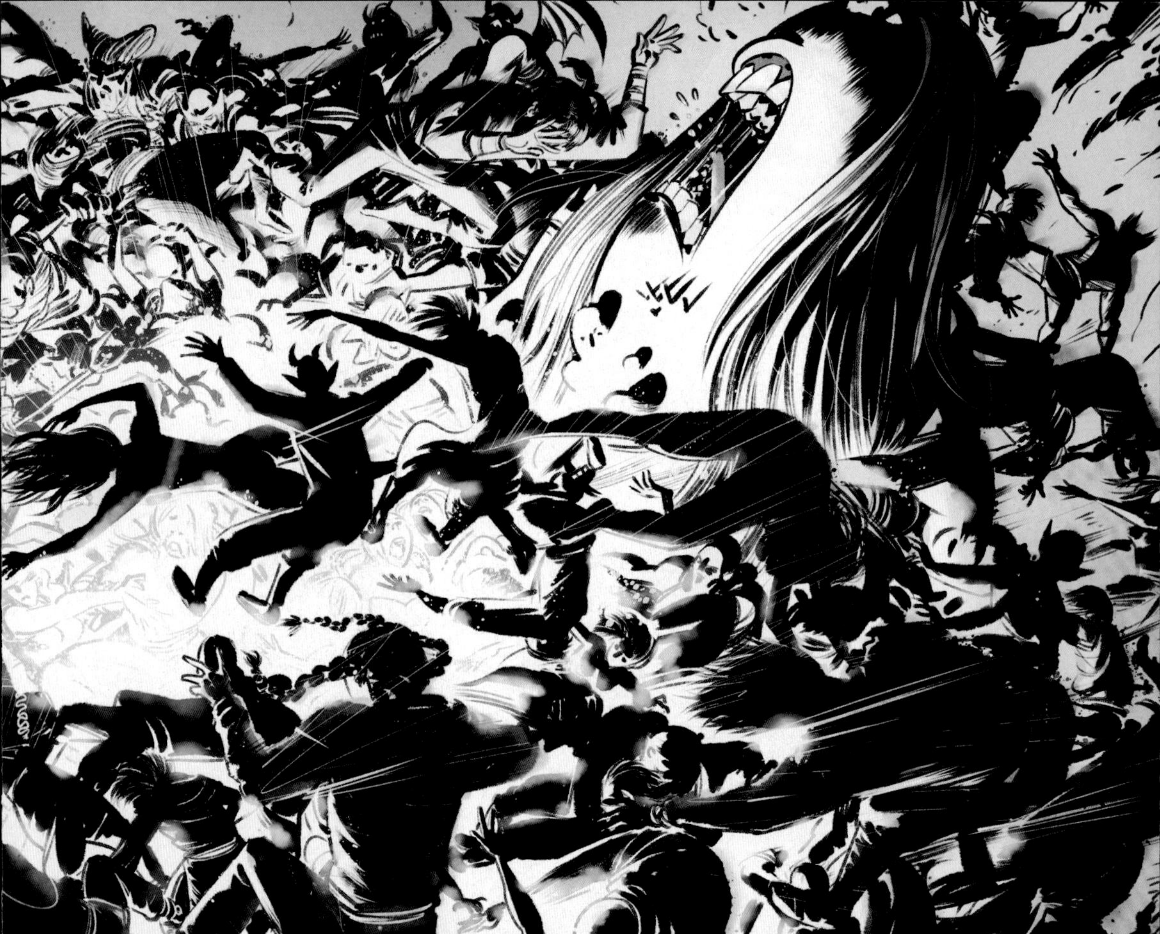

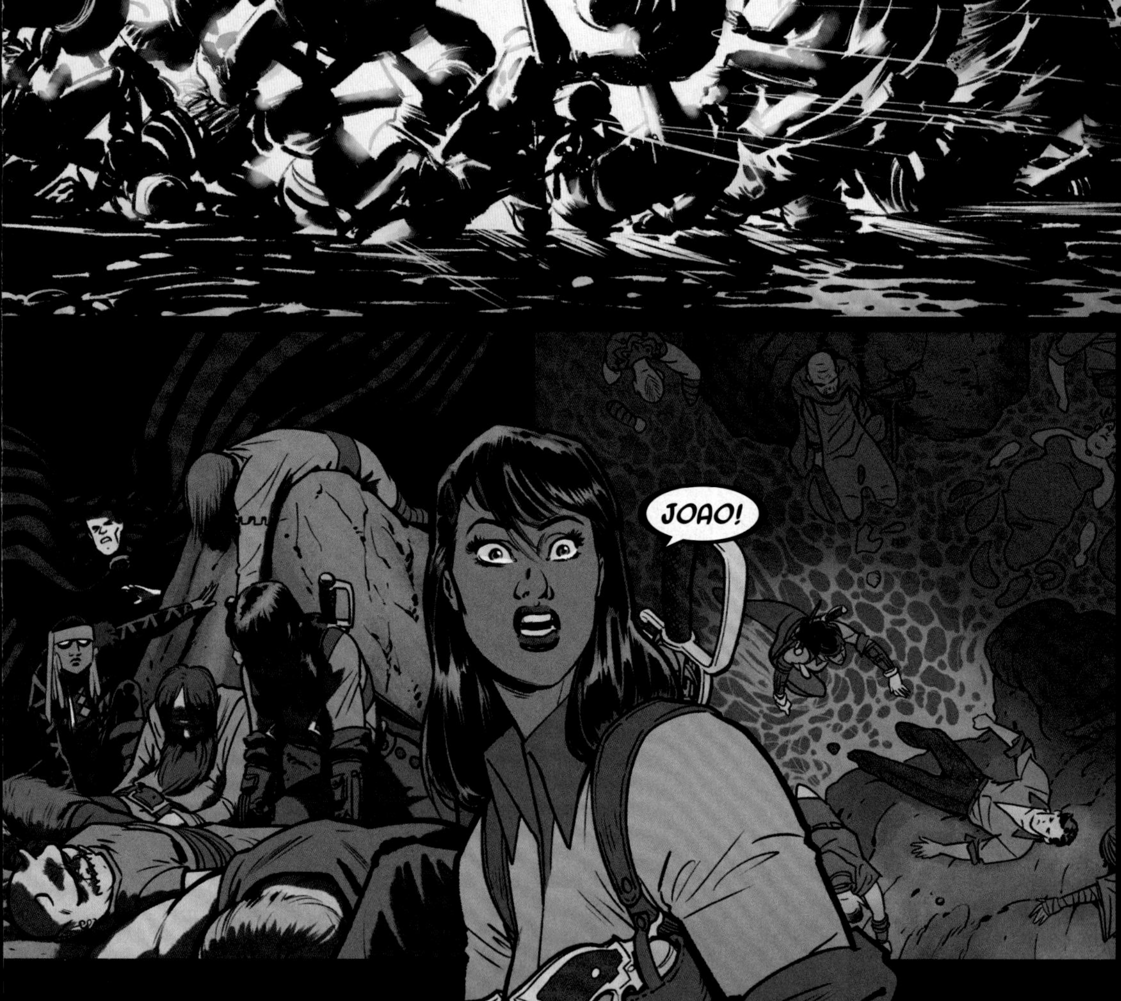
JOAO!

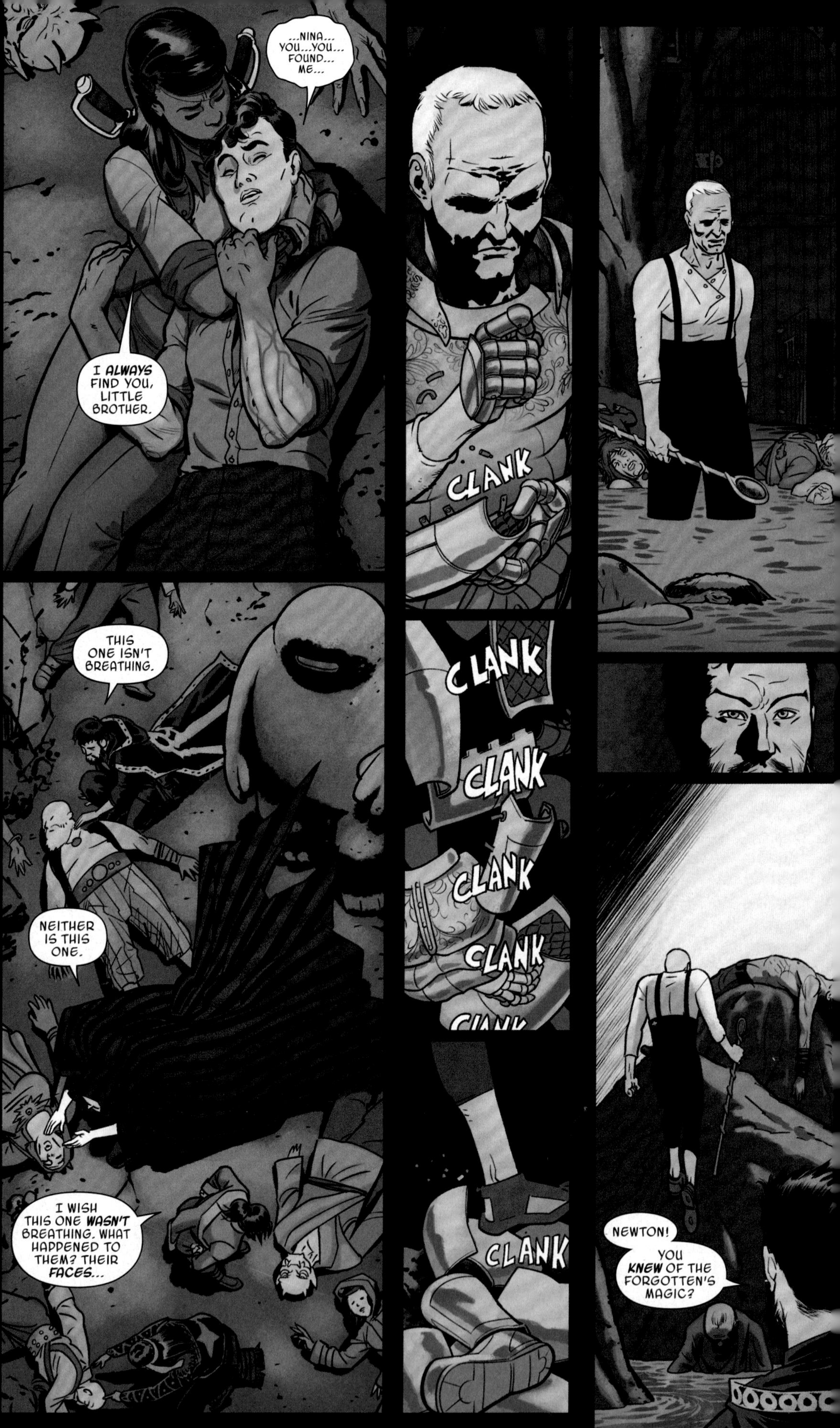
...NINA... YOU...YOU... FOUND... ME...
I ALWAYS FIND YOU, LITTLE BROTHER.
CLANK
THIS ONE ISN'T BREATHING.
NEITHER IS THIS ONE.
I WISH THIS ONE WASN'T BREATHING. WHAT HAPPENED TO THEM? THEIR FACES...
CLANK
CLANK
CLANK
CLANK
CLANK
NEWTON!
YOU KNEW OF THE FORGOTTEN'S MAGIC?

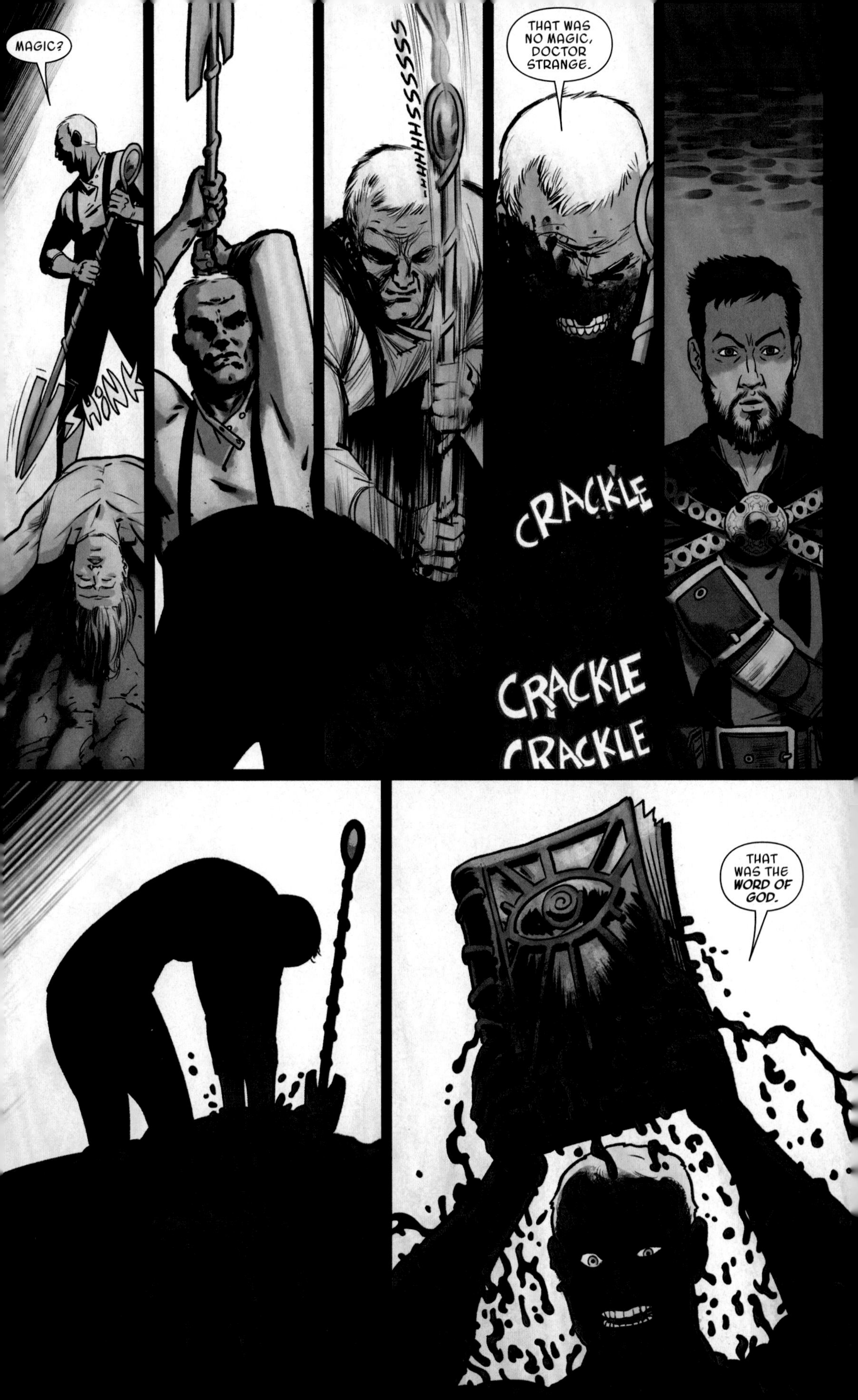
MAGIC?
SHONK
SSSSSSHHHHH—
THAT WAS NO MAGIC, DOCTOR STRANGE.
CRACKLE
CRACKLE
CRACKLE
THAT WAS THE WORD OF GOD.

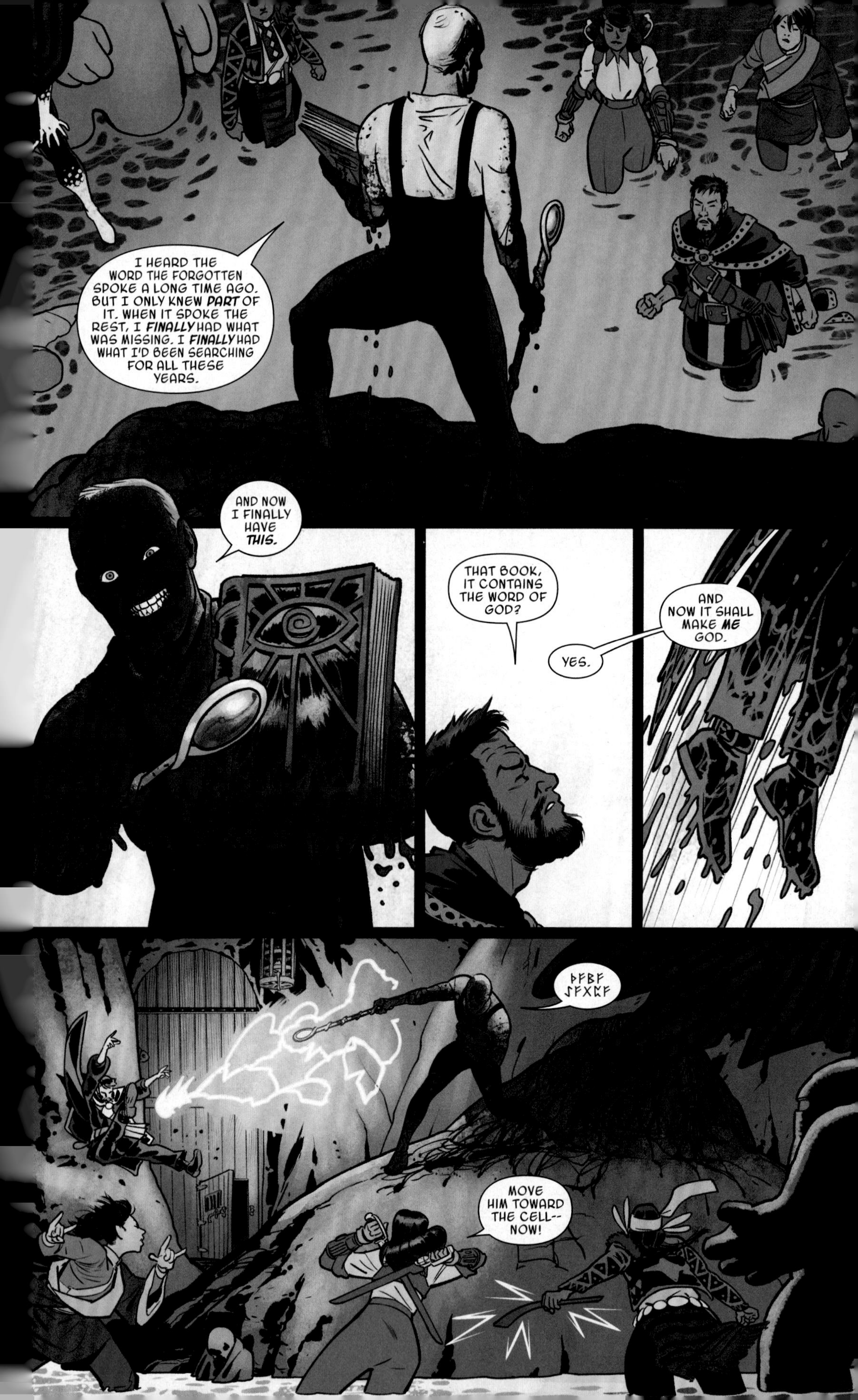
I HEARD THE WORD THE FORGOTTEN SPOKE A LONG TIME AGO. BUT I ONLY KNEW PART OF IT. WHEN IT SPOKE THE REST, I FINALLY HAD WHAT WAS MISSING. I FINALLY HAD WHAT I'D BEEN SEARCHING FOR ALL THESE YEARS.
AND NOW I FINALLY HAVE THIS.
THAT BOOK, IT CONTAINS THE WORD OF GOD?
YES.
AND NOW IT SHALL MAKE ME GOD.
MOVE HIM TOWARD THE CELL-- NOW!

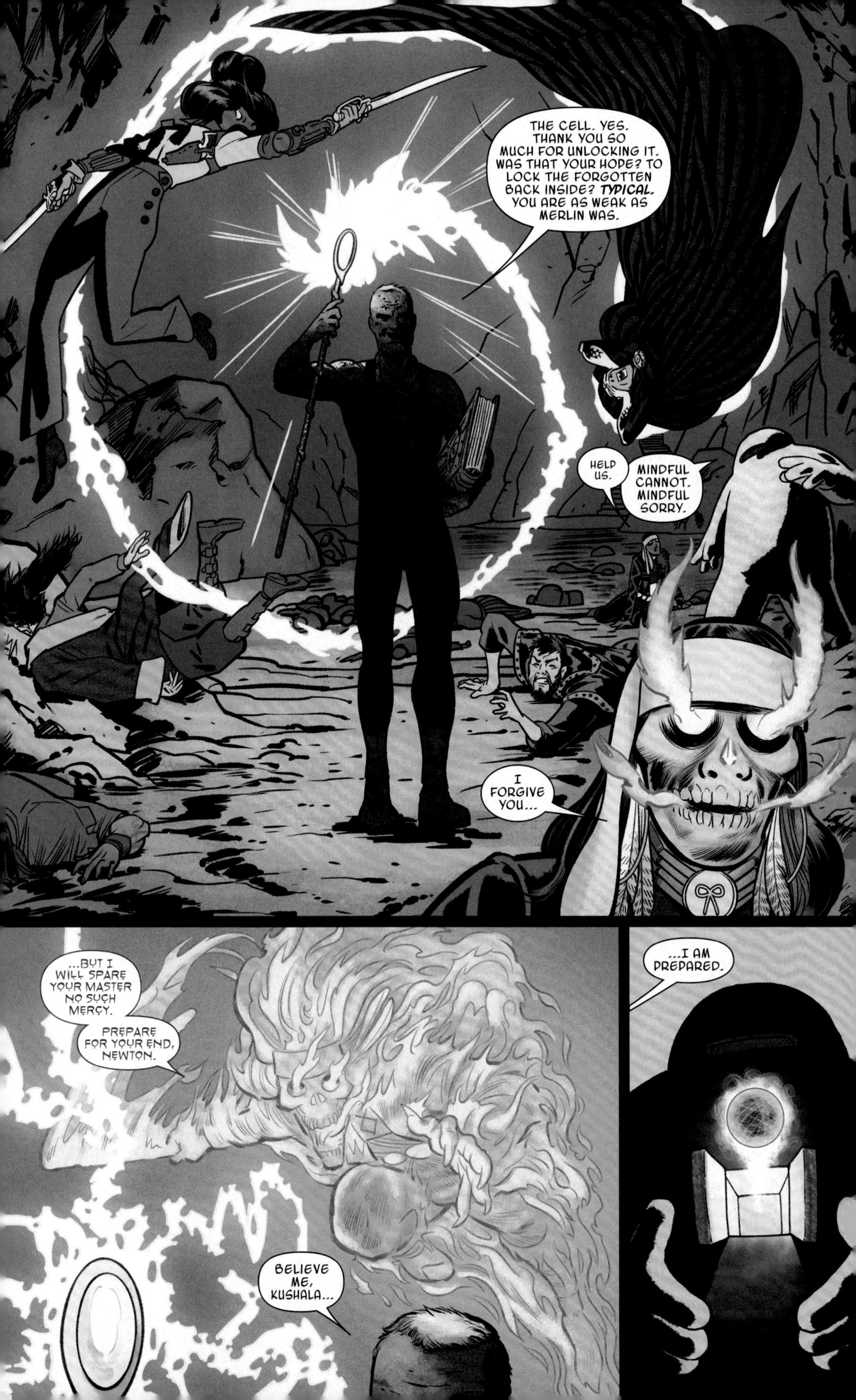
THE CELL. YES. THANK YOU SO MUCH FOR UNLOCKING IT. WAS THAT YOUR HOPE? TO LOCK THE FORGOTTEN BACK INSIDE? TYPICAL. YOU ARE AS WEAK AS MERLIN WAS.
HELD US.
MINDFUL CANNOT. MINDFUL SORRY.
I FORGIVE YOU...
...BUT I WILL SPARE YOUR MASTER NO SUCH MERCY.
PREPARE FOR YOUR END, NEWTON.
BELIEVE ME, KUSHALA...
...I AM PREPARED.

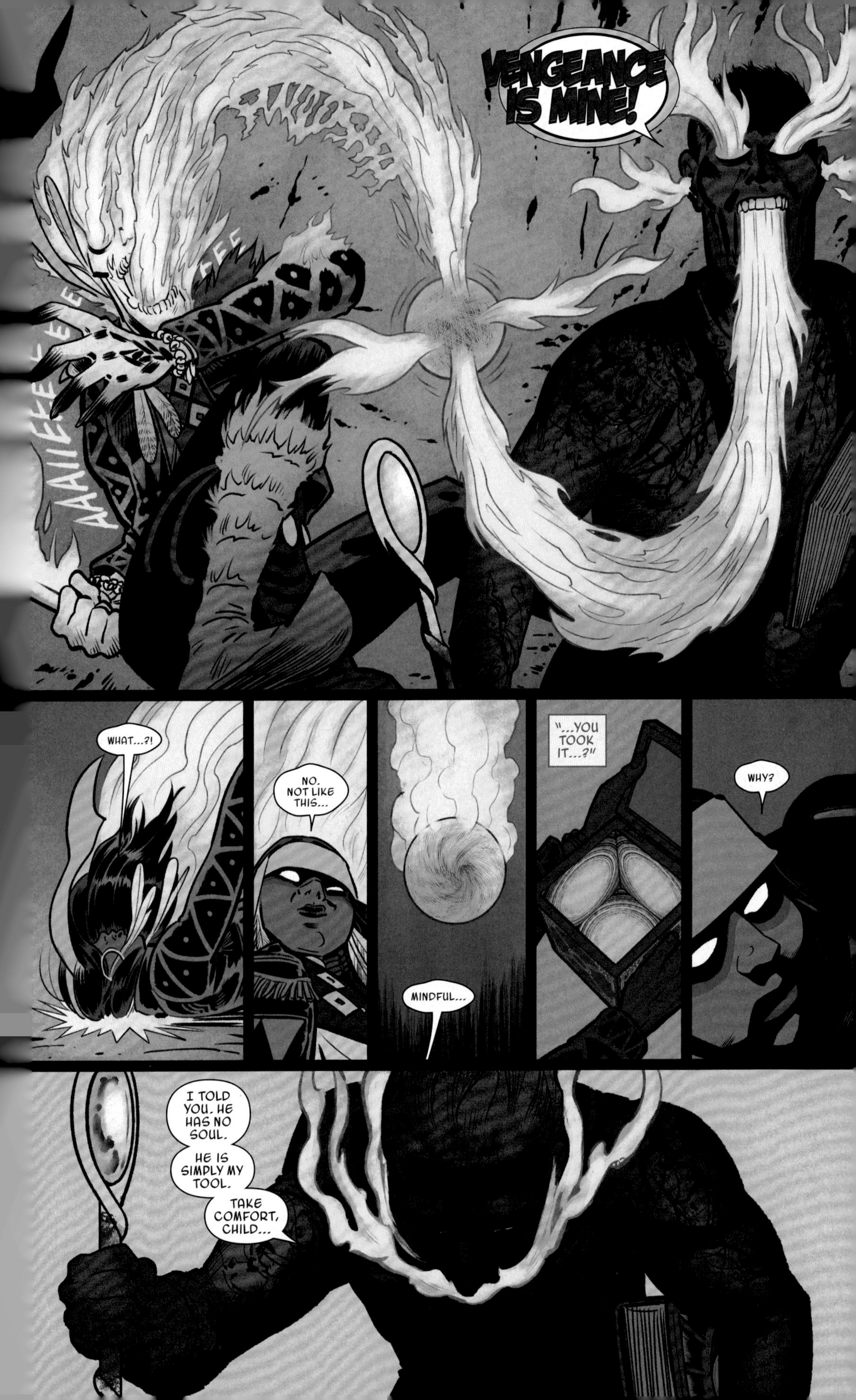
VENGEANCE IS MINE!
AAAIIEEEEEEEEE
WHAT...?!
NO. NOT LIKE THIS...
MINDFUL...
"...YOU TOOK IT...?"
WHY?
I TOLD YOU. HE HAS NO SOUL.
HE IS SIMPLY MY TOOL.
TAKE COMFORT, CHILD...

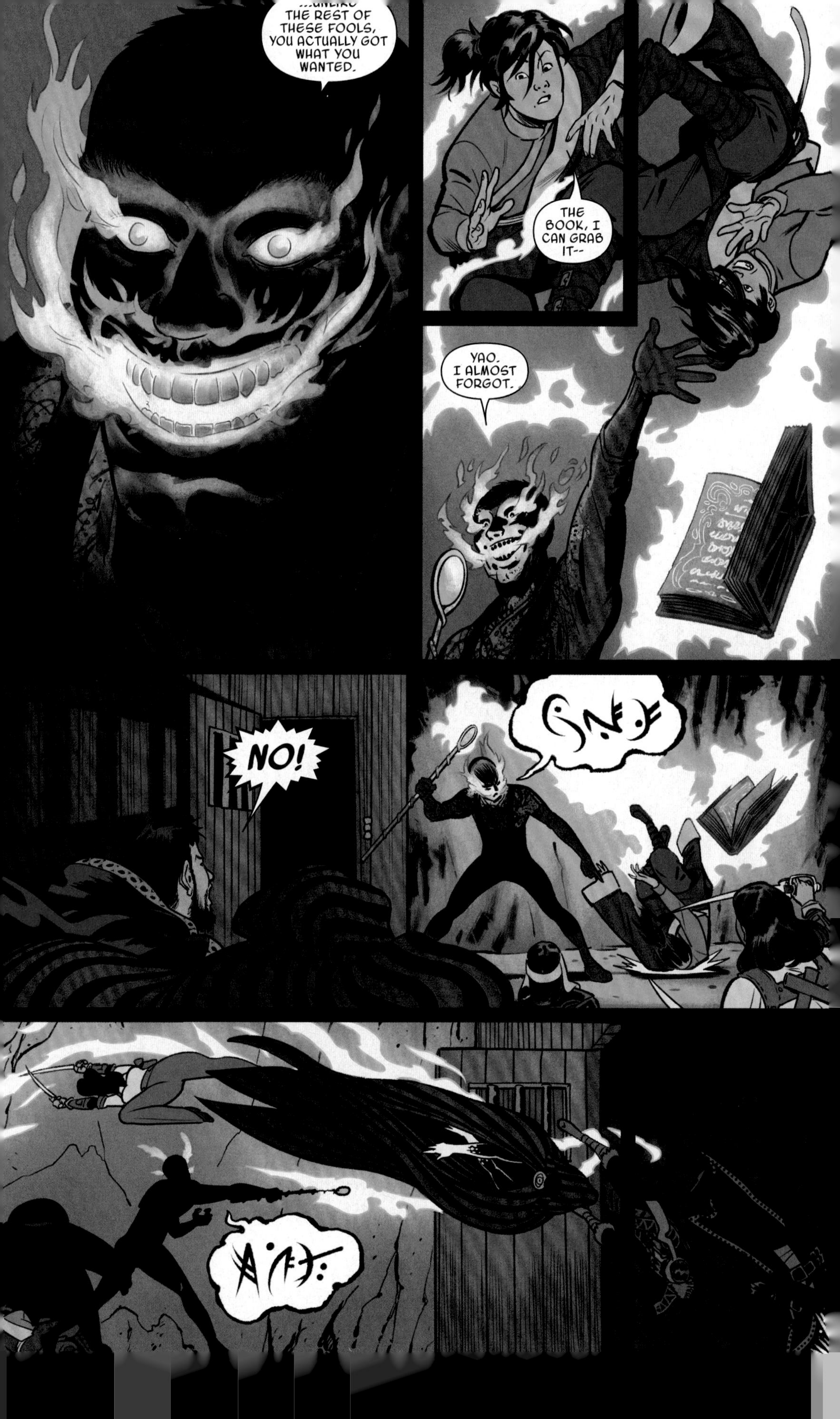
...UNLIKE THE REST OF THESE FOOLS, YOU ACTUALLY GOT WHAT YOU WANTED.
THE BOOK, I CAN GRAB IT--
YAO. I ALMOST FORGOT.
NO!

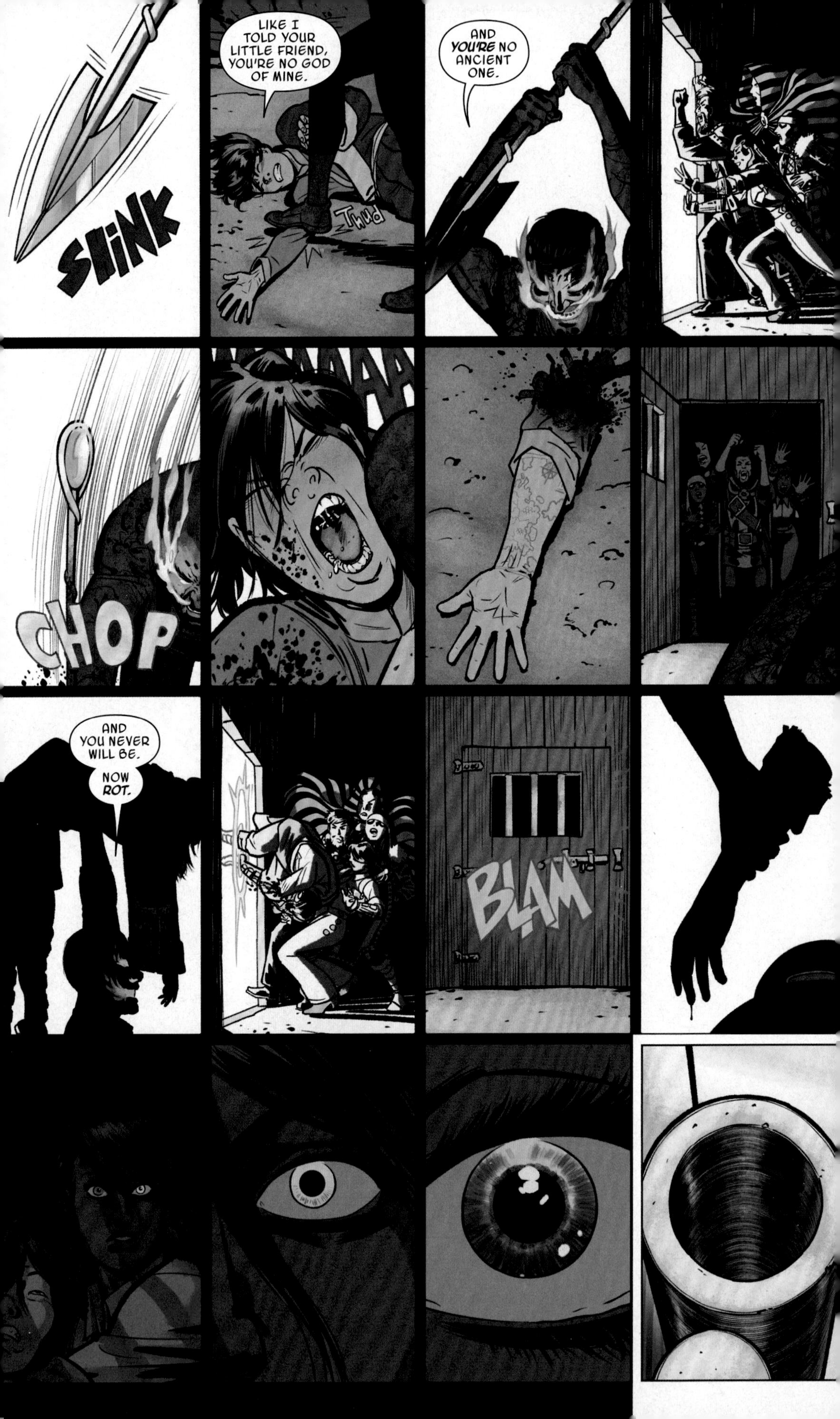
SHINK
LIKE I TOLD YOUR LITTLE FRIEND, YOU'RE NO GOD OF MINE.
THUD
AND *YOU'RE* NO ANCIENT ONE.
CHOP
AND YOU NEVER WILL BE.
NOW *ROT*.
BLAM

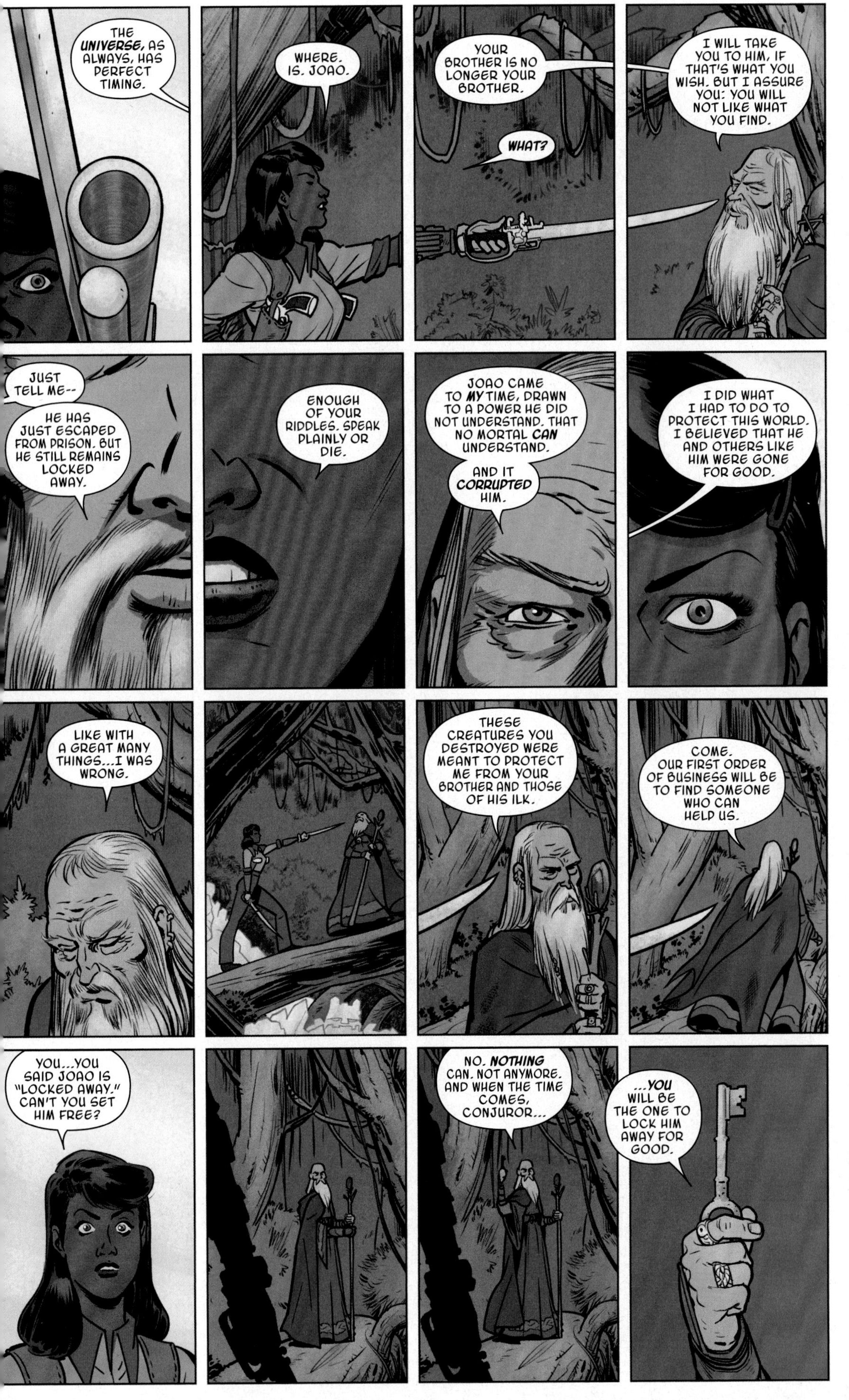

THE UNIVERSE, AS ALWAYS, HAS PERFECT TIMING.
WHERE. IS. JOAO.
YOUR BROTHER IS NO LONGER YOUR BROTHER.
WHAT?
I WILL TAKE YOU TO HIM, IF THAT'S WHAT YOU WISH. BUT I ASSURE YOU: YOU WILL NOT LIKE WHAT YOU FIND.
JUST TELL ME--
HE HAS JUST ESCAPED FROM PRISON. BUT HE STILL REMAINS LOCKED AWAY.
ENOUGH OF YOUR RIDDLES. SPEAK PLAINLY OR DIE.
JOAO CAME TO MY TIME, DRAWN TO A POWER HE DID NOT UNDERSTAND. THAT NO MORTAL CAN UNDERSTAND.
AND IT CORRUPTED HIM.
I DID WHAT I HAD TO DO TO PROTECT THIS WORLD. I BELIEVED THAT HE AND OTHERS LIKE HIM WERE GONE FOR GOOD.
LIKE WITH A GREAT MANY THINGS...I WAS WRONG.
THESE CREATURES YOU DESTROYED WERE MEANT TO PROTECT ME FROM YOUR BROTHER AND THOSE OF HIS ILK.
COME. OUR FIRST ORDER OF BUSINESS WILL BE TO FIND SOMEONE WHO CAN HELP US.
YOU...YOU SAID JOAO IS "LOCKED AWAY." CAN'T YOU SET HIM FREE?
NO. NOTHING CAN. NOT ANYMORE. AND WHEN THE TIME COMES, CONJUROR...
...YOU WILL BE THE ONE TO LOCK HIM AWAY FOR GOOD.

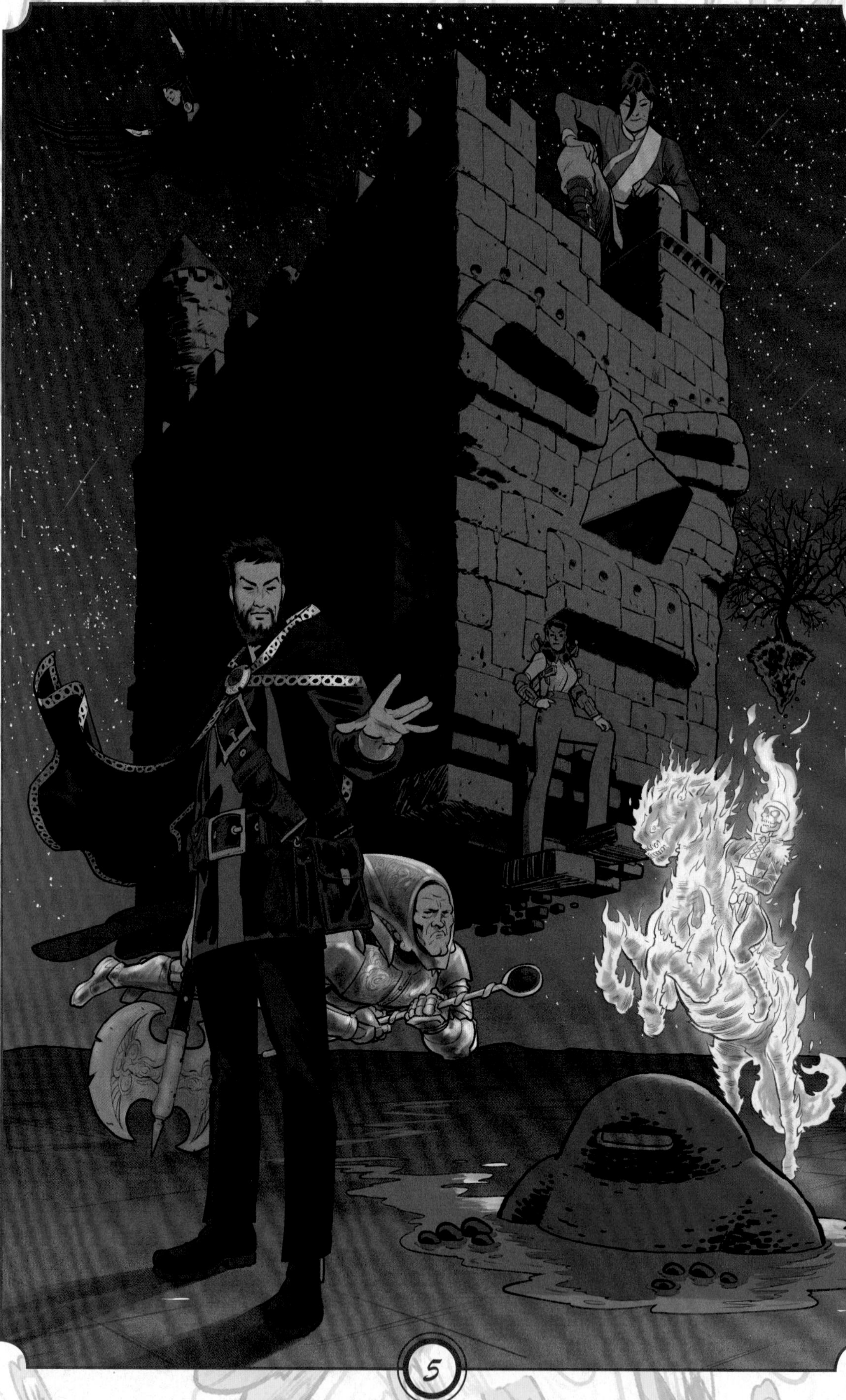

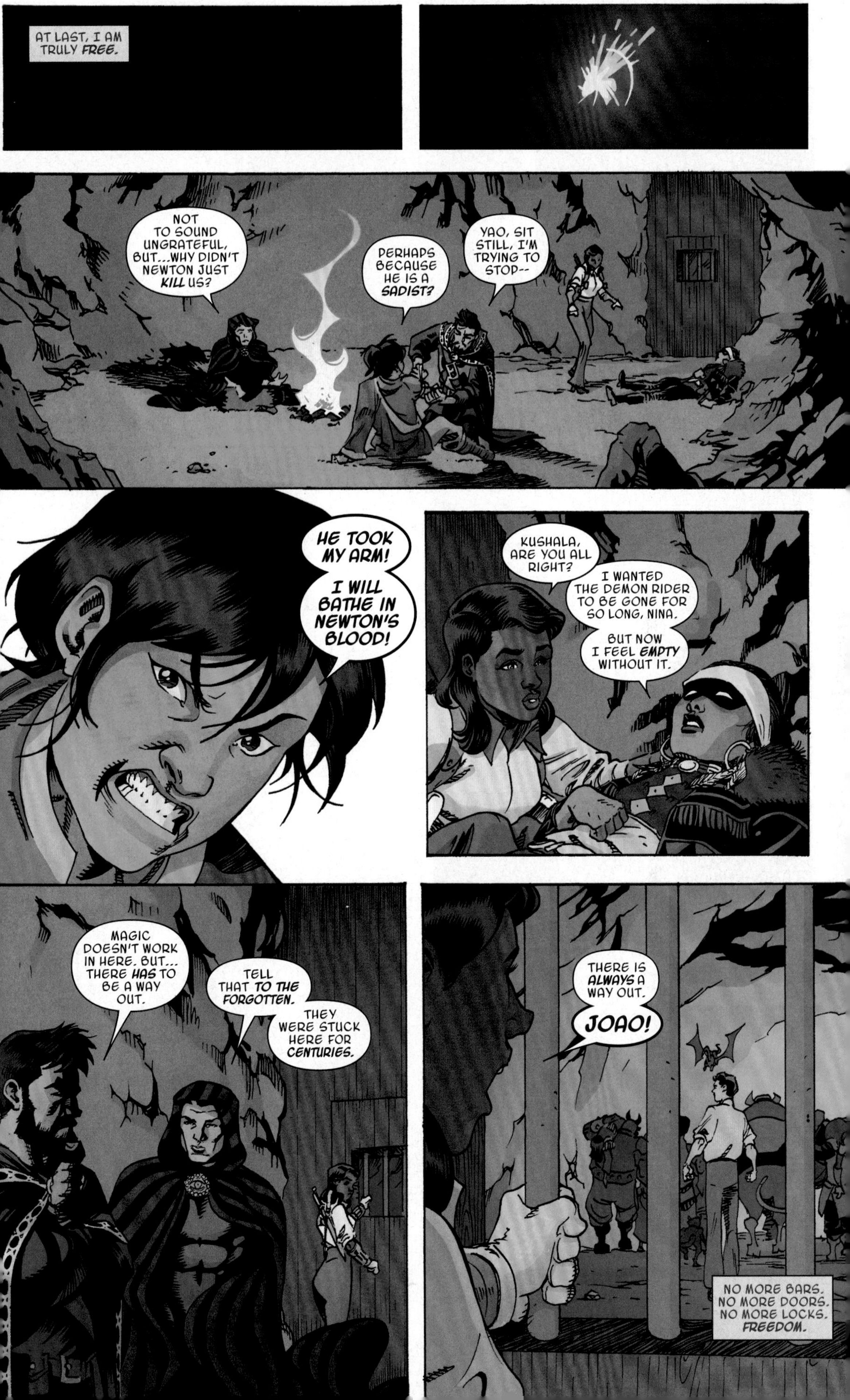
AT LAST, I AM TRULY FREE.
NOT TO SOUND UNGRATEFUL, BUT...WHY DIDN'T NEWTON JUST KILL US?
PERHAPS BECAUSE HE IS A SADIST?
YAO, SIT STILL, I'M TRYING TO STOP--
HE TOOK MY ARM!
I WILL BATHE IN NEWTON'S BLOOD!
KUSHALA, ARE YOU ALL RIGHT?
I WANTED THE DEMON RIDER TO BE GONE FOR SO LONG, NINA.
BUT NOW I FEEL EMPTY WITHOUT IT.
MAGIC DOESN'T WORK IN HERE. BUT... THERE HAS TO BE A WAY OUT.
TELL THAT TO THE FORGOTTEN.
THEY WERE STUCK HERE FOR CENTURIES.
THERE IS ALWAYS A WAY OUT.
JOAO!
NO MORE BARS. NO MORE DOORS. NO MORE LOCKS. FREEDOM.

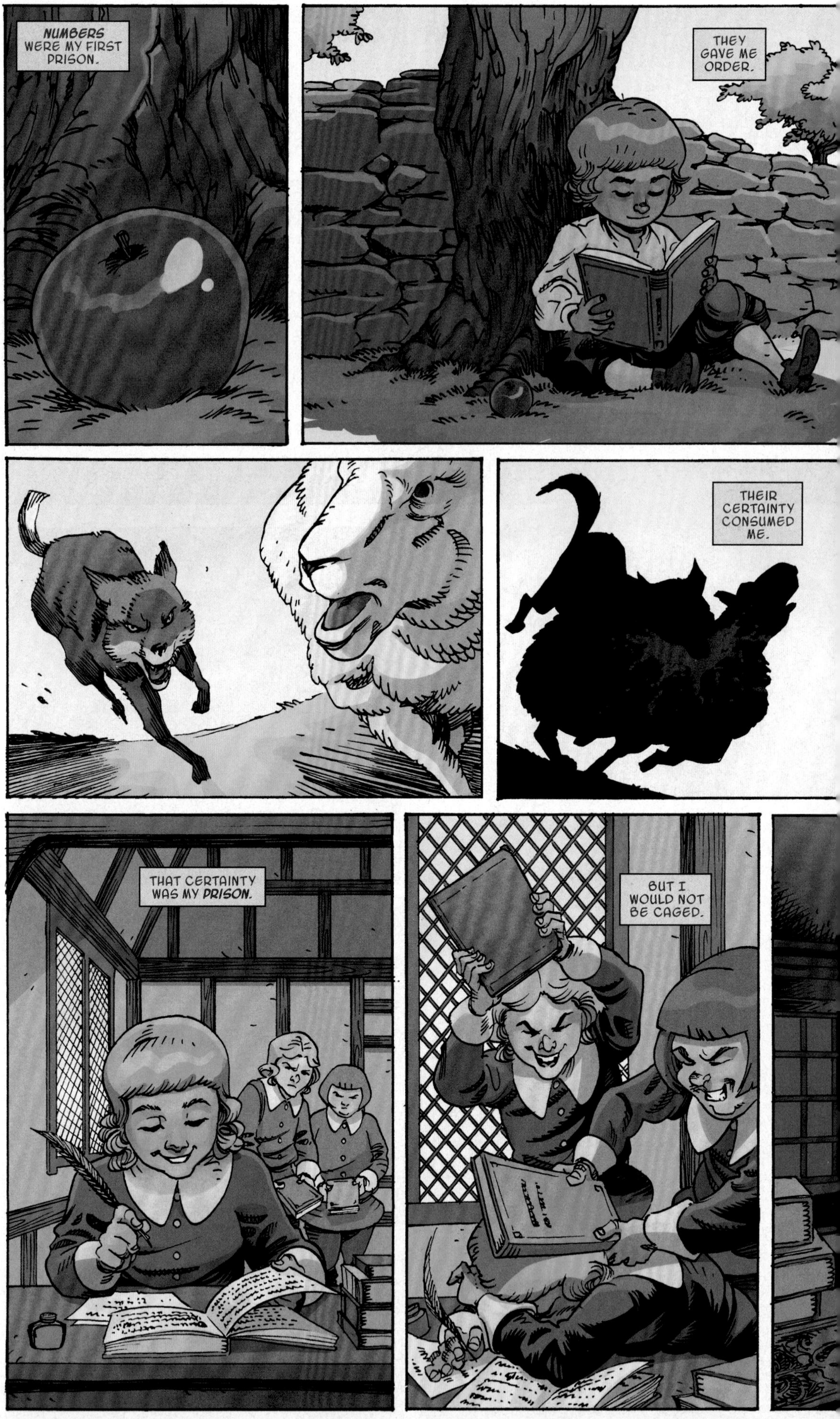
NUMBERS WERE MY FIRST PRISON.
THEY GAVE ME ORDER.
THEIR CERTAINTY CONSUMED ME.
THAT CERTAINTY WAS MY PRISON.
BUT I WOULD NOT BE CAGED.

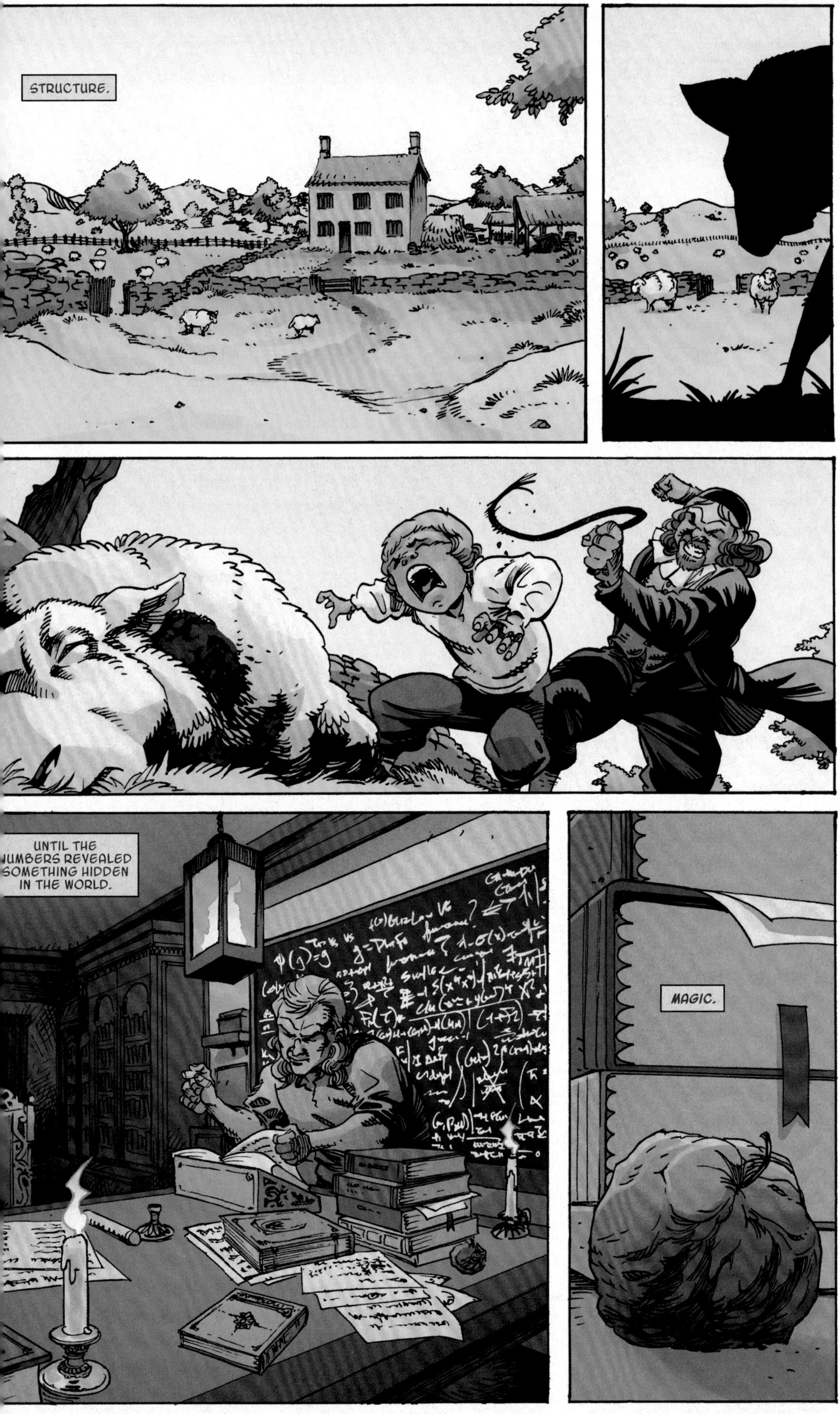
STRUCTURE.
UNTIL THE NUMBERS REVEALED SOMETHING HIDDEN IN THE WORLD.
MAGIC.

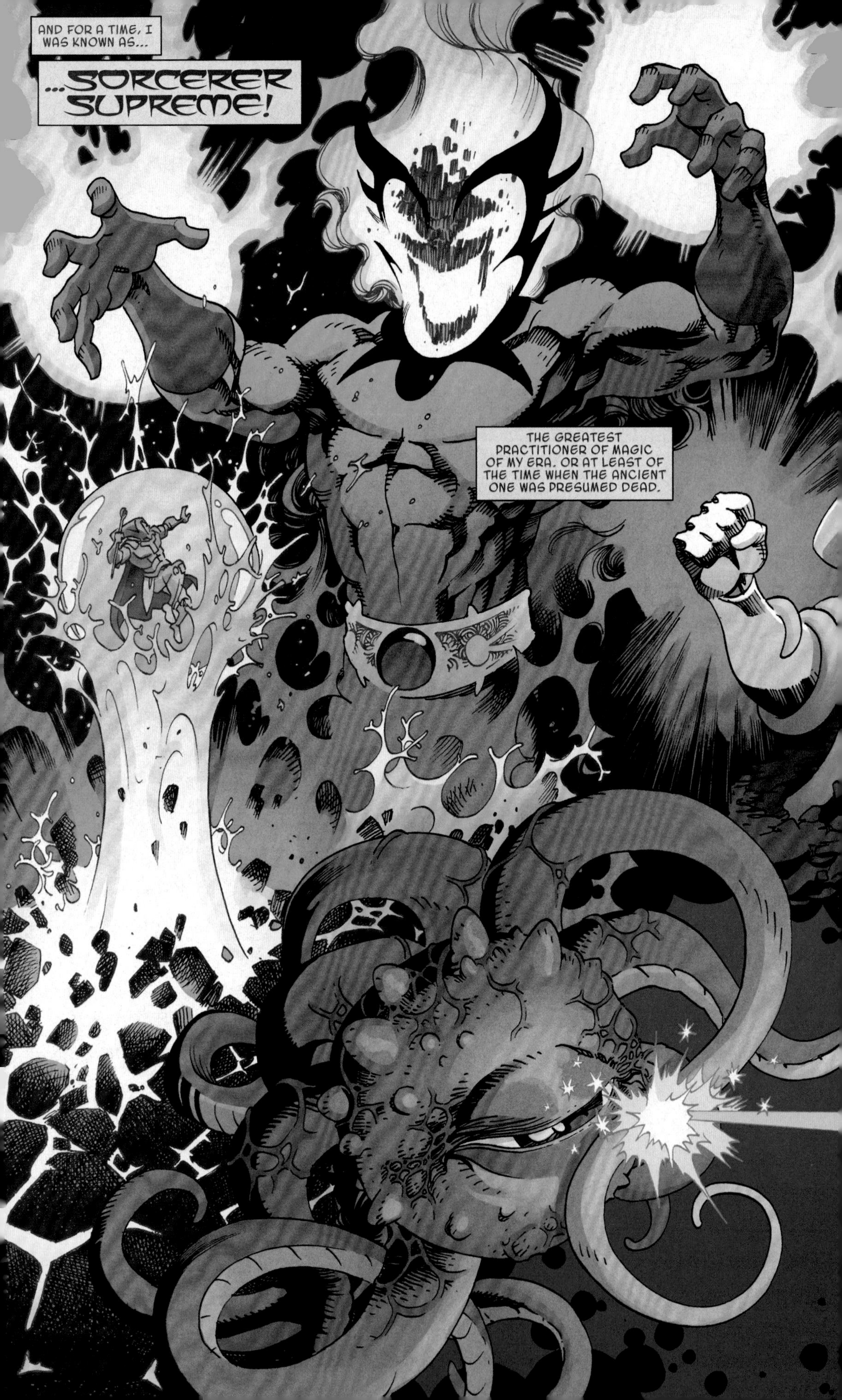

AND FOR A TIME, I WAS KNOWN AS...
...SORCERER SUPREME!
THE GREATEST PRACTITIONER OF MAGIC OF MY ERA. OR AT LEAST OF THE TIME WHEN THE ANCIENT ONE WAS PRESUMED DEAD.

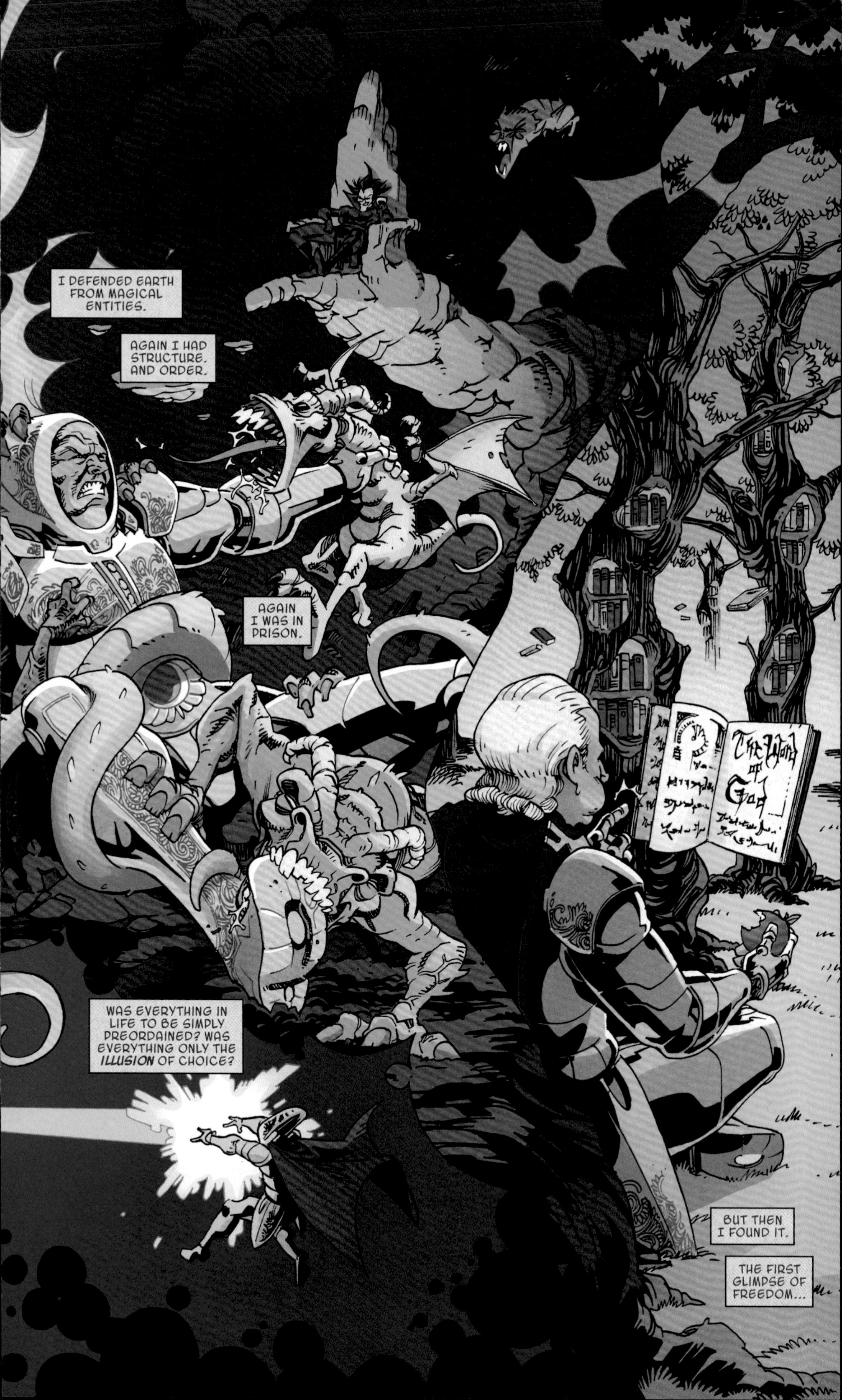
I DEFENDED EARTH FROM MAGICAL ENTITIES.
AGAIN I HAD STRUCTURE. AND ORDER.
AGAIN I WAS IN PRISON.
WAS EVERYTHING IN LIFE TO BE SIMPLY PREORDAINED? WAS EVERYTHING ONLY THE *ILLUSION* OF CHOICE?
BUT THEN I FOUND IT.
THE FIRST GLIMPSE OF FREEDOM...

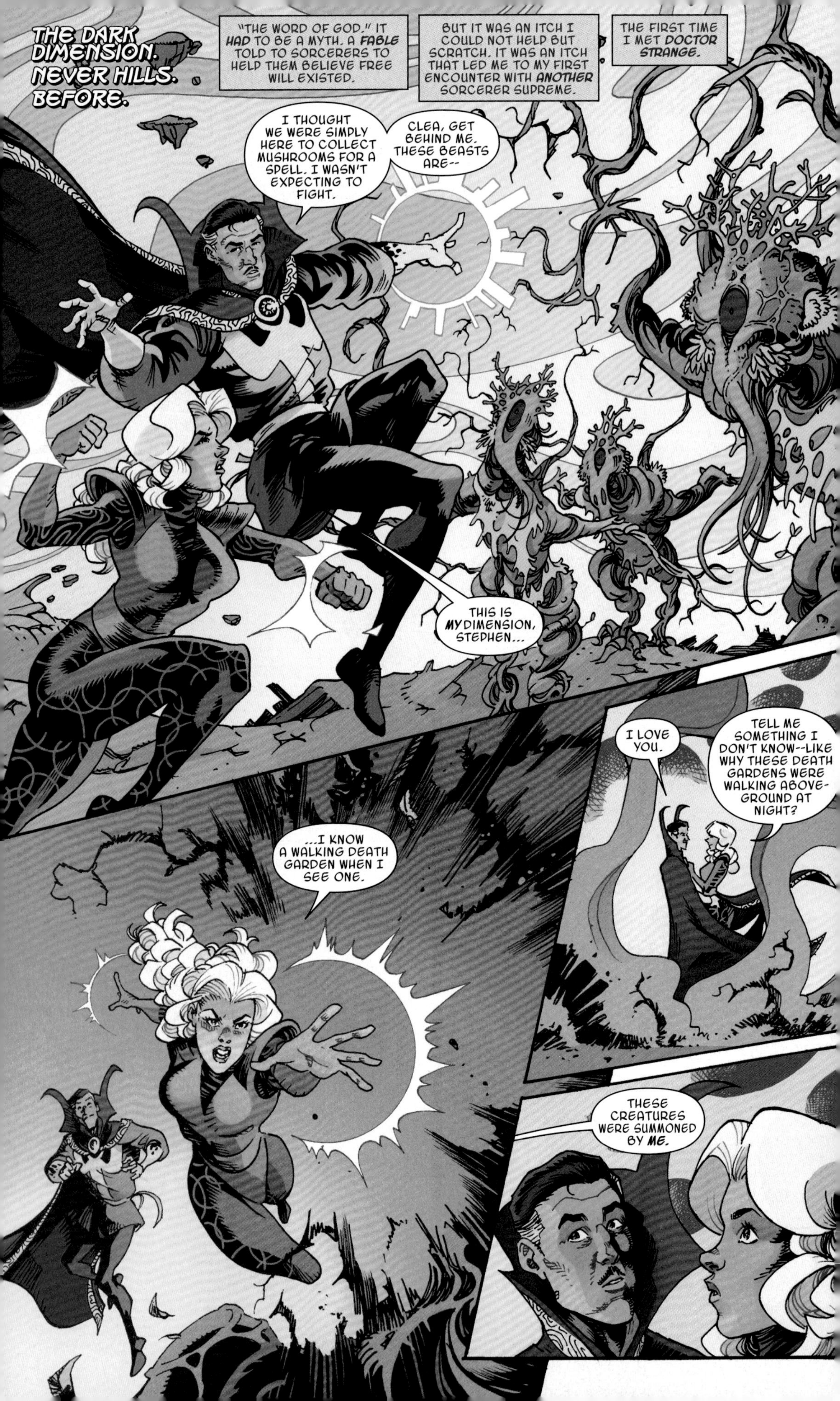
THE DARK DIMENSION. NEVER HILLS. BEFORE.
"THE WORD OF GOD." IT HAD TO BE A MYTH. A FABLE TOLD TO SORCERERS TO HELP THEM BELIEVE FREE WILL EXISTED.
BUT IT WAS AN ITCH I COULD NOT HELP BUT SCRATCH. IT WAS AN ITCH THAT LED ME TO MY FIRST ENCOUNTER WITH ANOTHER SORCERER SUPREME.
THE FIRST TIME I MET DOCTOR STRANGE.
I THOUGHT WE WERE SIMPLY HERE TO COLLECT MUSHROOMS FOR A SPELL. I WASN'T EXPECTING TO FIGHT.
CLEA, GET BEHIND ME. THESE BEASTS ARE--
THIS IS MY DIMENSION, STEPHEN...
...I KNOW A WALKING DEATH GARDEN WHEN I SEE ONE.
I LOVE YOU.
TELL ME SOMETHING I DON'T KNOW--LIKE WHY THESE DEATH GARDENS WERE WALKING ABOVE-GROUND AT NIGHT?
THESE CREATURES WERE SUMMONED BY ME.

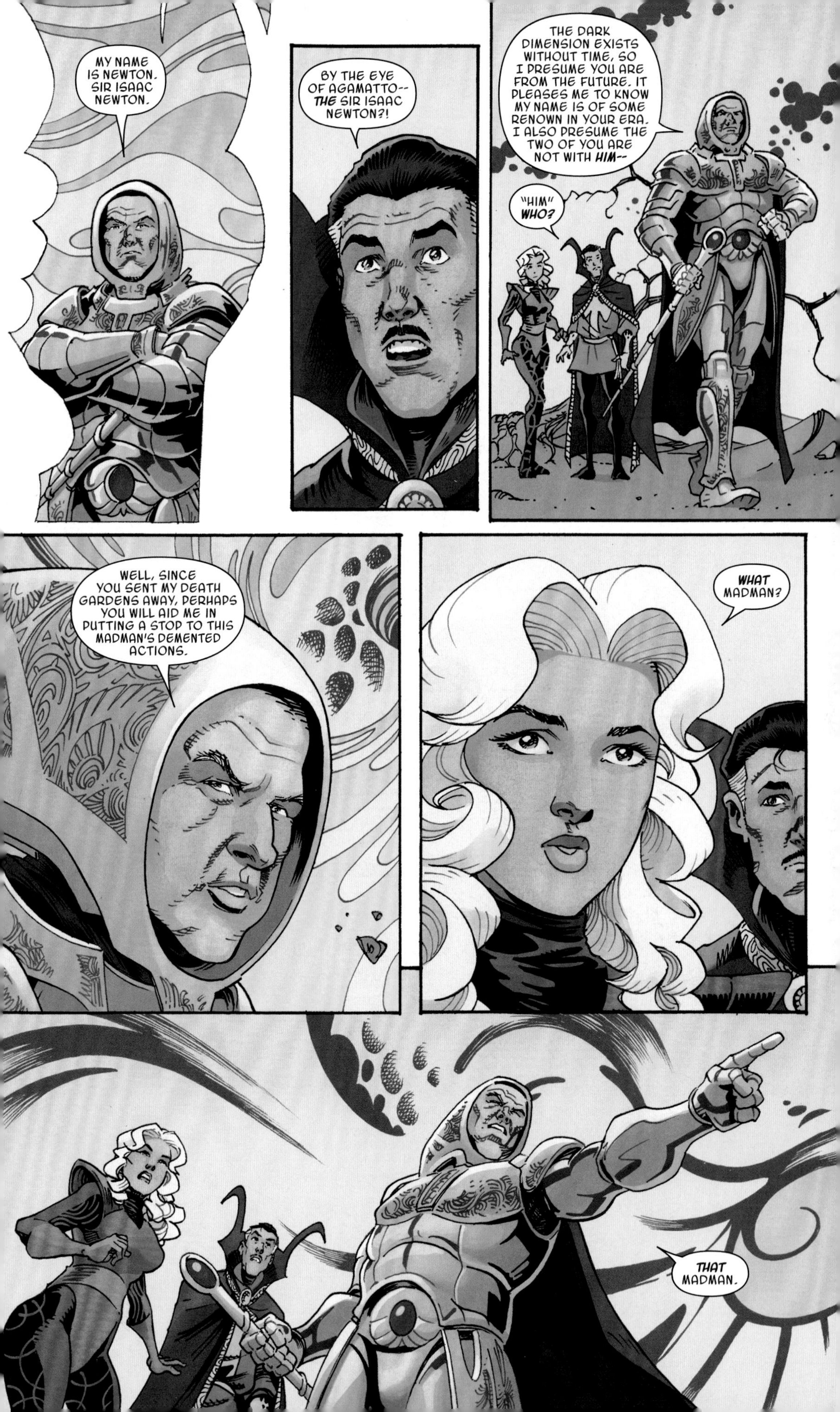
MY NAME IS NEWTON. SIR ISAAC NEWTON.
BY THE EYE OF AGAMATTO-- THE SIR ISAAC NEWTON?!
THE DARK DIMENSION EXISTS WITHOUT TIME, SO I PRESUME YOU ARE FROM THE FUTURE. IT PLEASES ME TO KNOW MY NAME IS OF SOME RENOWN IN YOUR ERA. I ALSO PRESUME THE TWO OF YOU ARE NOT WITH HIM--
"HIM" WHO?
WELL, SINCE YOU SENT MY DEATH GARDENS AWAY, PERHAPS YOU WILL AID ME IN PUTTING A STOP TO THIS MADMAN'S DEMENTED ACTIONS.
WHAT MADMAN?
THAT MADMAN.

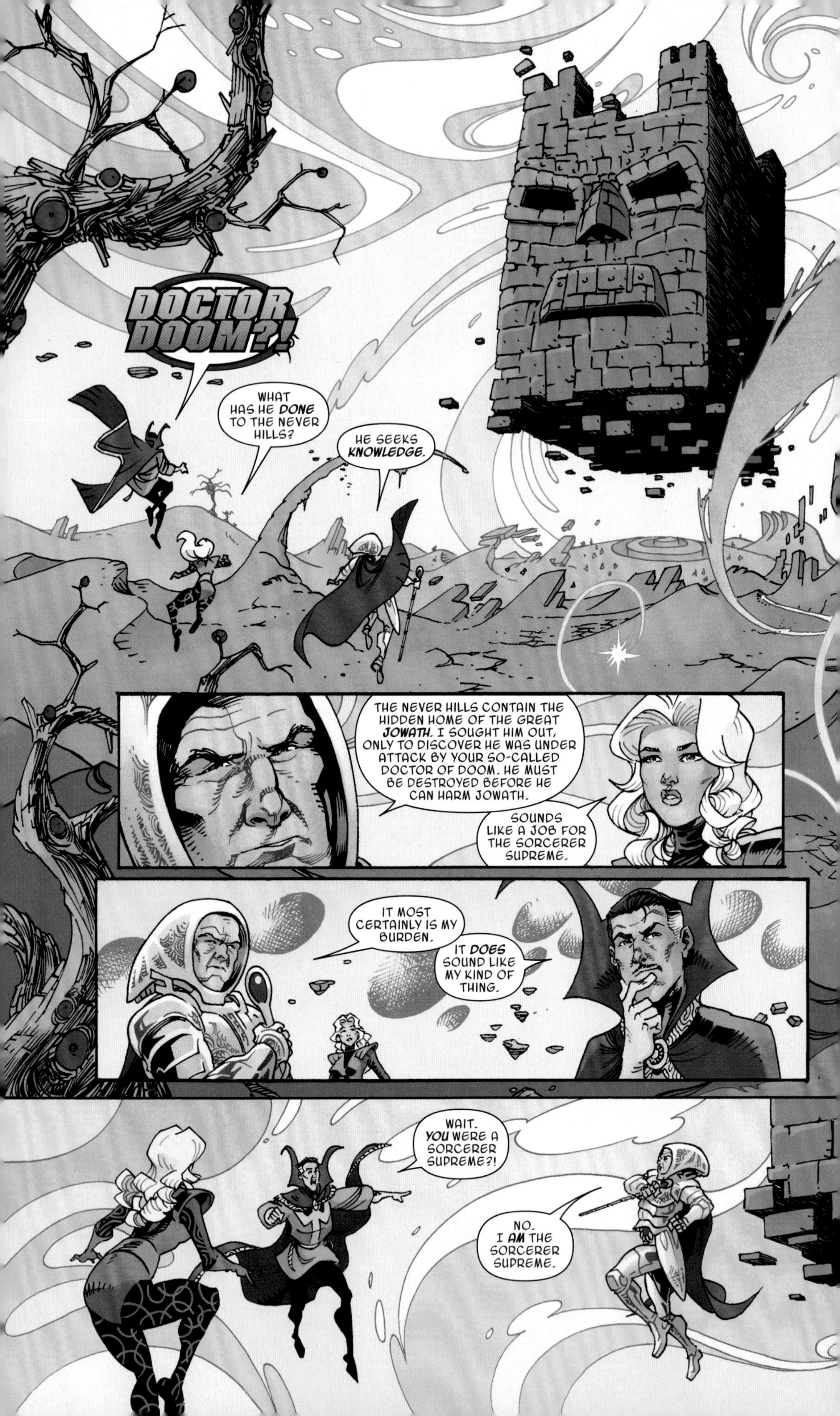

DOCTOR DOOM?!
WHAT HAS HE DONE TO THE NEVER HILLS?
HE SEEKS KNOWLEDGE.
THE NEVER HILLS CONTAIN THE HIDDEN HOME OF THE GREAT JOWATH. I SOUGHT HIM OUT, ONLY TO DISCOVER HE WAS UNDER ATTACK BY YOUR SO-CALLED DOCTOR OF DOOM. HE MUST BE DESTROYED BEFORE HE CAN HARM JOWATH.
SOUNDS LIKE A JOB FOR THE SORCERER SUPREME.
IT MOST CERTAINLY IS MY BURDEN.
IT DOES SOUND LIKE MY KIND OF THING.
WAIT. YOU WERE A SORCERER SUPREME?!
NO. I AM THE SORCERER SUPREME.

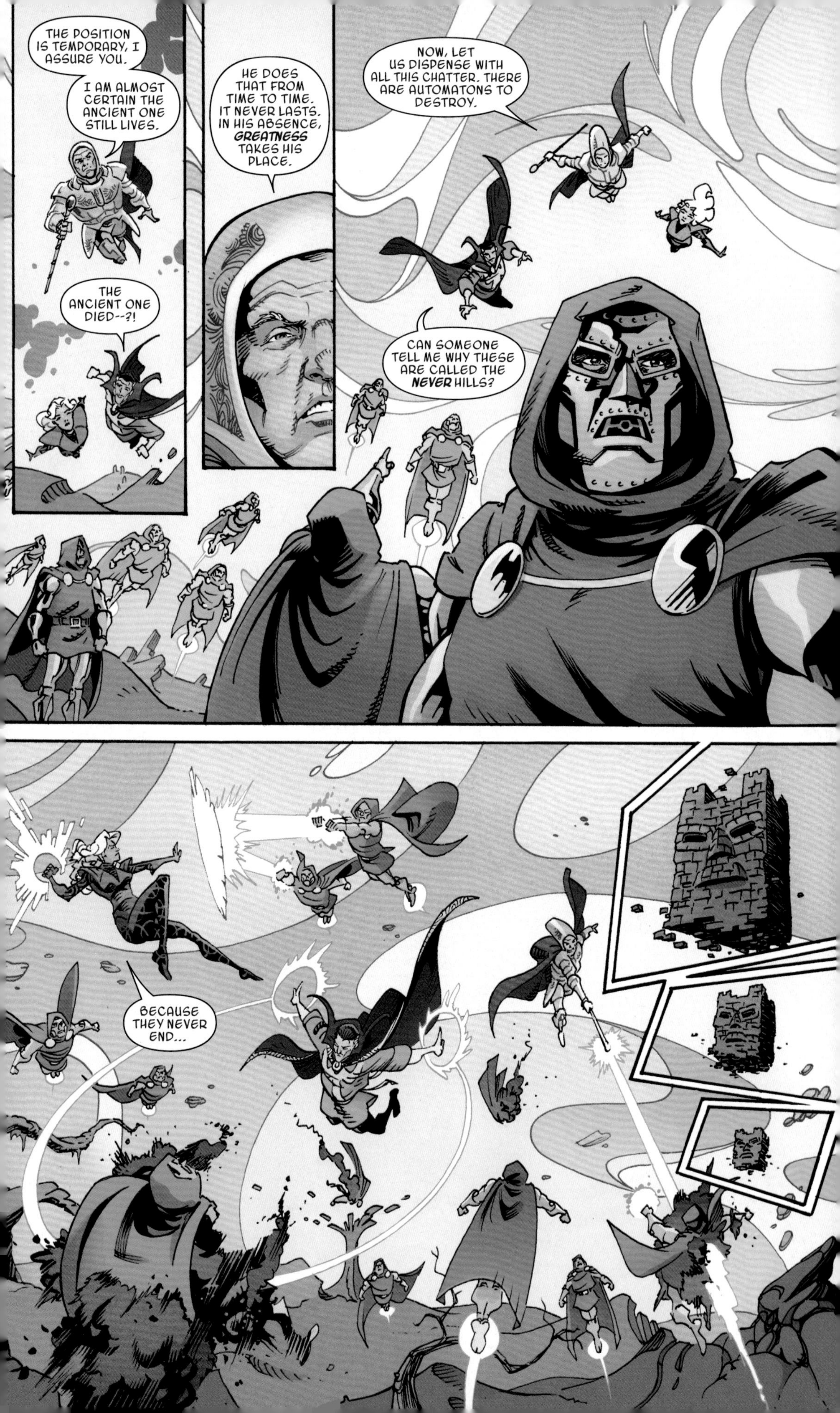
THE POSITION IS TEMPORARY, I ASSURE YOU.
I AM ALMOST CERTAIN THE ANCIENT ONE STILL LIVES.
THE ANCIENT ONE DIED--?!
HE DOES THAT FROM TIME TO TIME. IT NEVER LASTS. IN HIS ABSENCE, GREATNESS TAKES HIS PLACE.
NOW, LET US DISPENSE WITH ALL THIS CHATTER. THERE ARE AUTOMATONS TO DESTROY.
CAN SOMEONE TELL ME WHY THESE ARE CALLED THE NEVER HILLS?
BECAUSE THEY NEVER END...

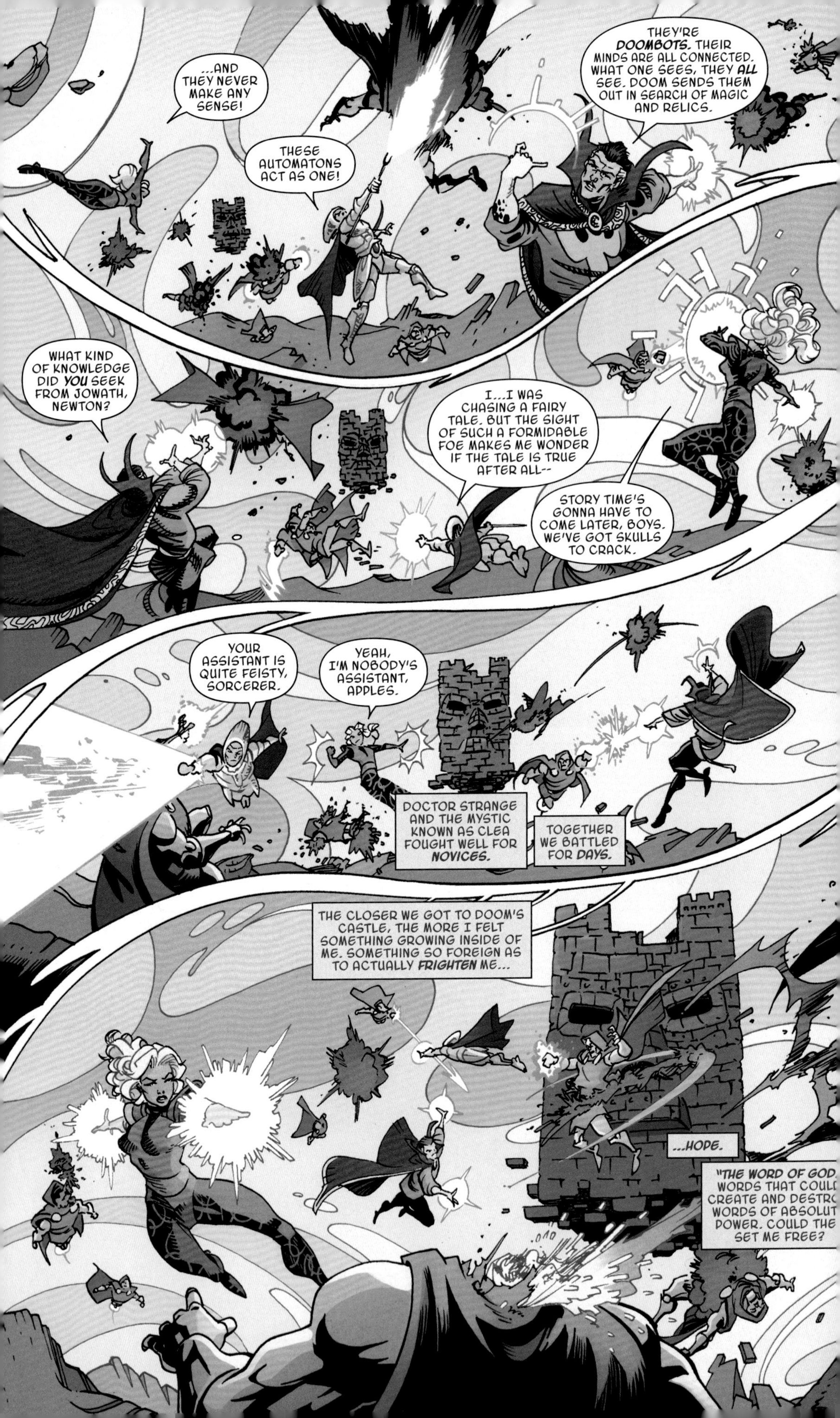

...AND THEY NEVER MAKE ANY SENSE!
THESE AUTOMATONS ACT AS ONE!
THEY'RE DOOMBOTS. THEIR MINDS ARE ALL CONNECTED. WHAT ONE SEES, THEY ALL SEE. DOOM SENDS THEM OUT IN SEARCH OF MAGIC AND RELICS.
WHAT KIND OF KNOWLEDGE DID YOU SEEK FROM JOWATH, NEWTON?
I...I WAS CHASING A FAIRY TALE. BUT THE SIGHT OF SUCH A FORMIDABLE FOE MAKES ME WONDER IF THE TALE IS TRUE AFTER ALL--
STORY TIME'S GONNA HAVE TO COME LATER, BOYS. WE'VE GOT SKULLS TO CRACK.
YOUR ASSISTANT IS QUITE FEISTY, SORCERER.
YEAH, I'M NOBODY'S ASSISTANT, APPLES.
DOCTOR STRANGE AND THE MYSTIC KNOWN AS CLEA FOUGHT WELL FOR NOVICES.
TOGETHER WE BATTLED FOR DAYS.
THE CLOSER WE GOT TO DOOM'S CASTLE, THE MORE I FELT SOMETHING GROWING INSIDE OF ME. SOMETHING SO FOREIGN AS TO ACTUALLY FRIGHTEN ME...
...HOPE.
"THE WORD OF GOD. WORDS THAT COULD CREATE AND DESTRO WORDS OF ABSOLUT POWER. COULD THE SET ME FREE?

I'LL HOLD THEM OFF. GO ASTRAL!

SHE IS RATHER WONDERFUL. SMART. POWERFUL. HELPFUL. PERHAPS I SHOULD ACQUIRE AN ASSISTANT OF MY OWN.

YEAH, I CAN STILL *HEAR* YOU, GENIUS.

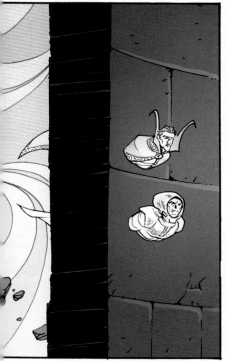

WRITE THEM DOWN... OR *DIE*, YOU CRETIN!

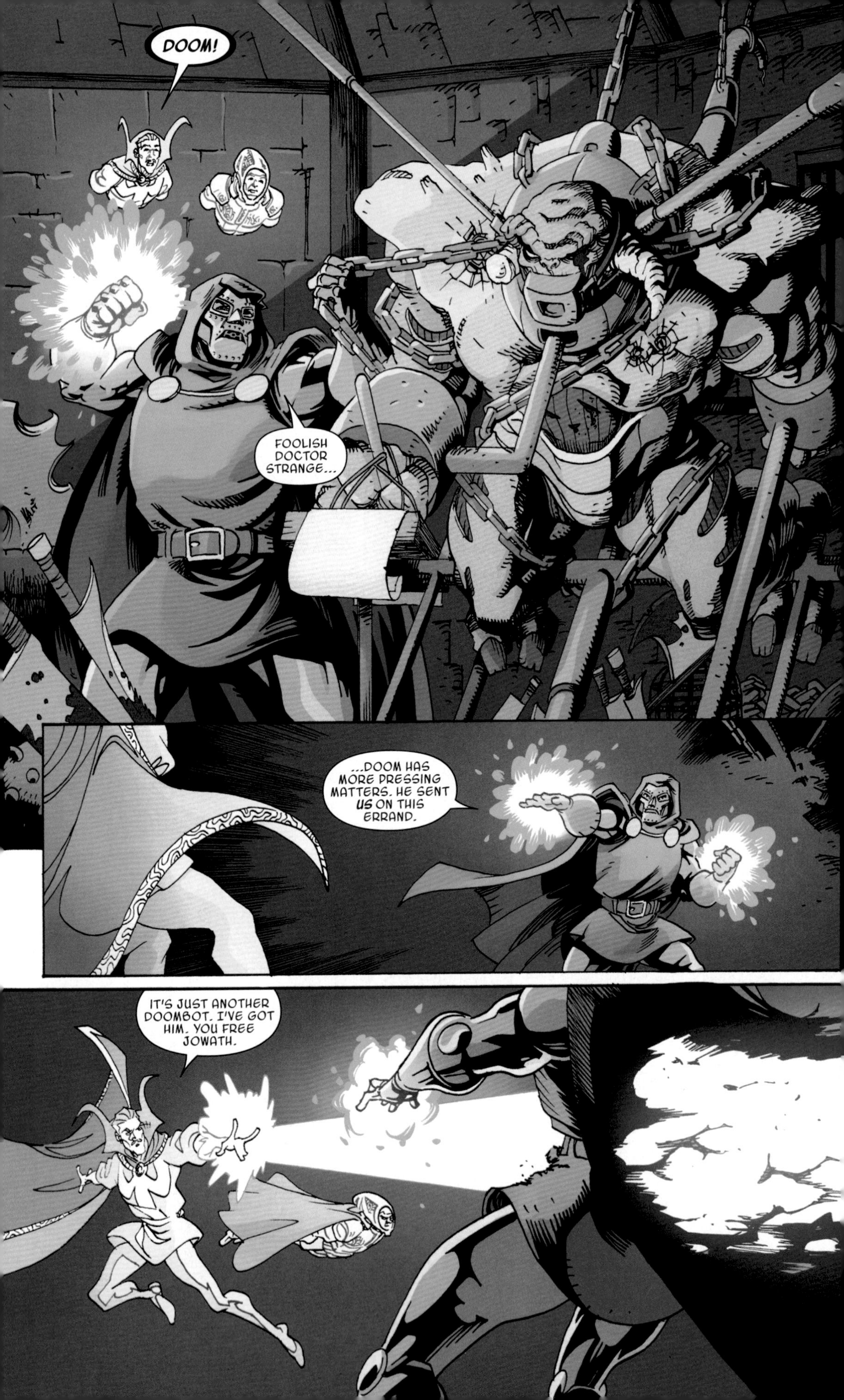
DOOM!
FOOLISH DOCTOR STRANGE...
...DOOM HAS MORE PRESSING MATTERS. HE SENT US ON THIS ERRAND.
IT'S JUST ANOTHER DOOMBOT. I'VE GOT HIM. YOU FREE JOWATH.

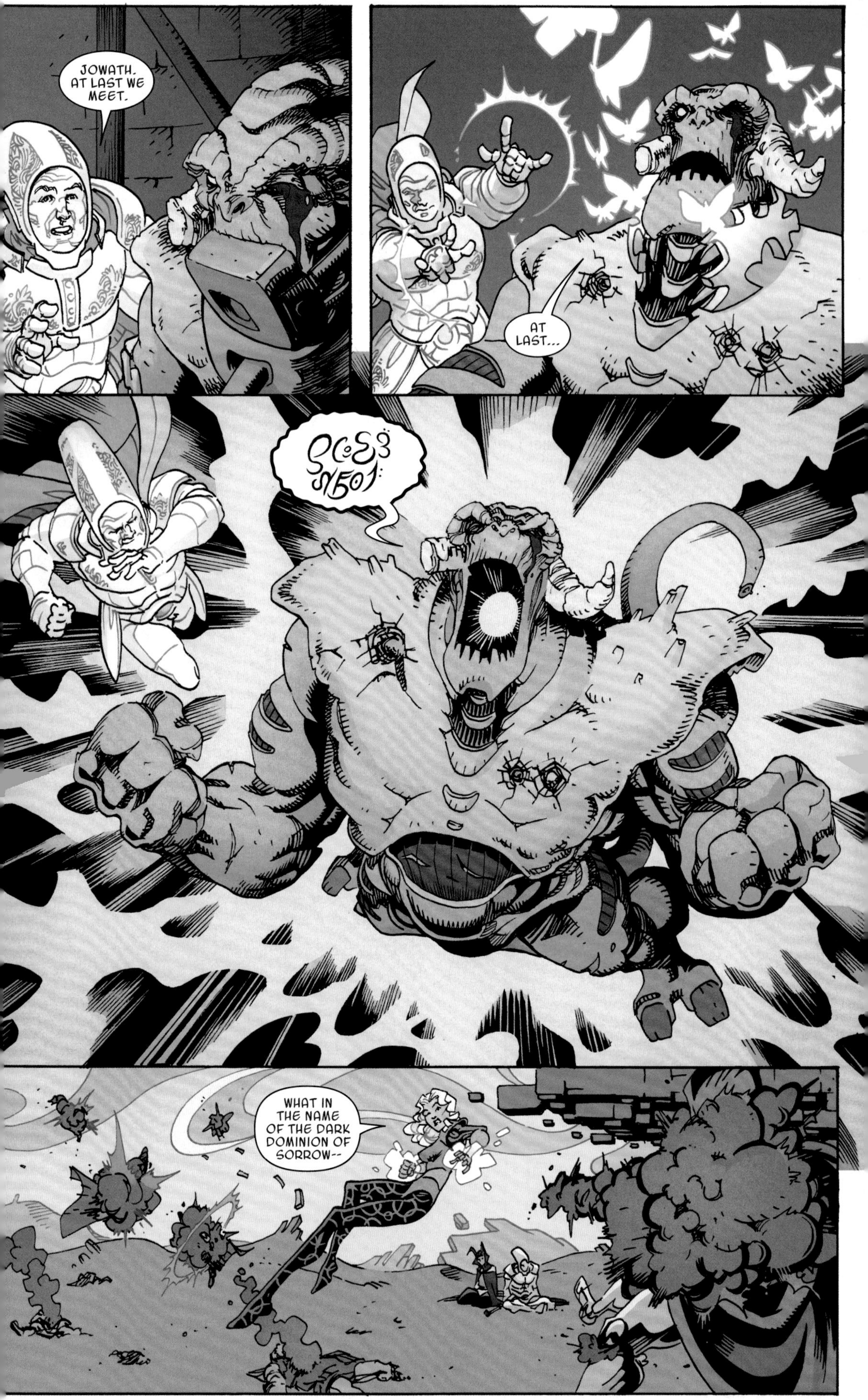
JOWATH. AT LAST WE MEET.
AT LAST...
WHAT IN THE NAME OF THE DARK DOMINION OF SORROW--

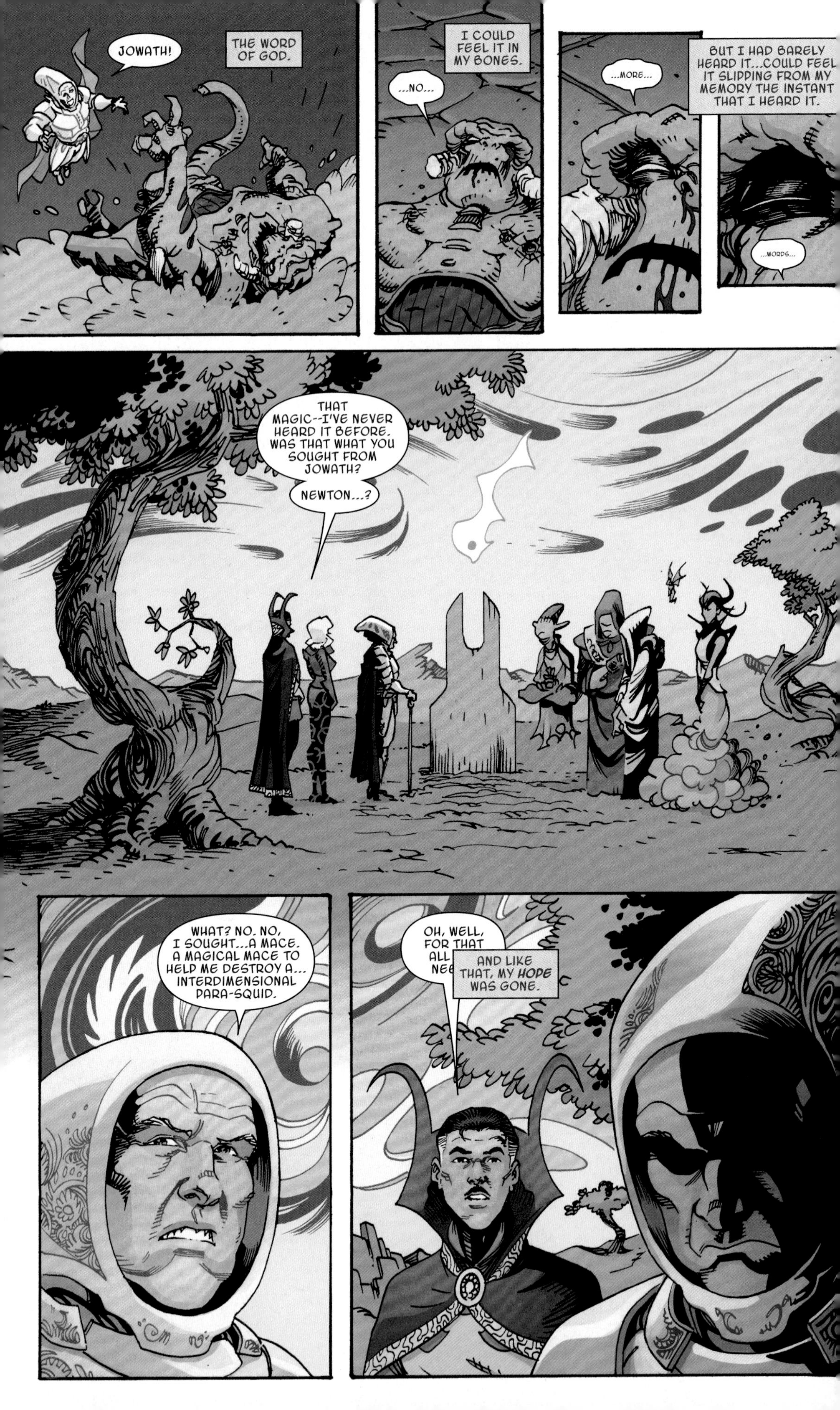
JOWATH!
THE WORD OF GOD.
I COULD FEEL IT IN MY BONES.
...NO...
...MORE...
BUT I HAD BARELY HEARD IT...COULD FEEL IT SLIPPING FROM MY MEMORY THE INSTANT THAT I HEARD IT.
...WORDS...
THAT MAGIC--I'VE NEVER HEARD IT BEFORE. WAS THAT WHAT YOU SOUGHT FROM JOWATH?
NEWTON...?
WHAT? NO. NO, I SOUGHT...A MACE. A MAGICAL MACE TO HELP ME DESTROY A... INTERDIMENSIONAL PARA-SQUID.
OH, WELL, FOR THAT ALL
AND LIKE THAT, MY *HOPE* WAS GONE.

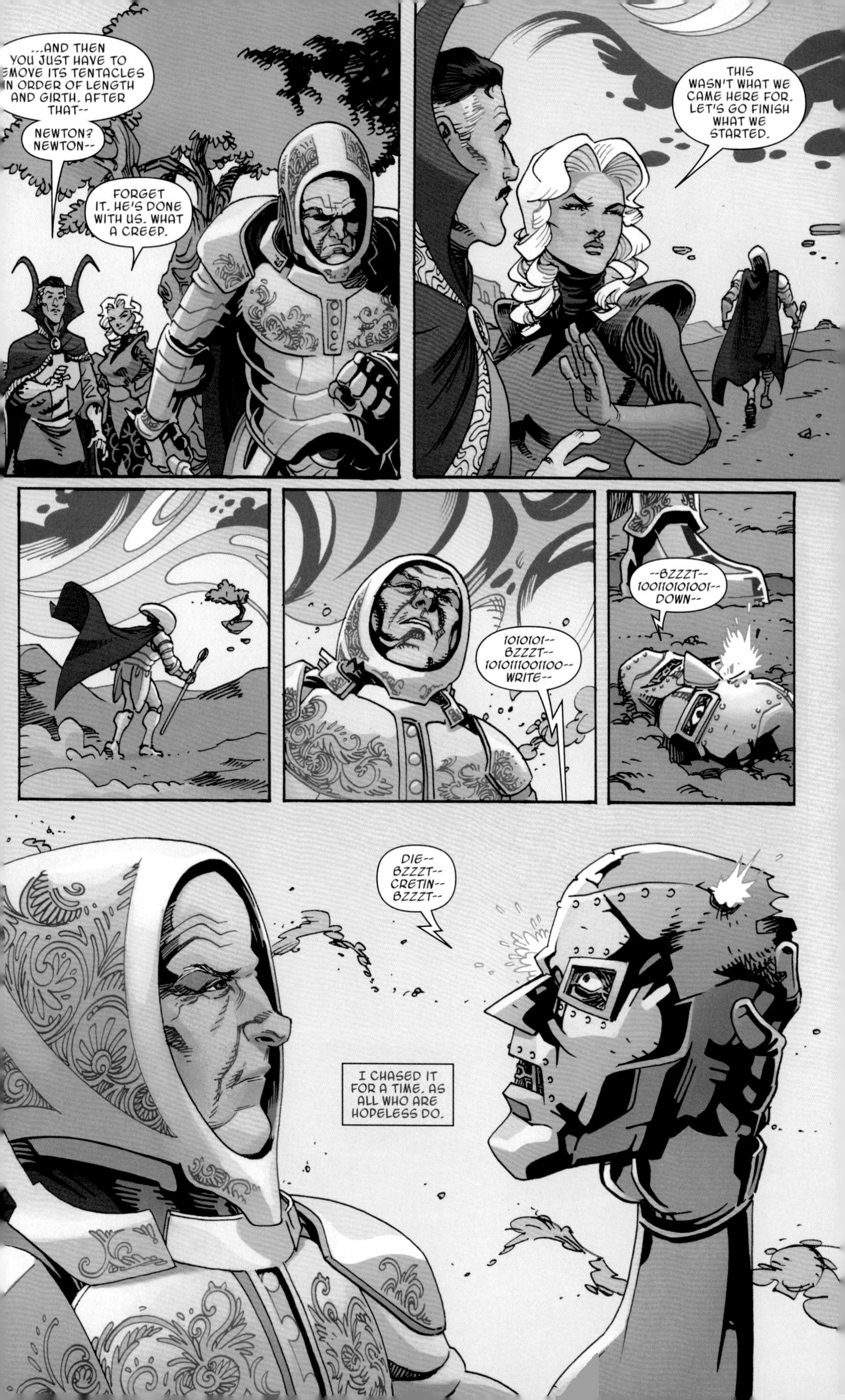
...AND THEN YOU JUST HAVE TO EMOVE ITS TENTACLES IN ORDER OF LENGTH AND GIRTH. AFTER THAT--
NEWTON? NEWTON--
FORGET IT. HE'S DONE WITH US. WHAT A CREEP.
THIS WASN'T WHAT WE CAME HERE FOR. LET'S GO FINISH WHAT WE STARTED.
1010101-- BZZZT-- 101011100110O-- WRITE--
--BZZZT-- 100110101001-- DOWN--
DIE-- BZZZT-- CRETIN-- BZZZT--
I CHASED IT FOR A TIME. AS ALL WHO ARE HOPELESS DO.

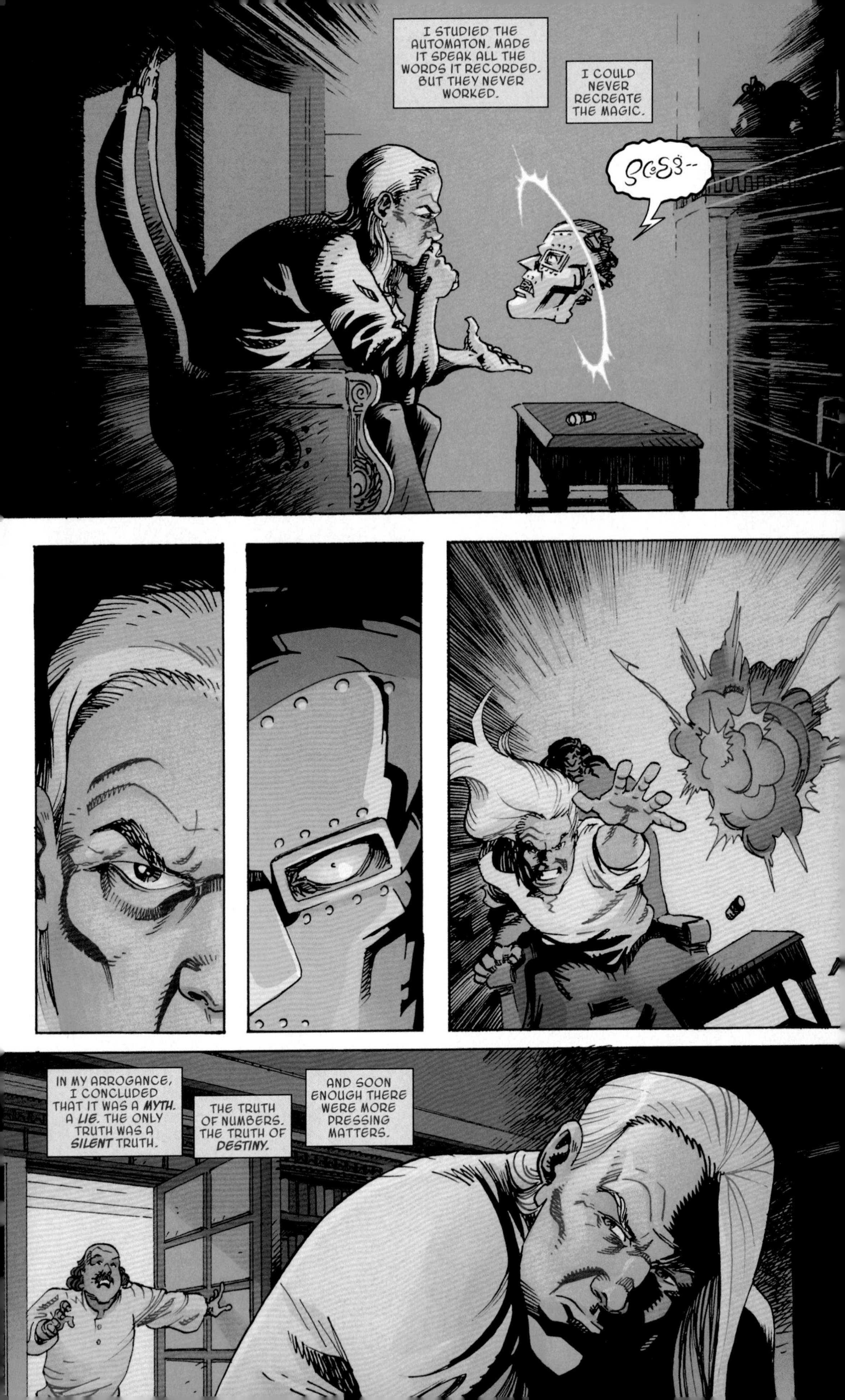
I STUDIED THE AUTOMATON. MADE IT SPEAK ALL THE WORDS IT RECORDED. BUT THEY NEVER WORKED.
I COULD NEVER RECREATE THE MAGIC.
IN MY ARROGANCE, I CONCLUDED THAT IT WAS A *MYTH*. A *LIE*. THE ONLY TRUTH WAS A *SILENT* TRUTH.
THE TRUTH OF NUMBERS. THE TRUTH OF *DESTINY*.
AND SOON ENOUGH THERE WERE MORE PRESSING MATTERS.

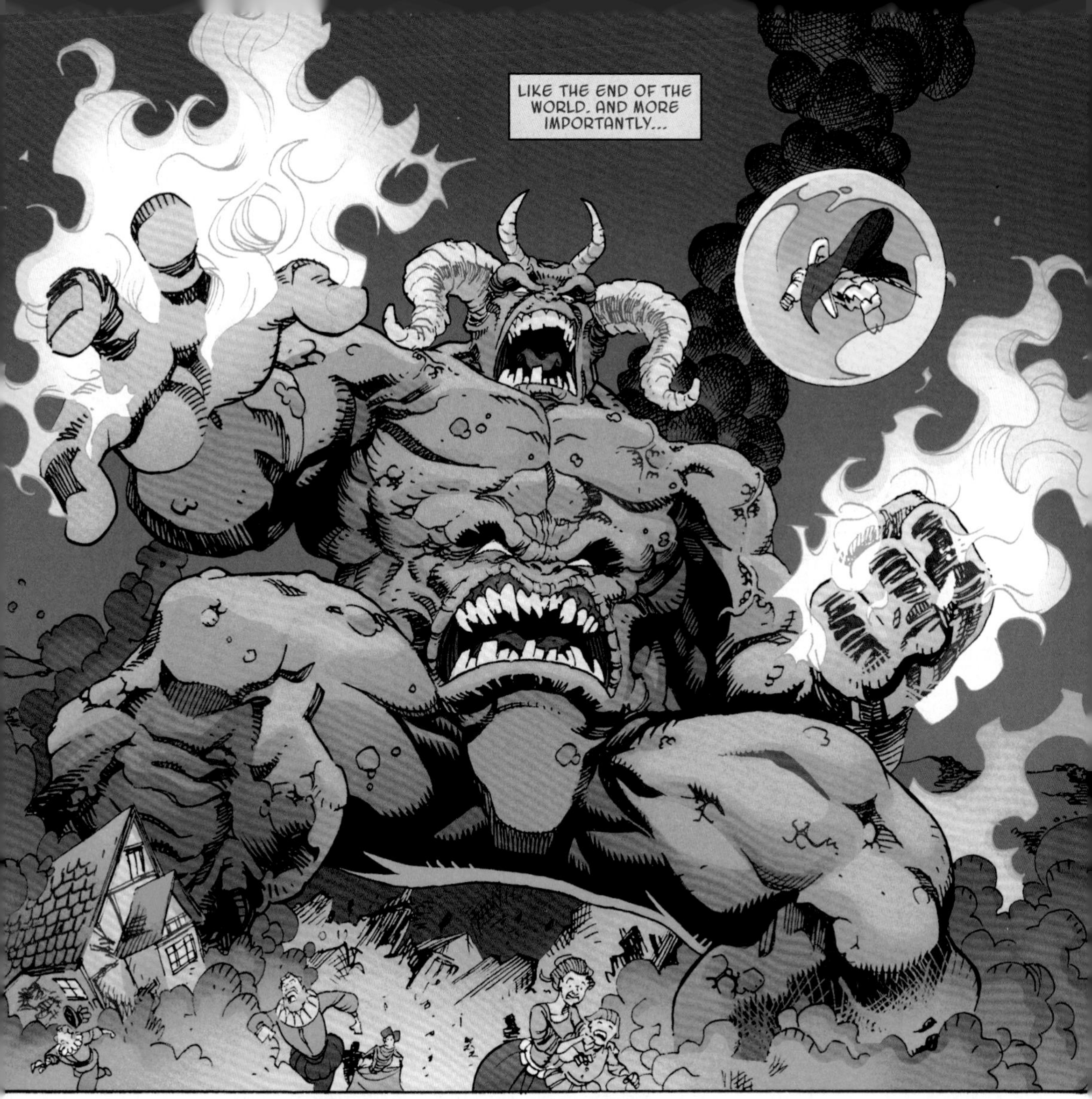

LIKE THE END OF THE WORLD. AND MORE IMPORTANTLY...

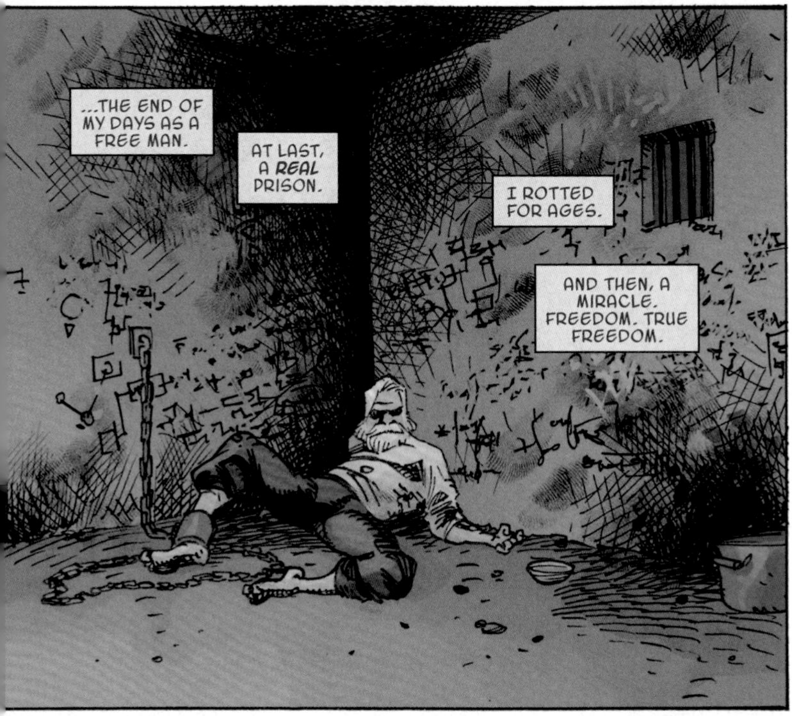

...THE END OF MY DAYS AS A FREE MAN.
AT LAST, A REAL PRISON.
I ROTTED FOR AGES.
AND THEN, A MIRACLE. FREEDOM. TRUE FREEDOM.

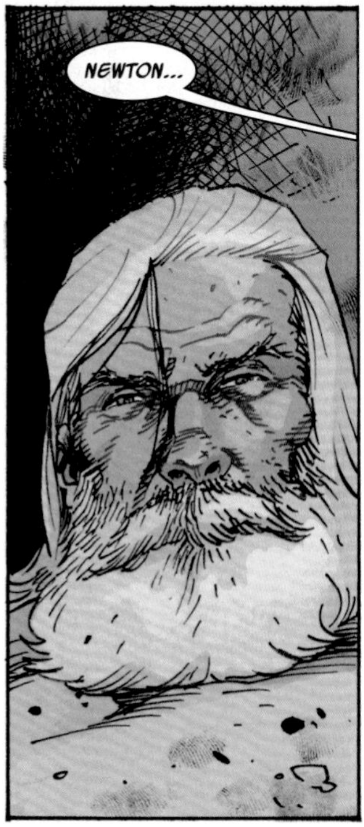

NEWTON...

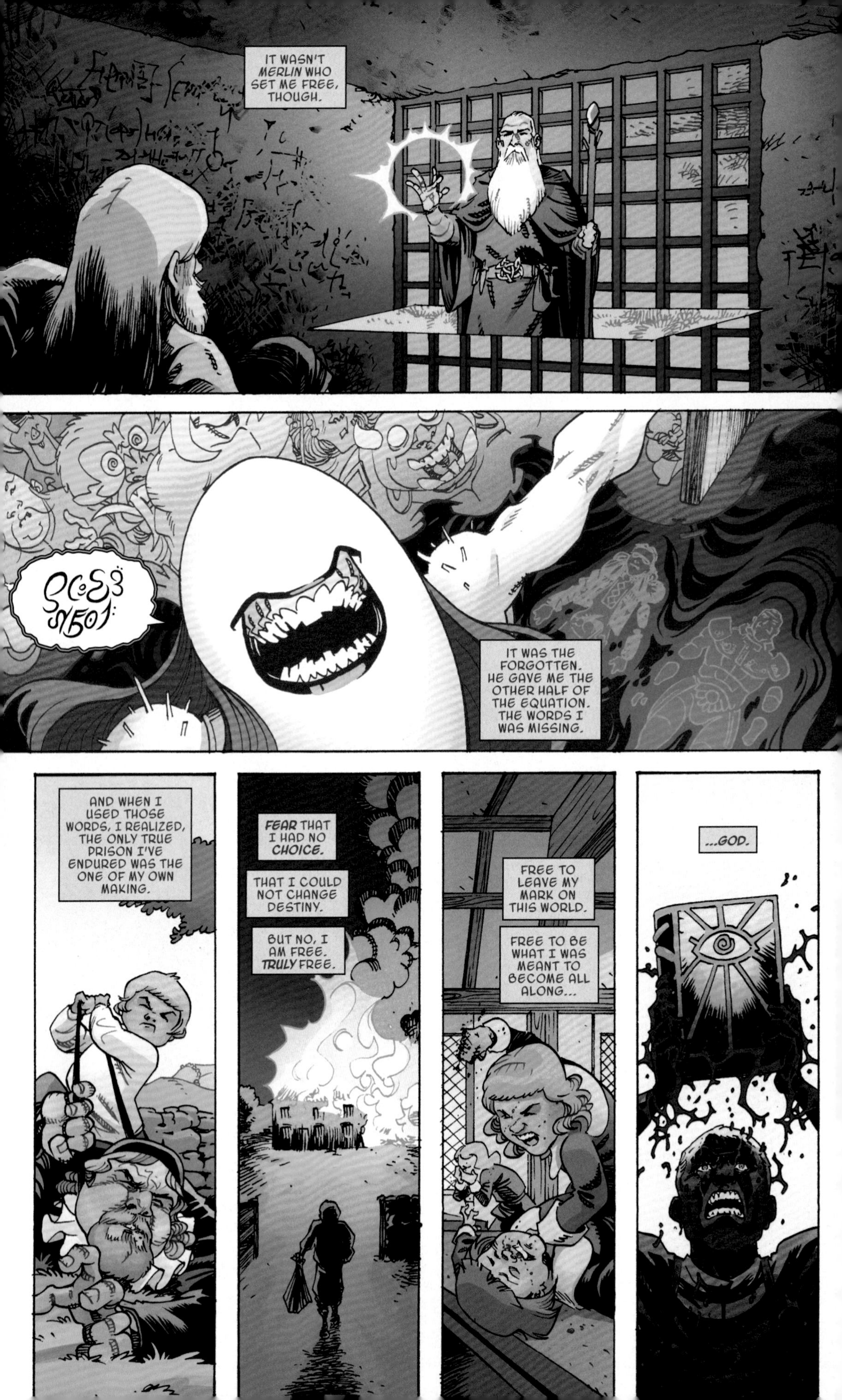
IT WASN'T MERLIN WHO SET ME FREE, THOUGH.
IT WAS THE FORGOTTEN. HE GAVE ME THE OTHER HALF OF THE EQUATION. THE WORDS I WAS MISSING.
AND WHEN I USED THOSE WORDS, I REALIZED, THE ONLY TRUE PRISON I'VE ENDURED WAS THE ONE OF MY OWN MAKING.
FEAR THAT I HAD NO CHOICE.
THAT I COULD NOT CHANGE DESTINY.
BUT NO, I AM FREE. TRULY FREE.
FREE TO LEAVE MY MARK ON THIS WORLD.
FREE TO BE WHAT I WAS MEANT TO BECOME ALL ALONG...
...GOD.

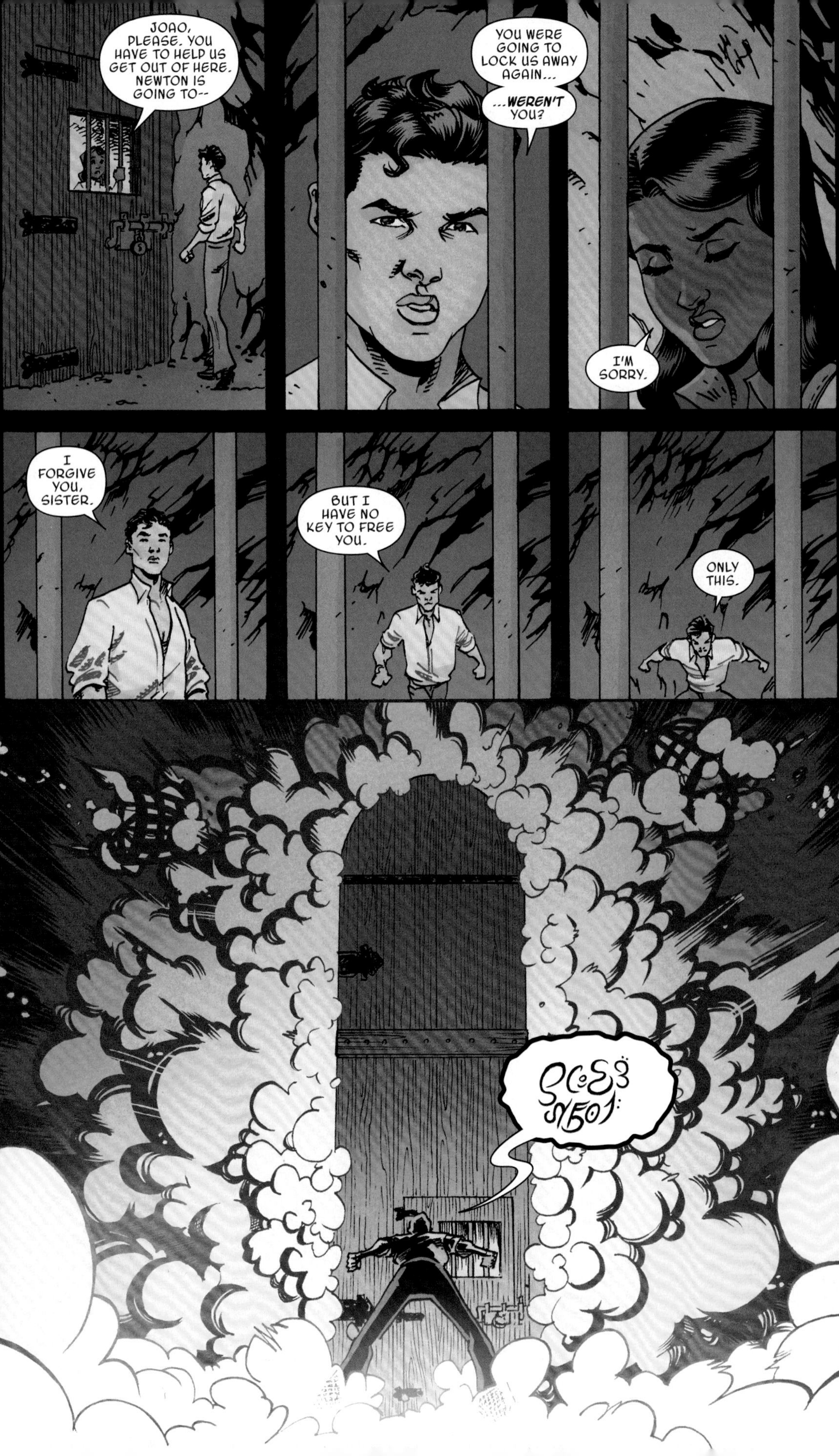
JOAO, PLEASE. YOU HAVE TO HELP US GET OUT OF HERE. NEWTON IS GOING TO--
YOU WERE GOING TO LOCK US AWAY AGAIN...
...WEREN'T YOU?
I'M SORRY.
I FORGIVE YOU, SISTER.
BUT I HAVE NO KEY TO FREE YOU.
ONLY THIS.

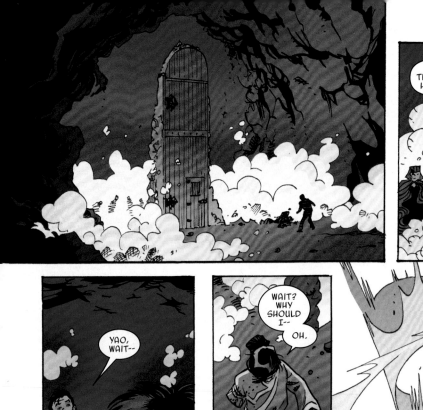

DID THAT JUST HAPPEN?

IT *CLEARLY* JUST HAPPENED. WHAT IS WRONG WITH YOU? WE'RE WASTING TIME. WE HAVE TO--

YAO, WAIT--

WAIT? WHY SHOULD I-- OH.

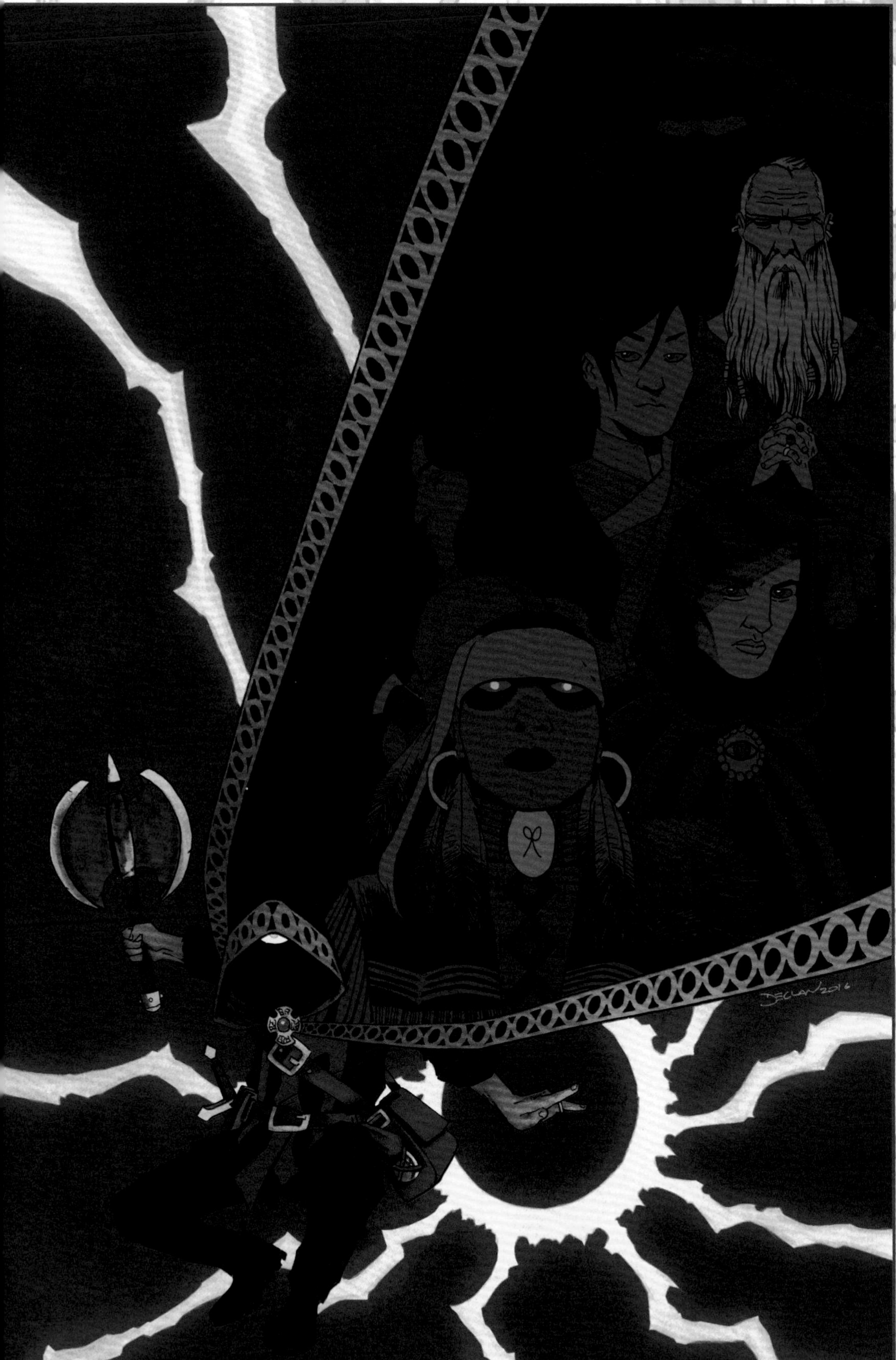
DECLAN 2016

NO. 3 VARIANT BY **DELCAN SHALVEY** & **JORDIE BELLAIRE**

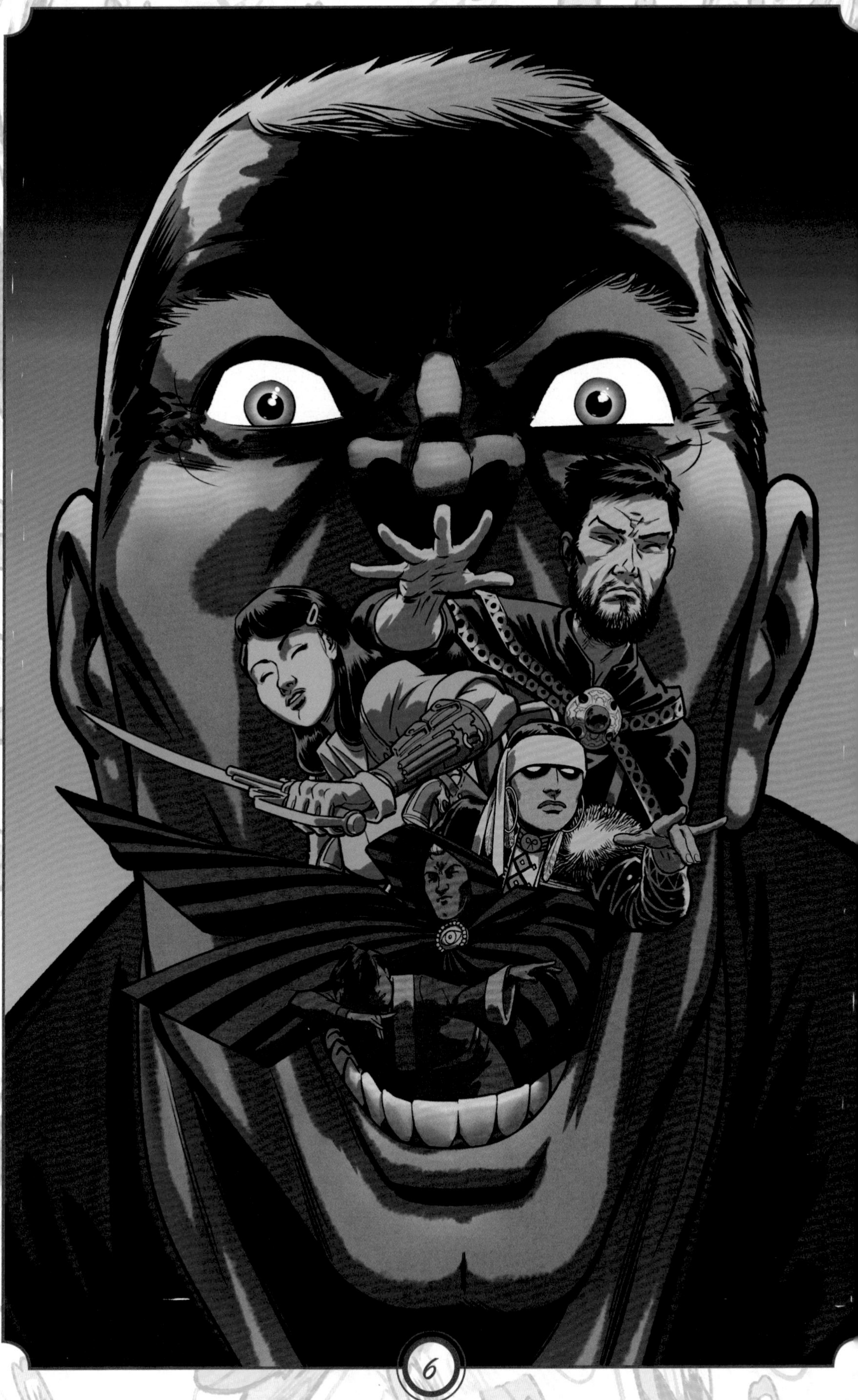

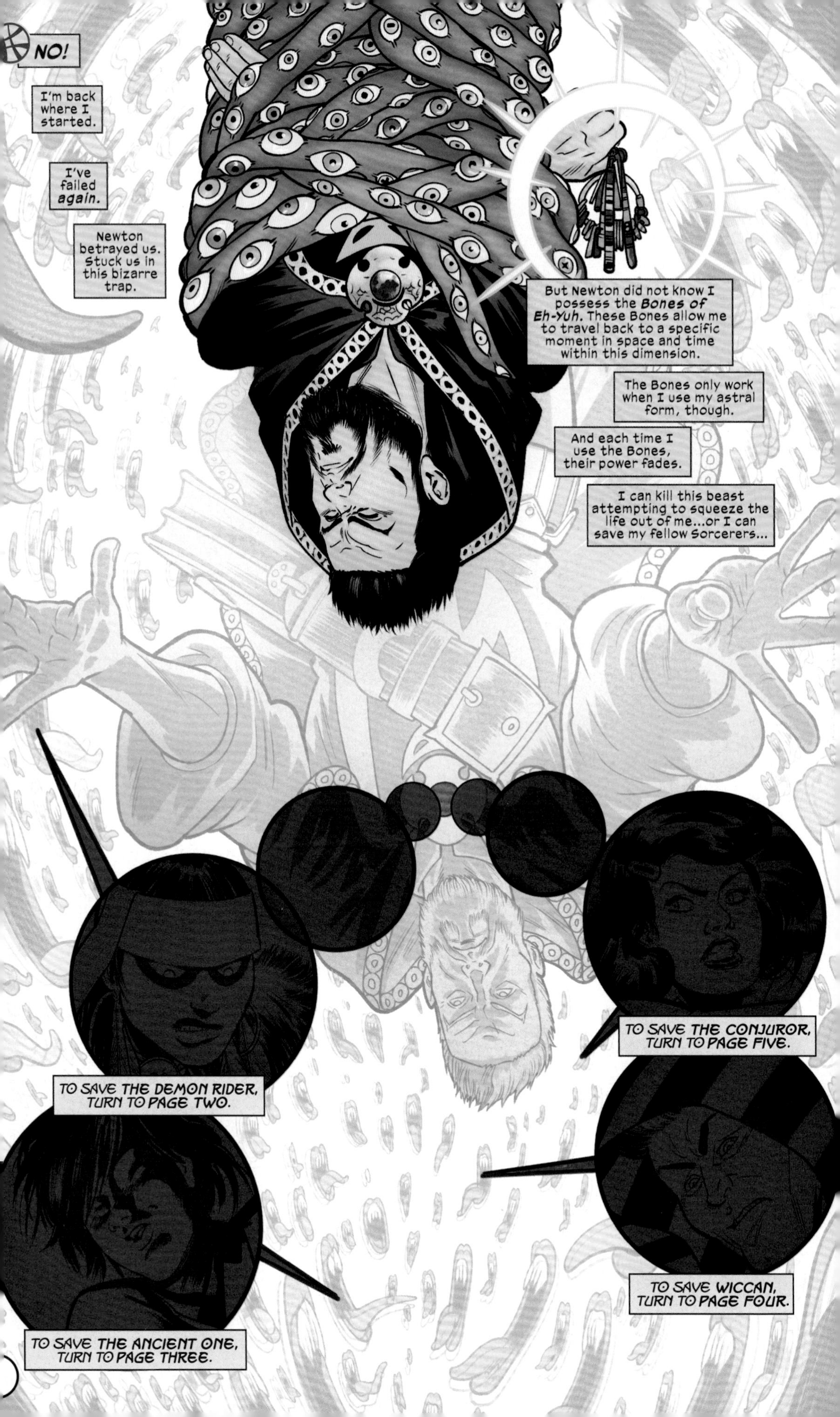
NO!
I'm back where I started.
I've failed *again.*
Newton betrayed us. Stuck us in this bizarre trap.
But Newton did not know I possess the *Bones of Eh-Yuh.* These Bones allow me to travel back to a specific moment in space and time within this dimension.
The Bones only work when I use my astral form, though.
And each time I use the Bones, their power fades.
I can kill this beast attempting to squeeze the life out of me...or I can save my fellow Sorcerers...
TO SAVE THE CONJUROR, TURN TO PAGE FIVE.
TO SAVE THE DEMON RIDER, TURN TO PAGE TWO.
TO SAVE WICCAN, TURN TO PAGE FOUR.
TO SAVE THE ANCIENT ONE, TURN TO PAGE THREE.

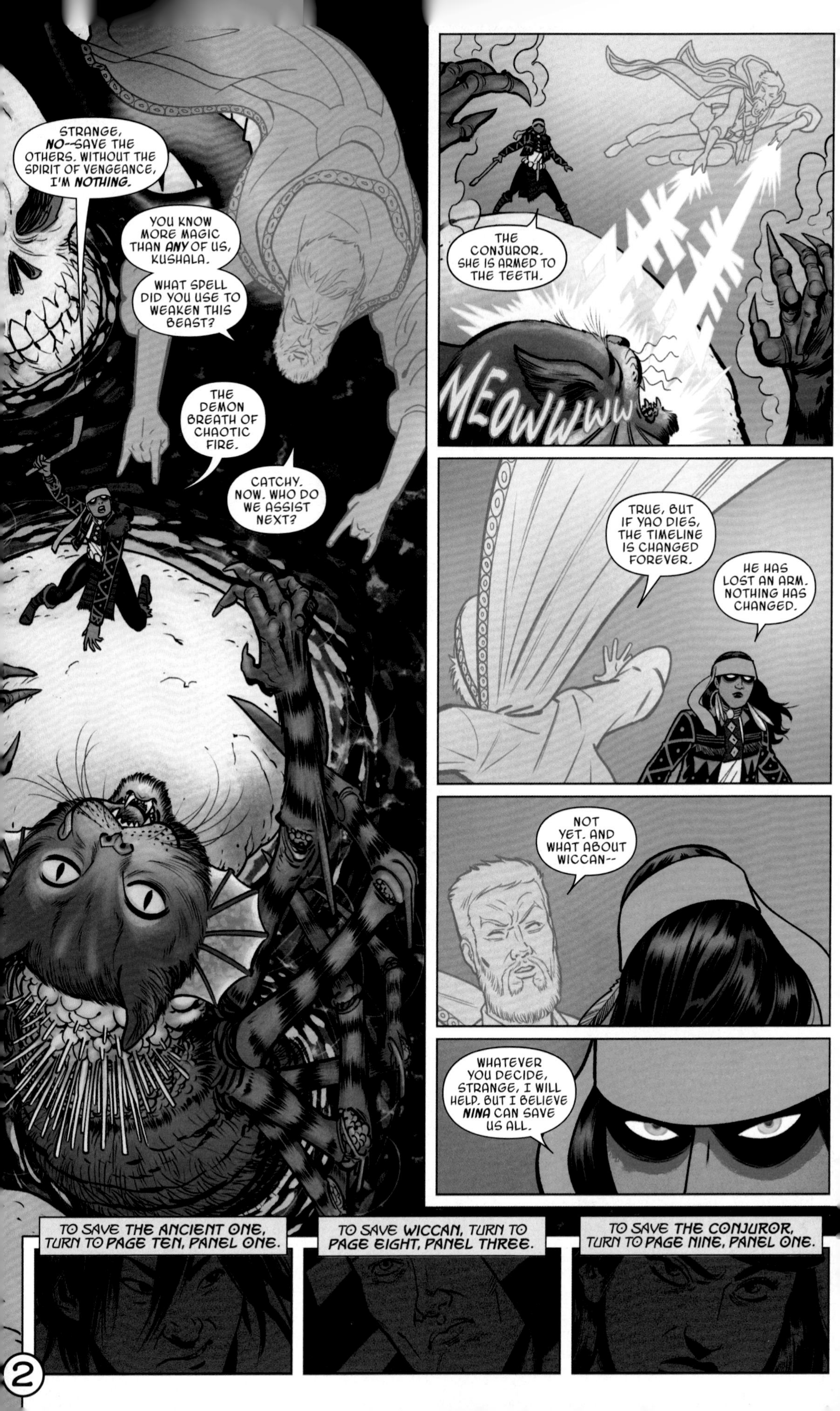
STRANGE, NO--SAVE THE OTHERS. WITHOUT THE SPIRIT OF VENGEANCE, I'M NOTHING.
YOU KNOW MORE MAGIC THAN ANY OF US, KUSHALA.
WHAT SPELL DID YOU USE TO WEAKEN THIS BEAST?
THE DEMON BREATH OF CHAOTIC FIRE.
CATCHY. NOW. WHO DO WE ASSIST NEXT?
THE CONJUROR. SHE IS ARMED TO THE TEETH.
MEOWWWWW
TRUE, BUT IF YAO DIES, THE TIMELINE IS CHANGED FOREVER.
HE HAS LOST AN ARM. NOTHING HAS CHANGED.
NOT YET. AND WHAT ABOUT WICCAN--
WHATEVER YOU DECIDE, STRANGE, I WILL HELP. BUT I BELIEVE NINA CAN SAVE US ALL.
TO SAVE THE ANCIENT ONE, TURN TO PAGE TEN, PANEL ONE.
TO SAVE WICCAN, TURN TO PAGE EIGHT, PANEL THREE.
TO SAVE THE CONJUROR, TURN TO PAGE NINE, PANEL ONE.
2

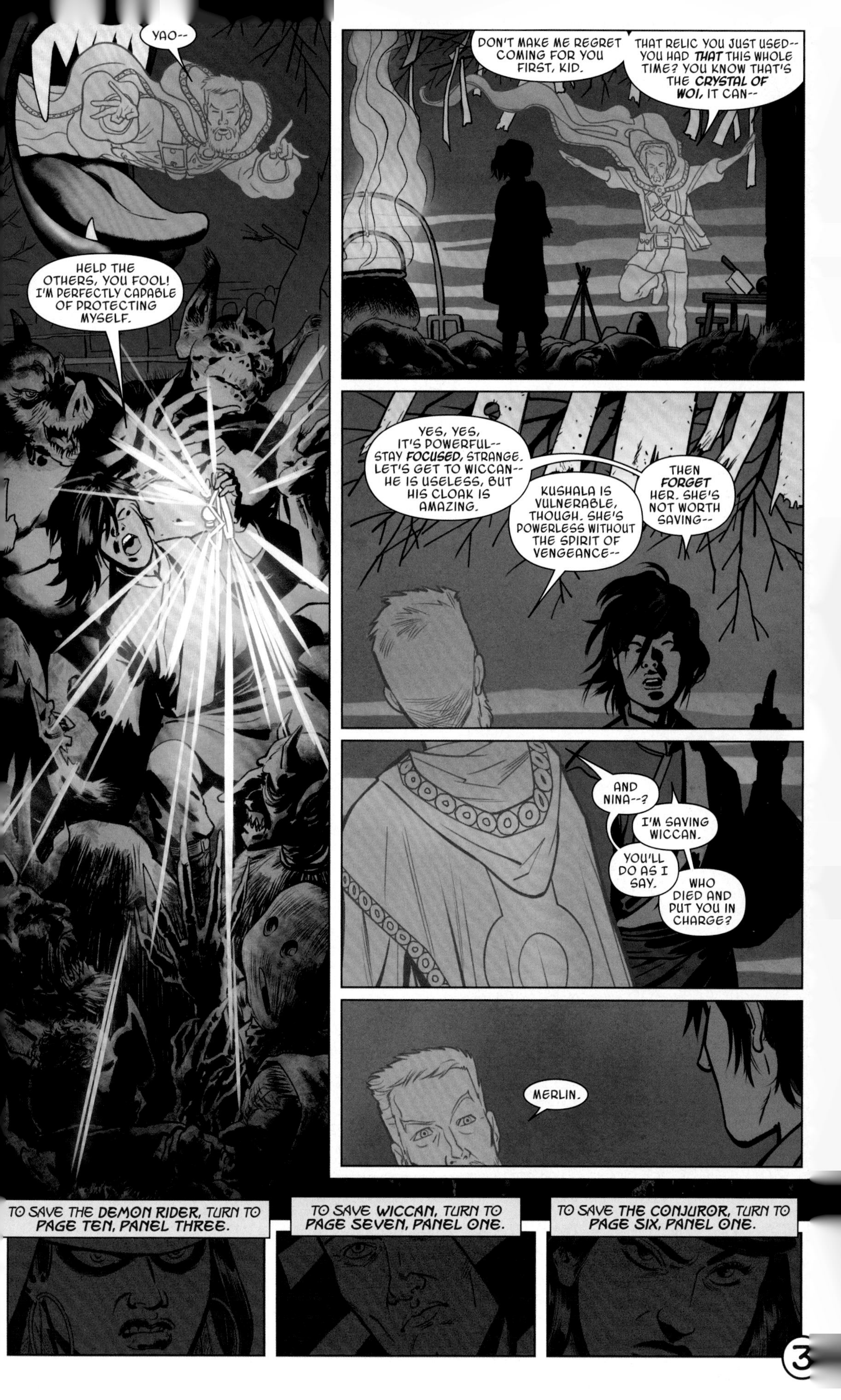

YAO--
HELP THE OTHERS, YOU FOOL! I'M PERFECTLY CAPABLE OF PROTECTING MYSELF.
DON'T MAKE ME REGRET COMING FOR YOU FIRST, KID.
THAT RELIC YOU JUST USED-- YOU HAD THAT THIS WHOLE TIME? YOU KNOW THAT'S THE CRYSTAL OF WOI, IT CAN--
YES, YES, IT'S POWERFUL-- STAY FOCUSED, STRANGE. LET'S GET TO WICCAN-- HE IS USELESS, BUT HIS CLOAK IS AMAZING.
KUSHALA IS VULNERABLE, THOUGH. SHE'S POWERLESS WITHOUT THE SPIRIT OF VENGEANCE--
THEN FORGET HER. SHE'S NOT WORTH SAVING--
AND NINA--?
I'M SAVING WICCAN.
YOU'LL DO AS I SAY.
WHO DIED AND PUT YOU IN CHARGE?
MERLIN.
TO SAVE THE DEMON RIDER, TURN TO PAGE TEN, PANEL THREE.
TO SAVE WICCAN, TURN TO PAGE SEVEN, PANEL ONE.
TO SAVE THE CONJUROR, TURN TO PAGE SIX, PANEL ONE.

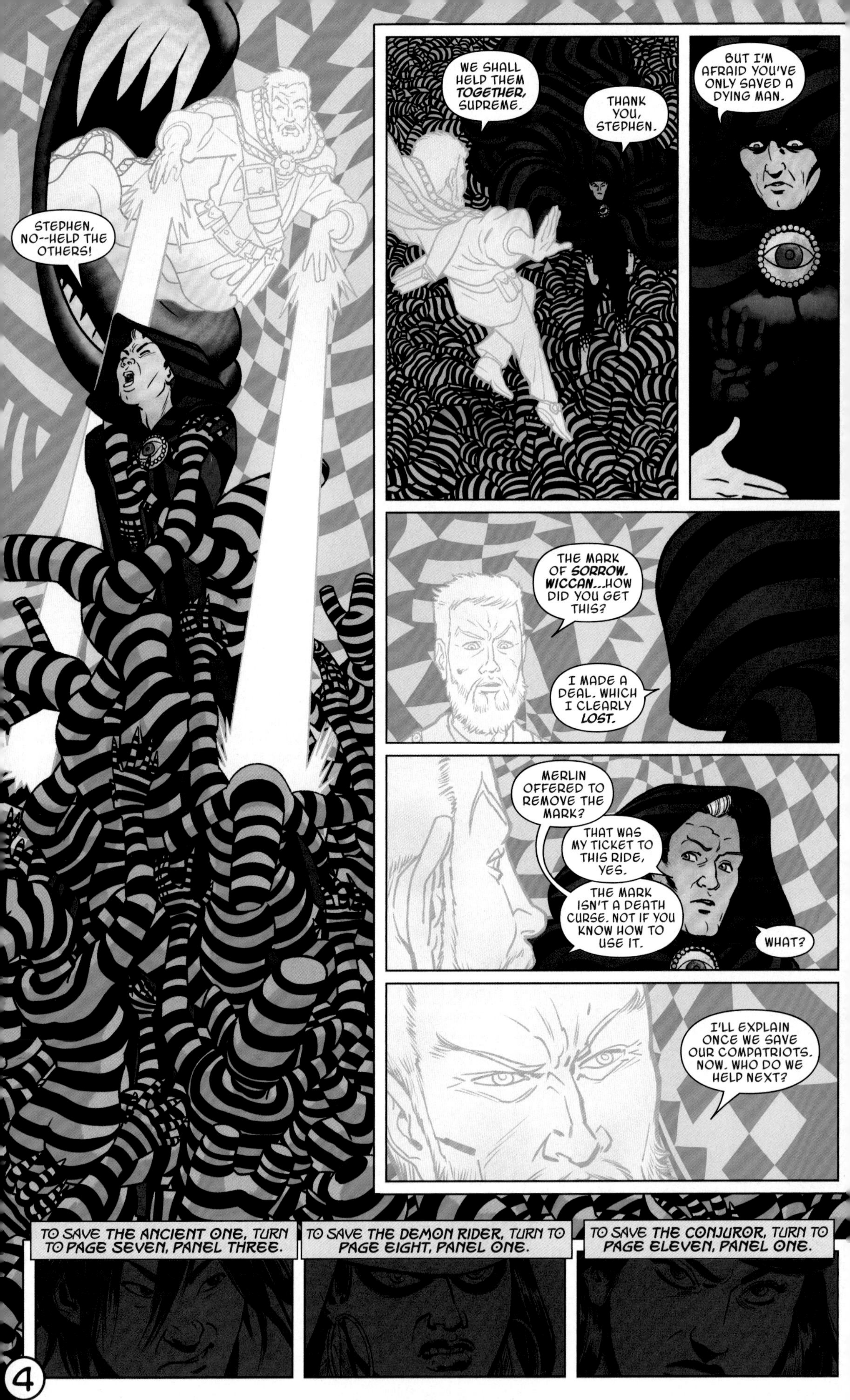

STEPHEN, NO--HELP THE OTHERS!
WE SHALL HELP THEM TOGETHER, SUPREME.
THANK YOU, STEPHEN.
BUT I'M AFRAID YOU'VE ONLY SAVED A DYING MAN.
THE MARK OF SORROW. WICCAN...HOW DID YOU GET THIS?
I MADE A DEAL. WHICH I CLEARLY LOST.
MERLIN OFFERED TO REMOVE THE MARK?
THAT WAS MY TICKET TO THIS RIDE, YES.
THE MARK ISN'T A DEATH CURSE. NOT IF YOU KNOW HOW TO USE IT.
WHAT?
I'LL EXPLAIN ONCE WE SAVE OUR COMPATRIOTS. NOW. WHO DO WE HELP NEXT?
TO SAVE THE ANCIENT ONE, TURN TO PAGE SEVEN, PANEL THREE.
TO SAVE THE DEMON RIDER, TURN TO PAGE EIGHT, PANEL ONE.
TO SAVE THE CONJUROR, TURN TO PAGE ELEVEN, PANEL ONE.

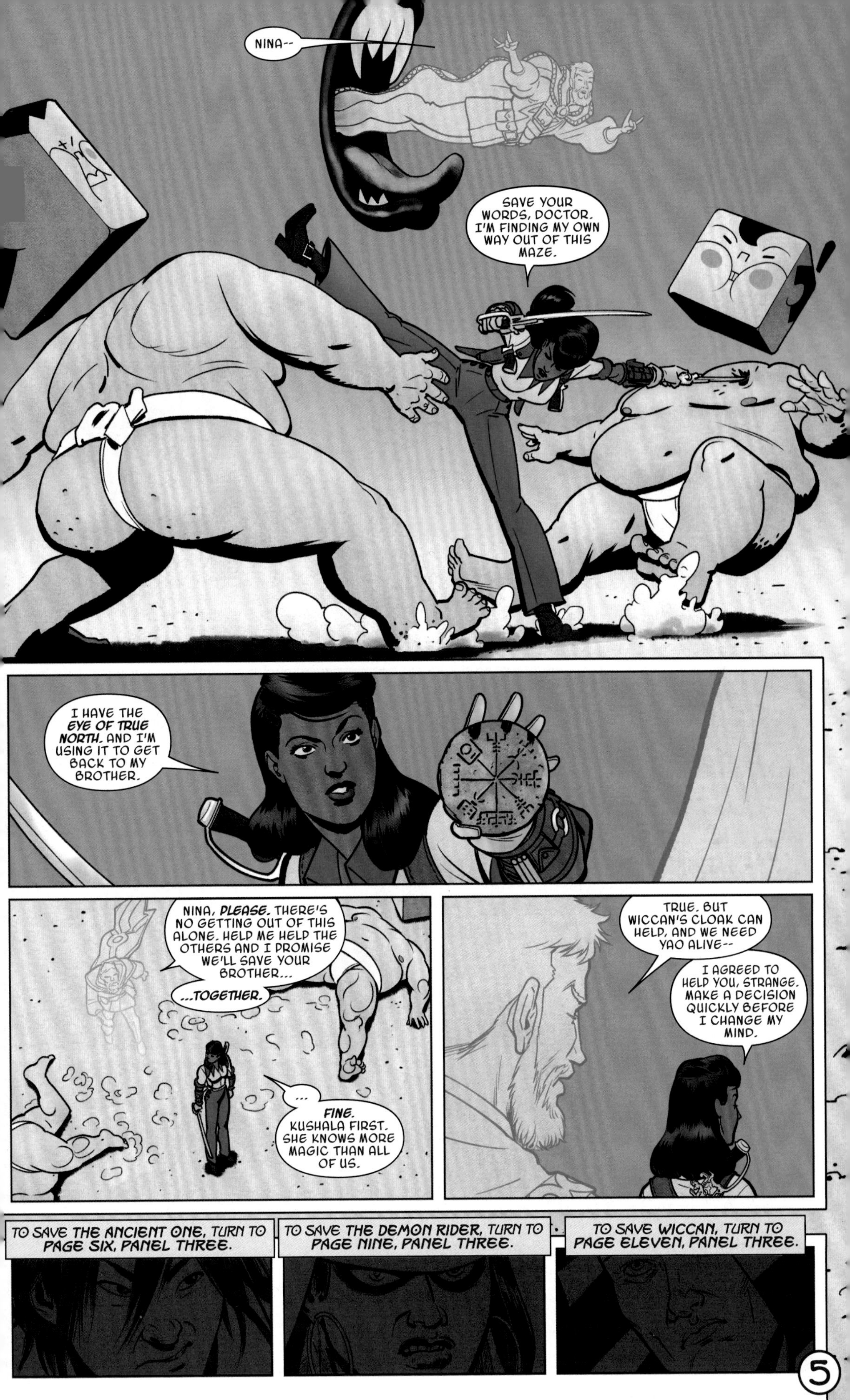

NINA--
SAVE YOUR WORDS, DOCTOR. I'M FINDING MY OWN WAY OUT OF THIS MAZE.
I HAVE THE EYE OF TRUE NORTH. AND I'M USING IT TO GET BACK TO MY BROTHER.
NINA, PLEASE. THERE'S NO GETTING OUT OF THIS ALONE. HELP ME HELP THE OTHERS AND I PROMISE WE'LL SAVE YOUR BROTHER...
...TOGETHER.
...
FINE. KUSHALA FIRST. SHE KNOWS MORE MAGIC THAN ALL OF US.
TRUE. BUT WICCAN'S CLOAK CAN HELP, AND WE NEED YAO ALIVE--
I AGREED TO HELP YOU, STRANGE. MAKE A DECISION QUICKLY BEFORE I CHANGE MY MIND.
TO SAVE THE ANCIENT ONE, TURN TO PAGE SIX, PANEL THREE.
TO SAVE THE DEMON RIDER, TURN TO PAGE NINE, PANEL THREE.
TO SAVE WICCAN, TURN TO PAGE ELEVEN, PANEL THREE.

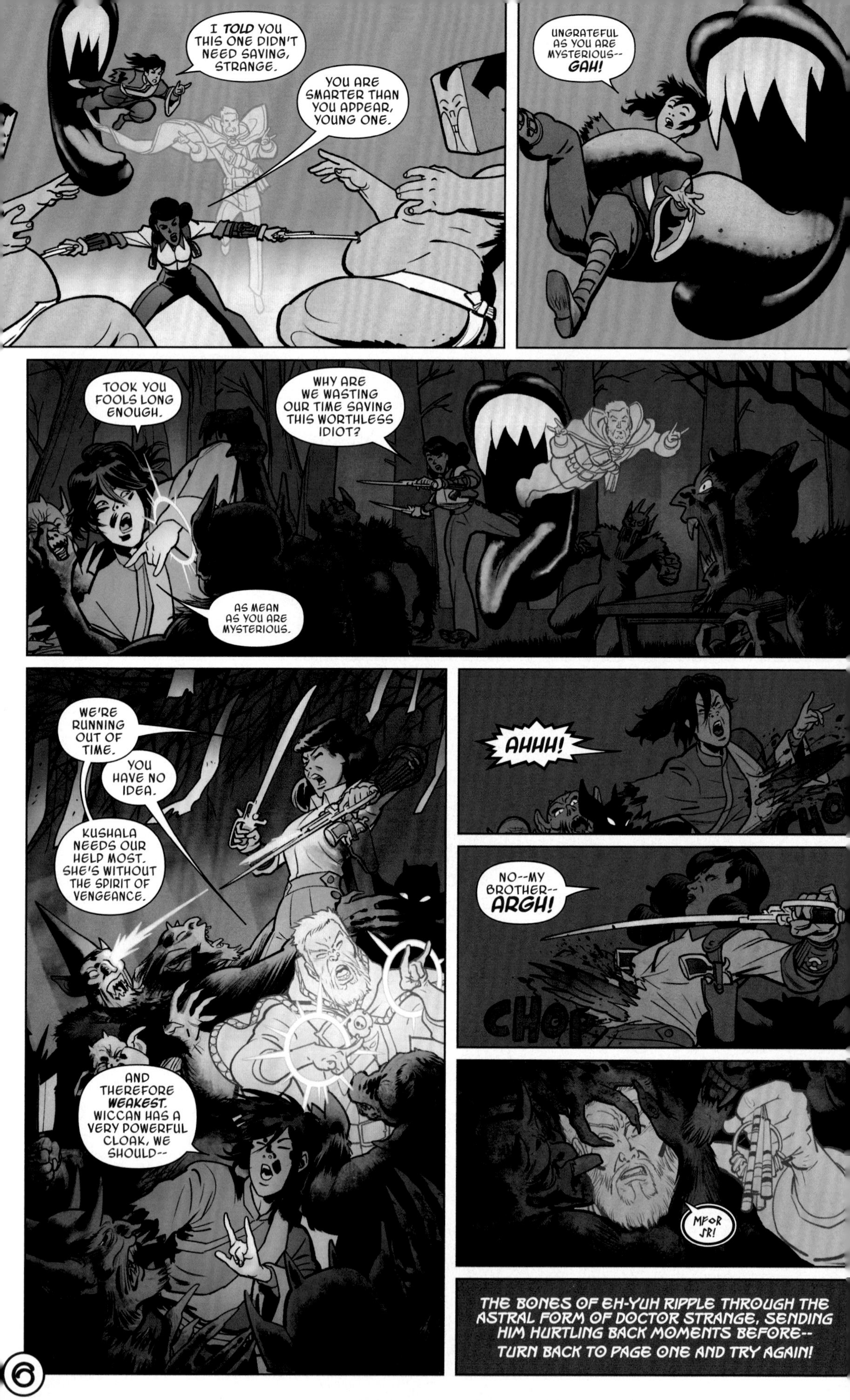

I *TOLD* YOU THIS ONE DIDN'T NEED SAVING, STRANGE.
YOU ARE SMARTER THAN YOU APPEAR, YOUNG ONE.
UNGRATEFUL AS YOU ARE MYSTERIOUS-- **GAH!**
TOOK YOU FOOLS LONG ENOUGH.
WHY ARE WE WASTING OUR TIME SAVING THIS WORTHLESS IDIOT?
AS MEAN AS YOU ARE MYSTERIOUS.
WE'RE RUNNING OUT OF TIME.
YOU HAVE NO IDEA.
KUSHALA NEEDS OUR HELP MOST. SHE'S WITHOUT THE SPIRIT OF VENGEANCE.
AND THEREFORE *WEAKEST.* WICCAN HAS A VERY POWERFUL CLOAK, WE SHOULD--
AHHH!
CHOP
NO--MY BROTHER-- **ARGH!**
CHOP
MFOR SR!
THE BONES OF EH-YUH RIPPLE THROUGH THE ASTRAL FORM OF DOCTOR STRANGE, SENDING HIM HURTLING BACK MOMENTS BEFORE--
TURN BACK TO PAGE ONE AND TRY AGAIN!

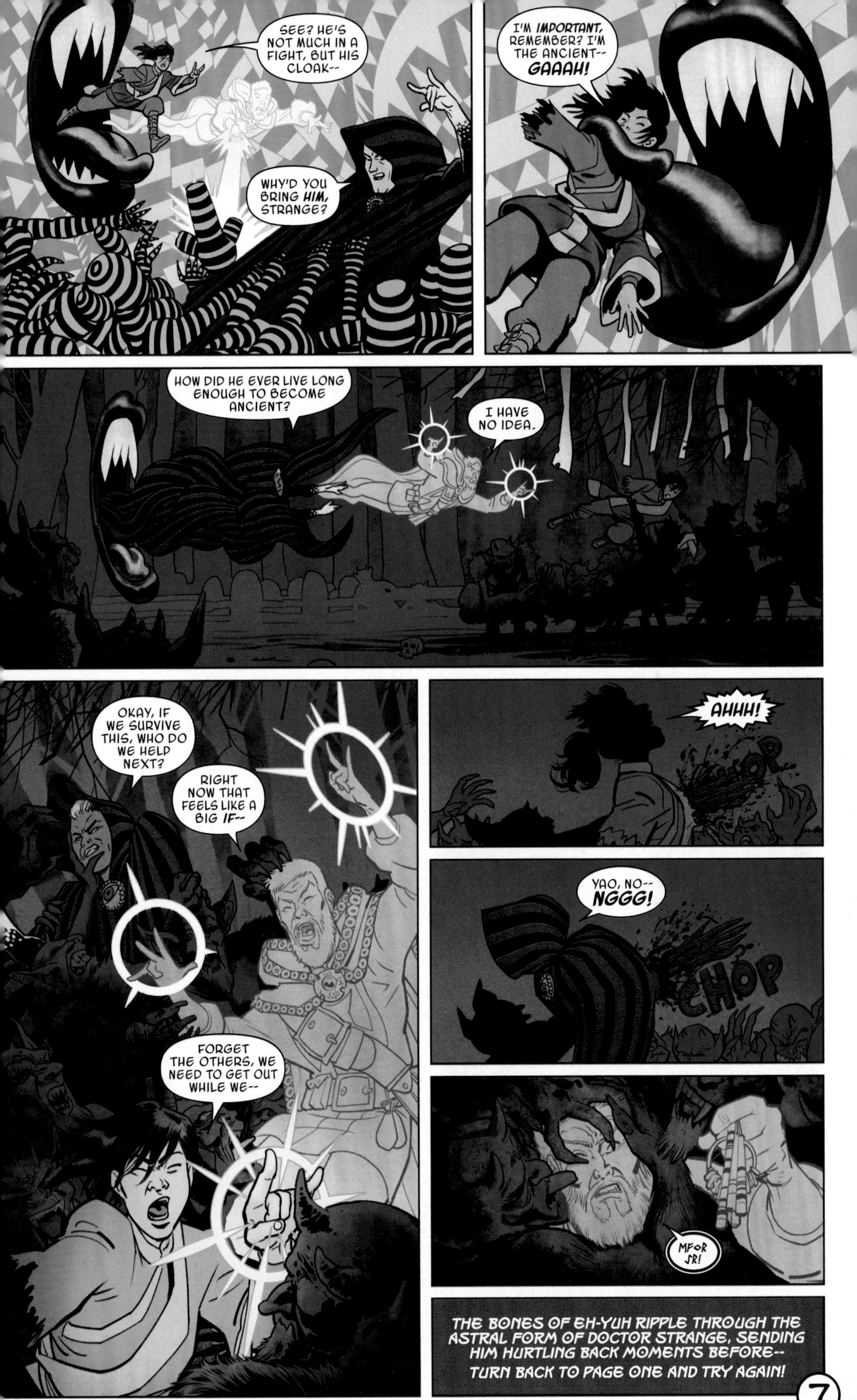
SEE? HE'S NOT MUCH IN A FIGHT, BUT HIS CLOAK--
WHY'D YOU BRING HIM, STRANGE?
I'M IMPORTANT, REMEMBER? I'M THE ANCIENT-- GAAAH!
HOW DID HE EVER LIVE LONG ENOUGH TO BECOME ANCIENT?
I HAVE NO IDEA.
OKAY, IF WE SURVIVE THIS, WHO DO WE HELP NEXT?
RIGHT NOW THAT FEELS LIKE A BIG IF--
FORGET THE OTHERS, WE NEED TO GET OUT WHILE WE--
AHHH!
YAO, NO-- NGGG!
CHOP
MFOR SR!
THE BONES OF EH-YUH RIPPLE THROUGH THE ASTRAL FORM OF DOCTOR STRANGE, SENDING HIM HURTLING BACK MOMENTS BEFORE--
TURN BACK TO PAGE ONE AND TRY AGAIN!

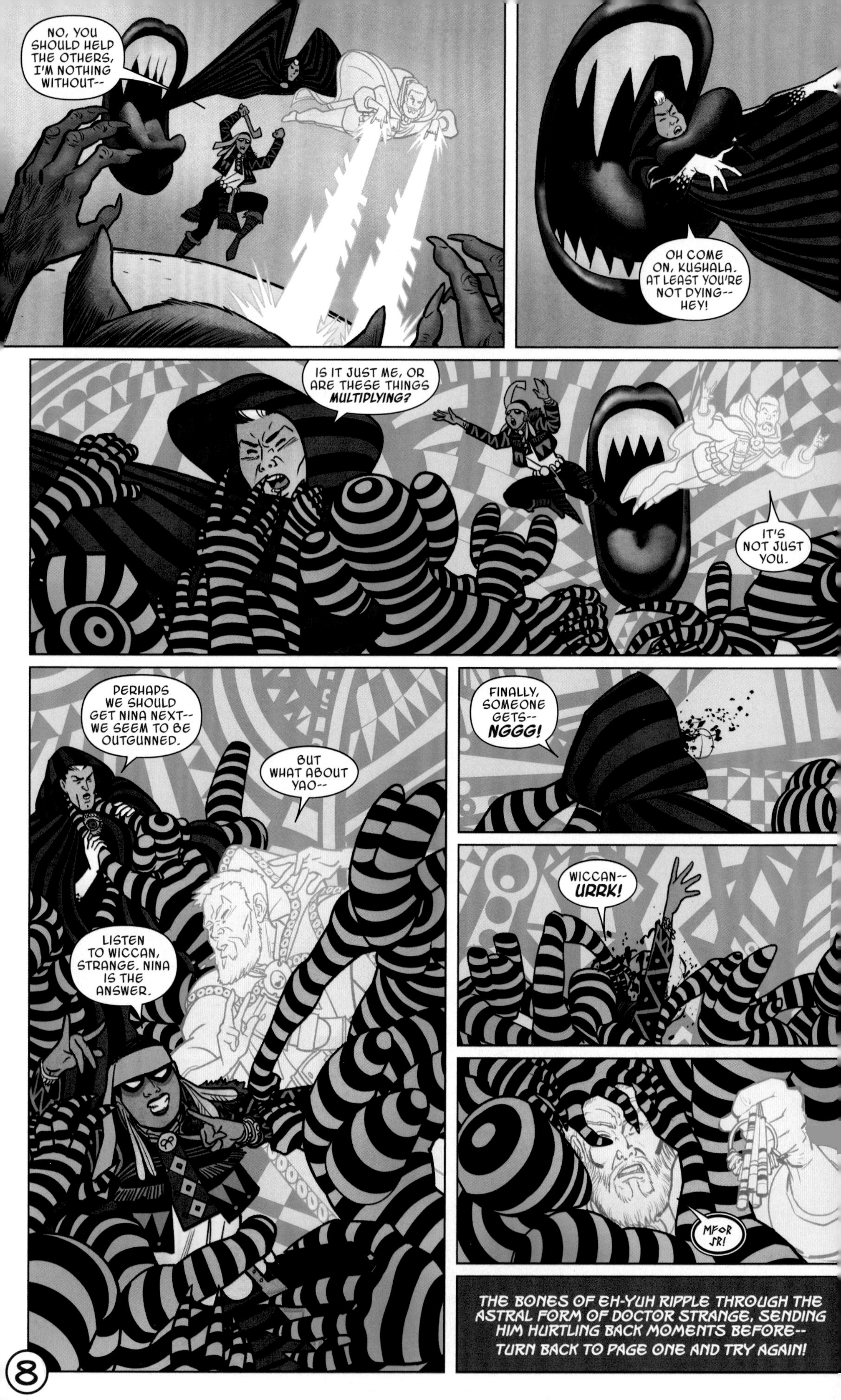
NO, YOU SHOULD HELP THE OTHERS, I'M NOTHING WITHOUT--
OH COME ON, KUSHALA. AT LEAST YOU'RE NOT DYING-- HEY!
IS IT JUST ME, OR ARE THESE THINGS *MULTIPLYING?*
IT'S NOT JUST YOU.
PERHAPS WE SHOULD GET NINA NEXT-- WE SEEM TO BE OUTGUNNED.
BUT WHAT ABOUT YAO--
LISTEN TO WICCAN, STRANGE. NINA IS THE ANSWER.
FINALLY, SOMEONE GETS-- **NGGG!**
WICCAN-- **URRK!**
MFOR JR!
THE BONES OF EH-YUH RIPPLE THROUGH THE ASTRAL FORM OF DOCTOR STRANGE, SENDING HIM HURTLING BACK MOMENTS BEFORE--
TURN BACK TO PAGE ONE AND TRY AGAIN!

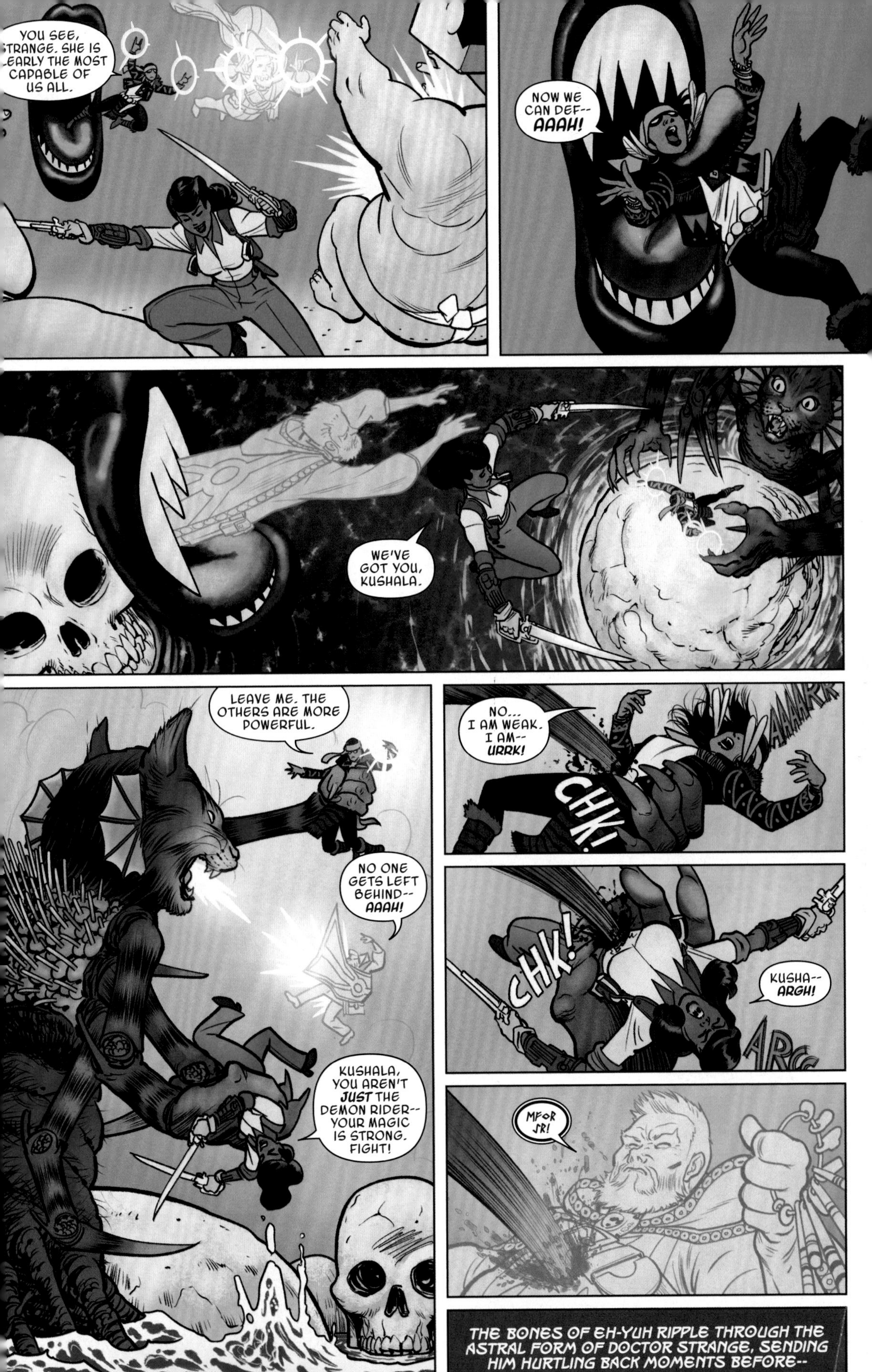
YOU SEE, STRANGE. SHE IS CLEARLY THE MOST CAPABLE OF US ALL.
NOW WE CAN DEF-- AAAH!
WE'VE GOT YOU, KUSHALA.
LEAVE ME. THE OTHERS ARE MORE POWERFUL.
NO ONE GETS LEFT BEHIND-- AAAH!
KUSHALA, YOU AREN'T JUST THE DEMON RIDER-- YOUR MAGIC IS STRONG. FIGHT!
NO... I AM WEAK. I AM-- URRK!
AAAARK
CHK!
CHK!
KUSHA-- ARGH!
ARG
MFOR JR!
THE BONES OF EH-YUH RIPPLE THROUGH THE ASTRAL FORM OF DOCTOR STRANGE, SENDING HIM HURTLING BACK MOMENTS BEFORE--
TURN BACK TO PAGE ONE AND TRY AGAIN!

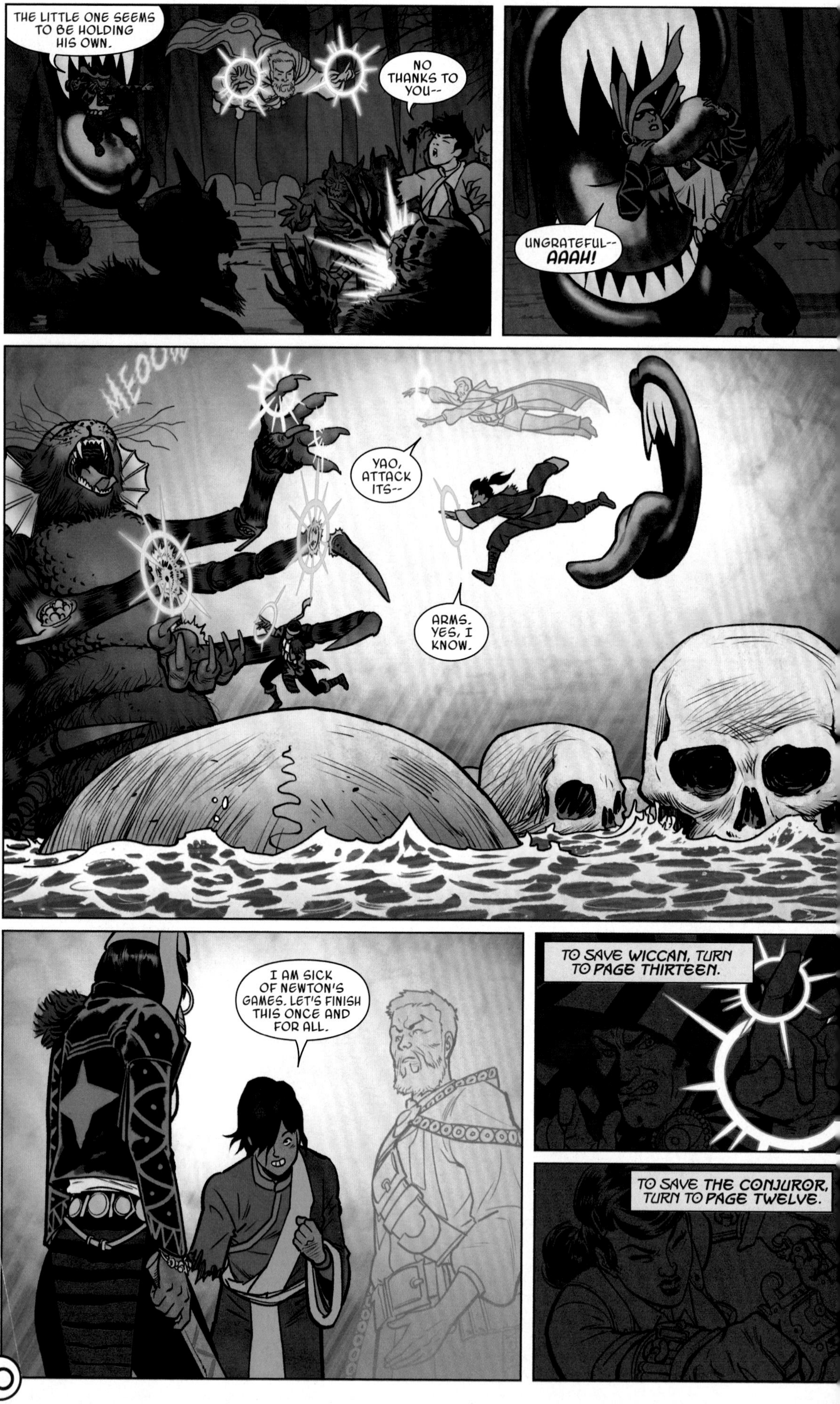
THE LITTLE ONE SEEMS TO BE HOLDING HIS OWN.
NO THANKS TO YOU--
UNGRATEFUL-- AAAH!
MEOOW
YAO, ATTACK ITS--
ARMS. YES, I KNOW.
I AM SICK OF NEWTON'S GAMES. LET'S FINISH THIS ONCE AND FOR ALL.
TO SAVE WICCAN, TURN TO PAGE THIRTEEN.
TO SAVE THE CONJUROR, TURN TO PAGE TWELVE.

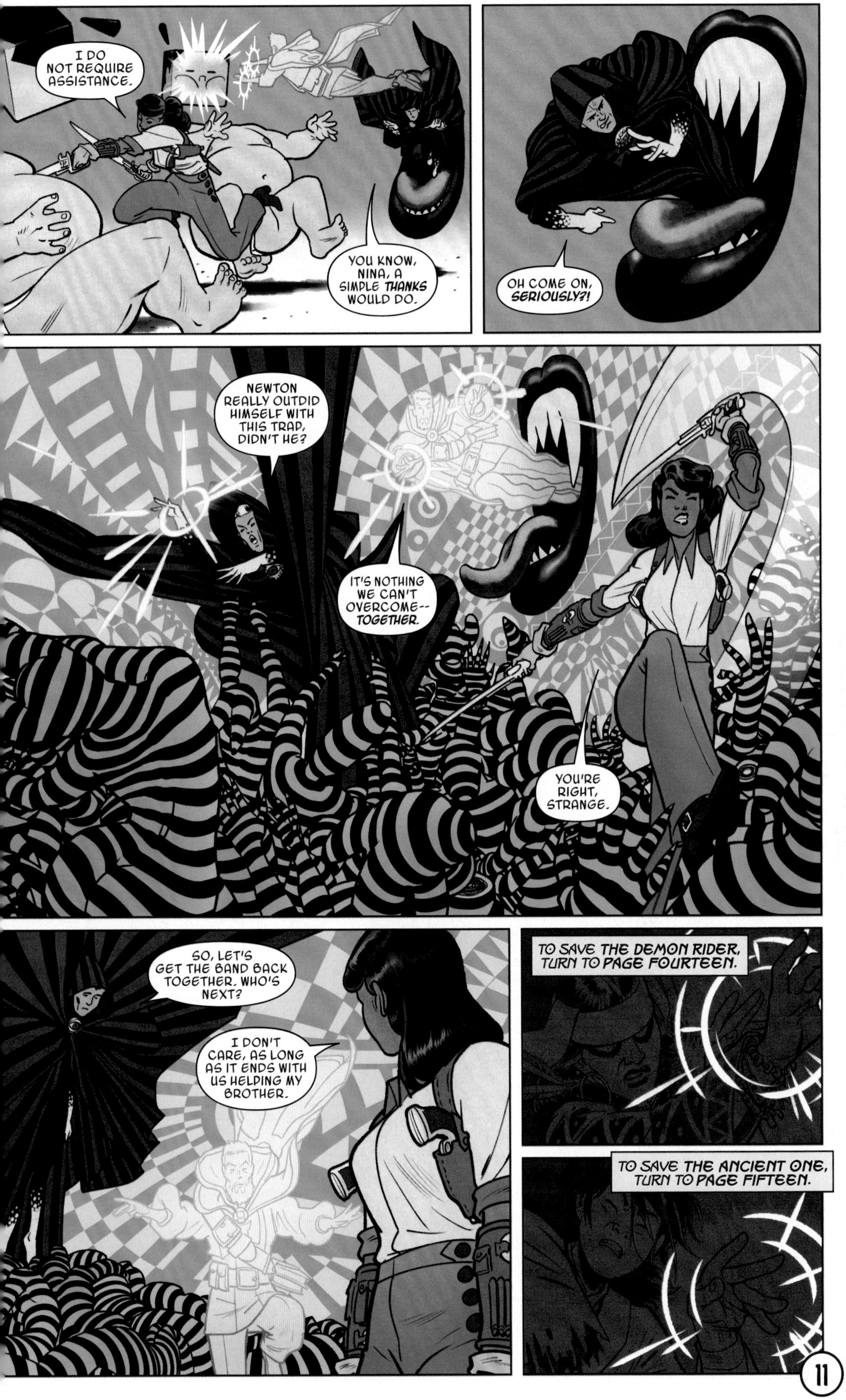
I DO NOT REQUIRE ASSISTANCE.
YOU KNOW, NINA, A SIMPLE THANKS WOULD DO.
OH COME ON, SERIOUSLY?!
NEWTON REALLY OUTDID HIMSELF WITH THIS TRAP, DIDN'T HE?
IT'S NOTHING WE CAN'T OVERCOME-- TOGETHER.
YOU'RE RIGHT, STRANGE.
SO, LET'S GET THE BAND BACK TOGETHER. WHO'S NEXT?
I DON'T CARE, AS LONG AS IT ENDS WITH US HELPING MY BROTHER.
TO SAVE THE DEMON RIDER, TURN TO PAGE FOURTEEN.
TO SAVE THE ANCIENT ONE, TURN TO PAGE FIFTEEN.

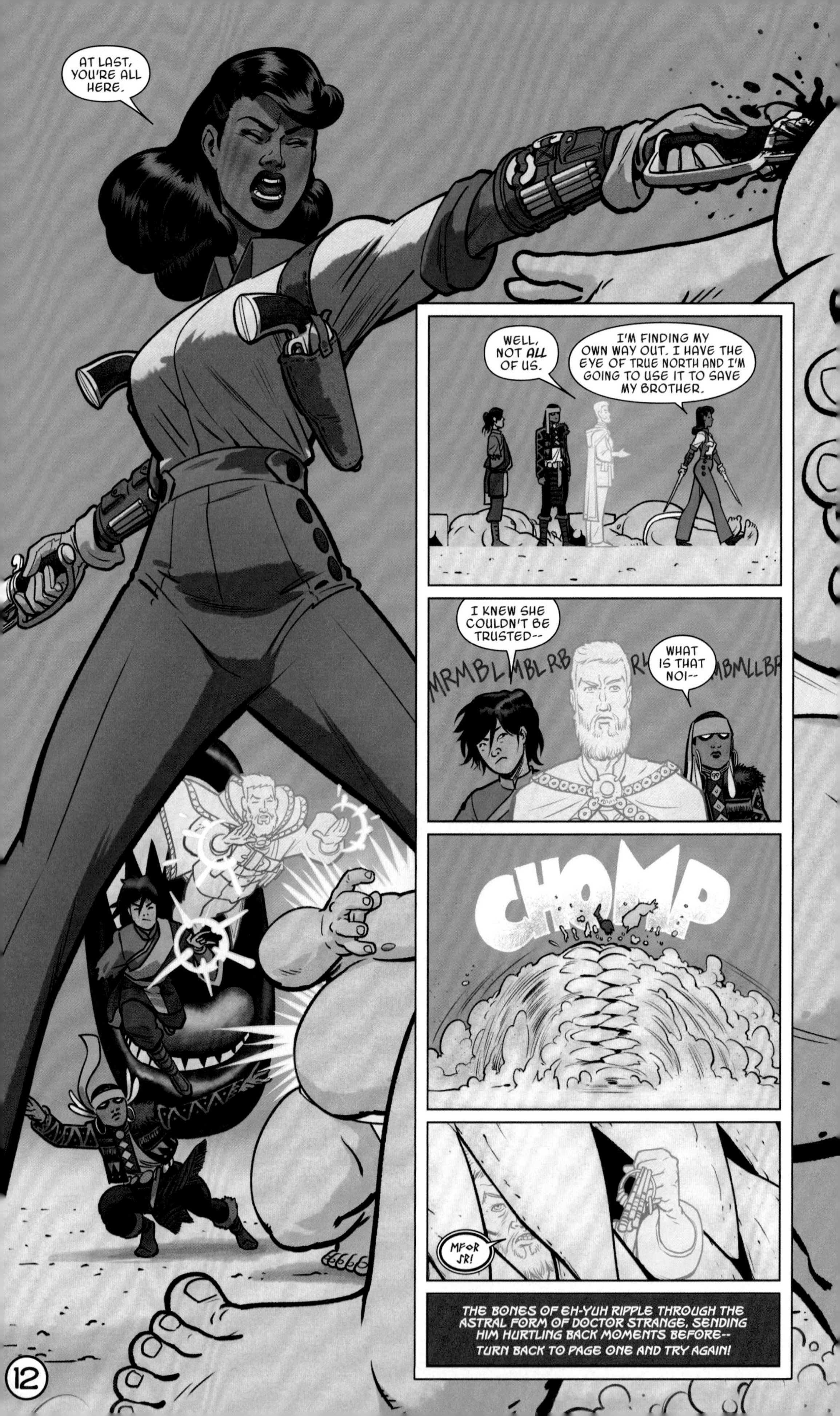
AT LAST, YOU'RE ALL HERE.
WELL, NOT ALL OF US.
I'M FINDING MY OWN WAY OUT. I HAVE THE EYE OF TRUE NORTH AND I'M GOING TO USE IT TO SAVE MY BROTHER.
I KNEW SHE COULDN'T BE TRUSTED--
MRMBLMBLRB
WHAT IS THAT NOI--
CHOMP
MFOR SR!
THE BONES OF EH-YUH RIPPLE THROUGH THE ASTRAL FORM OF DOCTOR STRANGE, SENDING HIM HURTLING BACK MOMENTS BEFORE--
TURN BACK TO PAGE ONE AND TRY AGAIN!

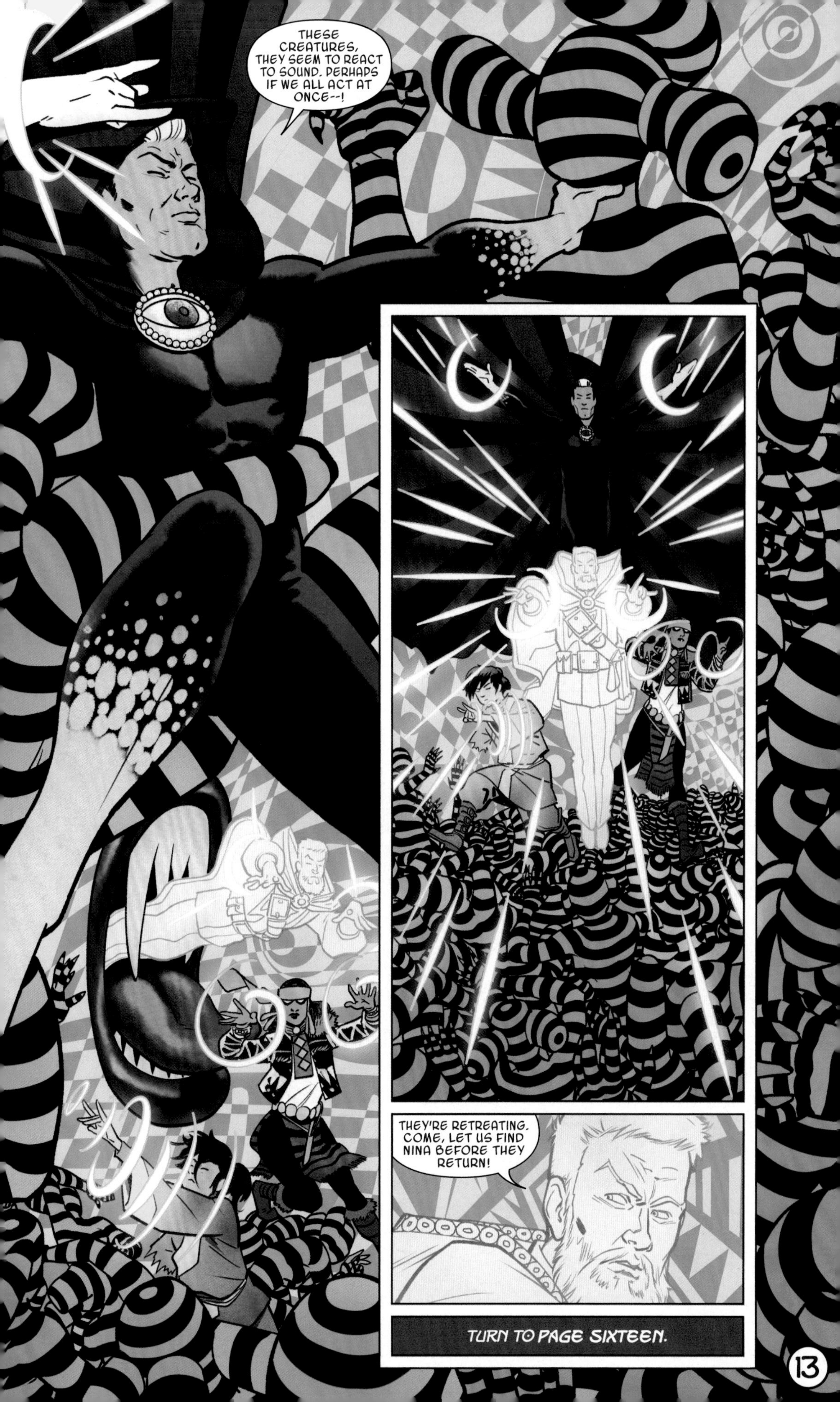
THESE CREATURES, THEY SEEM TO REACT TO SOUND. PERHAPS IF WE ALL ACT AT ONCE--!
THEY'RE RETREATING. COME, LET US FIND NINA BEFORE THEY RETURN!
TURN TO PAGE SIXTEEN.
13

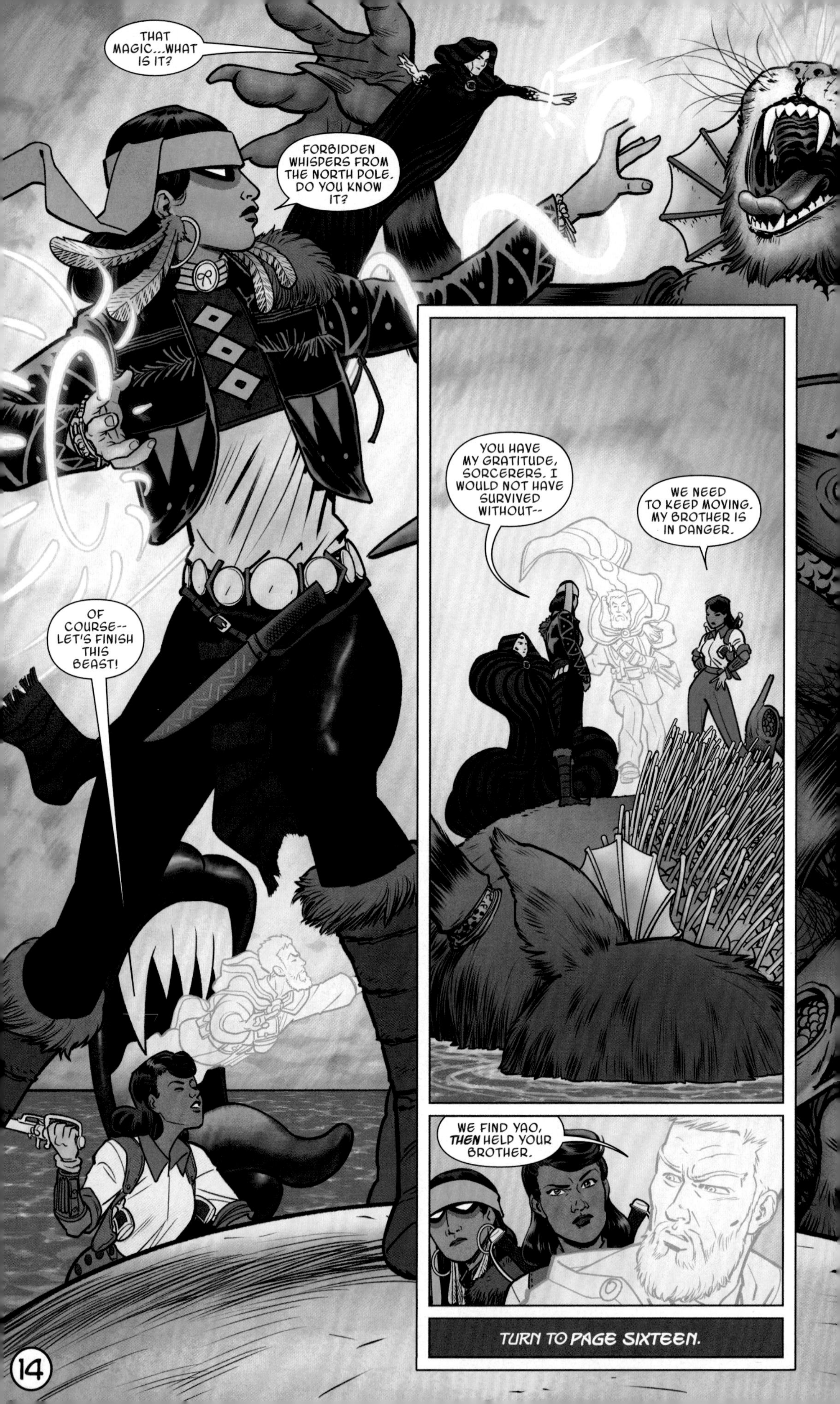

THAT MAGIC...WHAT IS IT?
FORBIDDEN WHISPERS FROM THE NORTH POLE. DO YOU KNOW IT?
OF COURSE-- LET'S FINISH THIS BEAST!
YOU HAVE MY GRATITUDE, SORCERERS. I WOULD NOT HAVE SURVIVED WITHOUT--
WE NEED TO KEEP MOVING. MY BROTHER IS IN DANGER.
WE FIND YAO, THEN HELP YOUR BROTHER.

TURN TO PAGE SIXTEEN.

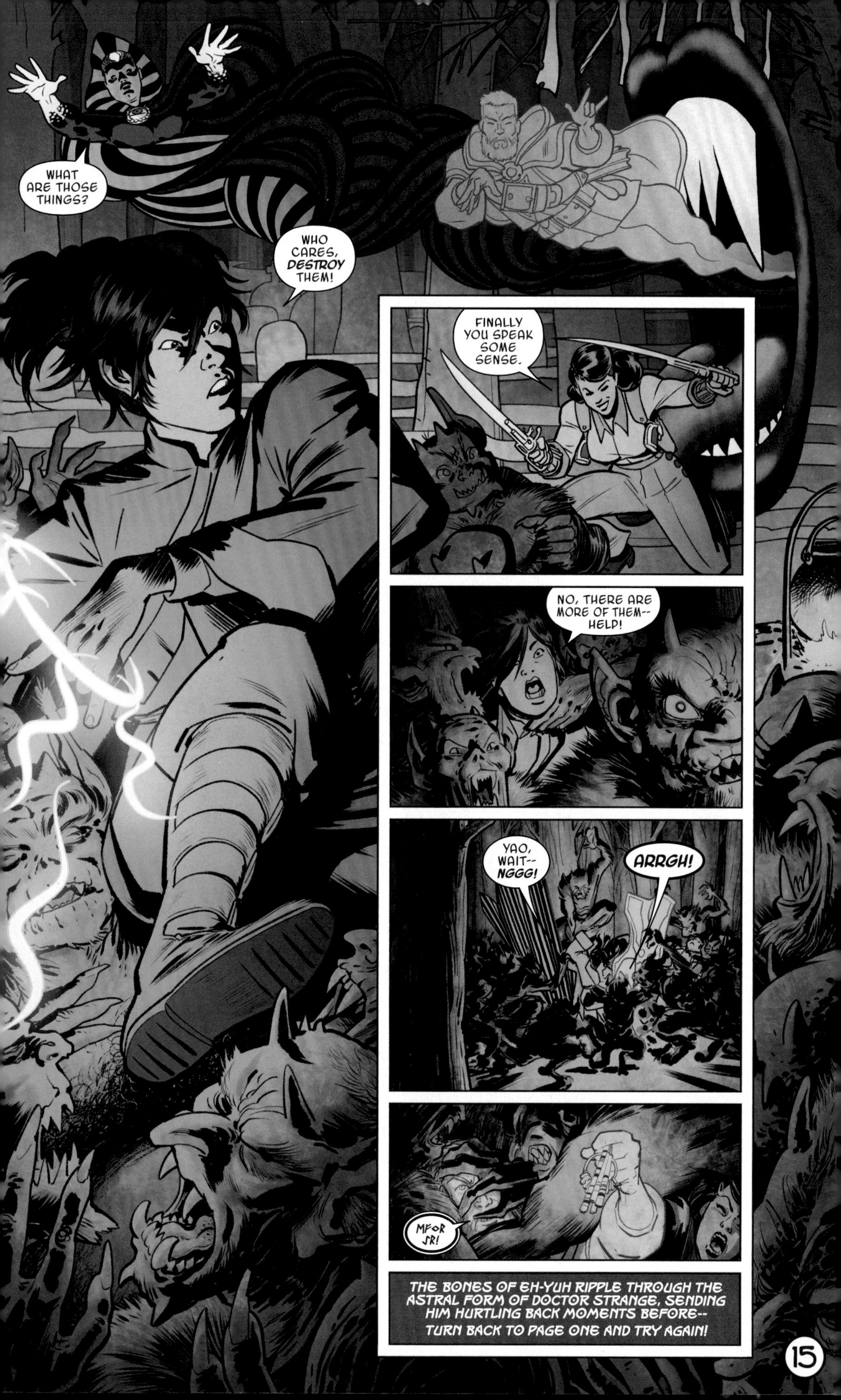
WHAT ARE THOSE THINGS?
WHO CARES, DESTROY THEM!
FINALLY YOU SPEAK SOME SENSE.
NO, THERE ARE MORE OF THEM-- HELP!
YAO, WAIT-- NGGG!
ARRGH!
MFOR SR!
THE BONES OF EH-YUH RIPPLE THROUGH THE ASTRAL FORM OF DOCTOR STRANGE, SENDING HIM HURTLING BACK MOMENTS BEFORE-- TURN BACK TO PAGE ONE AND TRY AGAIN!

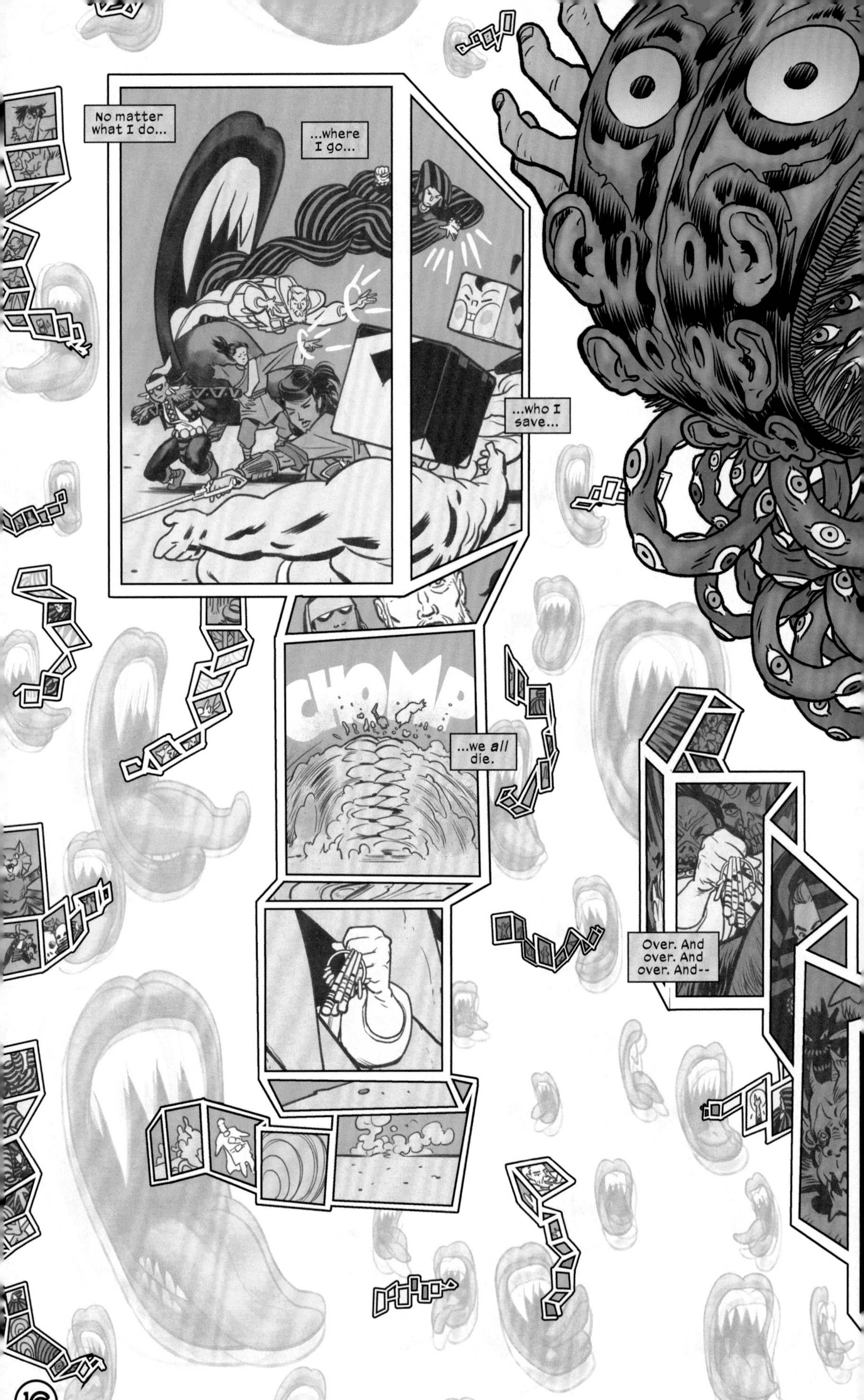

No matter what I do...
...where I go...
...who I save...
CHOMP
...we all die.
Over. And over. And over. And--

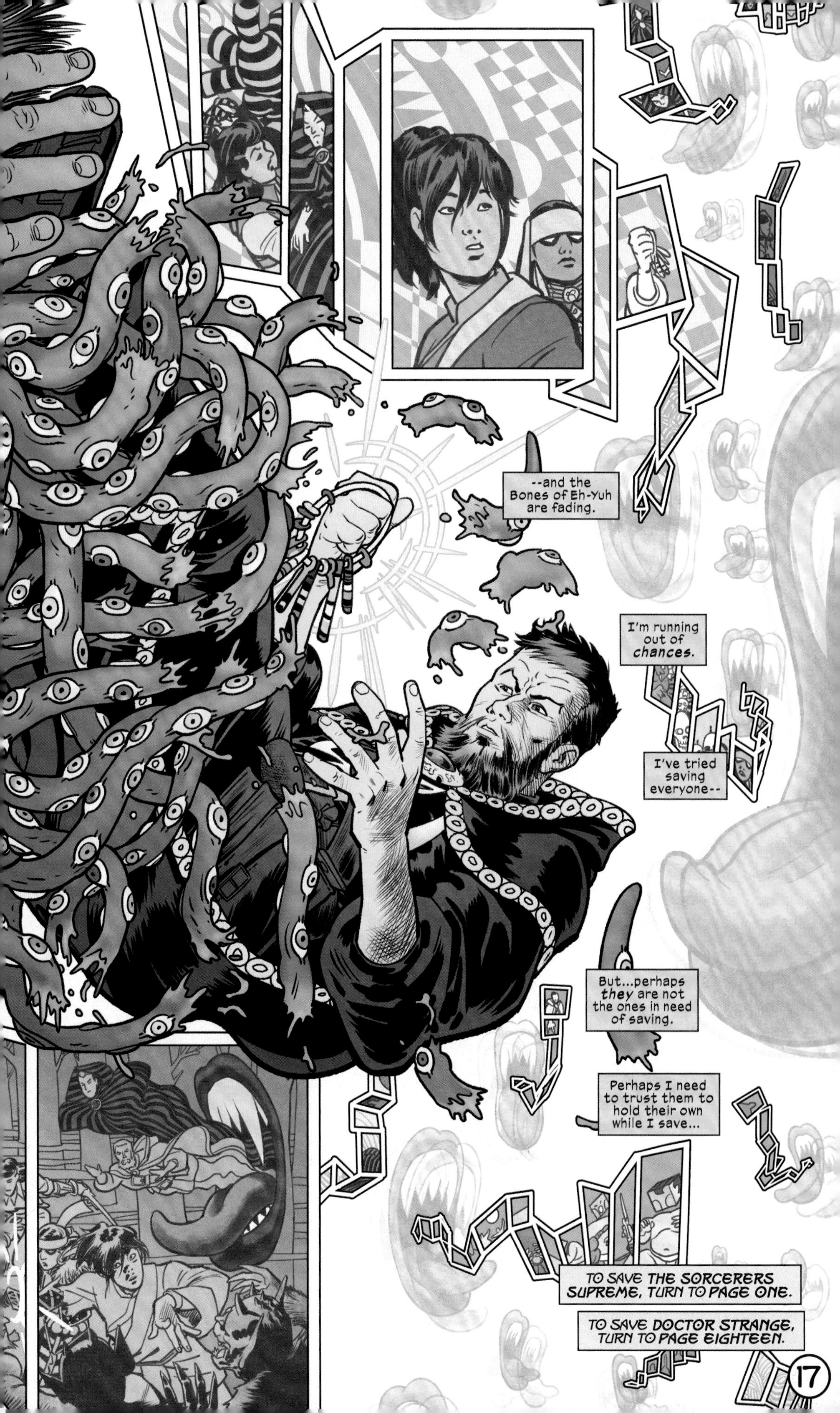

--and the Bones of Eh-Yuh are fading.
I'm running out of *chances*.
I've tried saving everyone--
But...perhaps *they* are not the ones in need of saving.
Perhaps I need to trust them to hold their own while I save...

TO SAVE THE SORCERERS SUPREME, TURN TO PAGE ONE.

TO SAVE DOCTOR STRANGE, TURN TO PAGE EIGHTEEN.

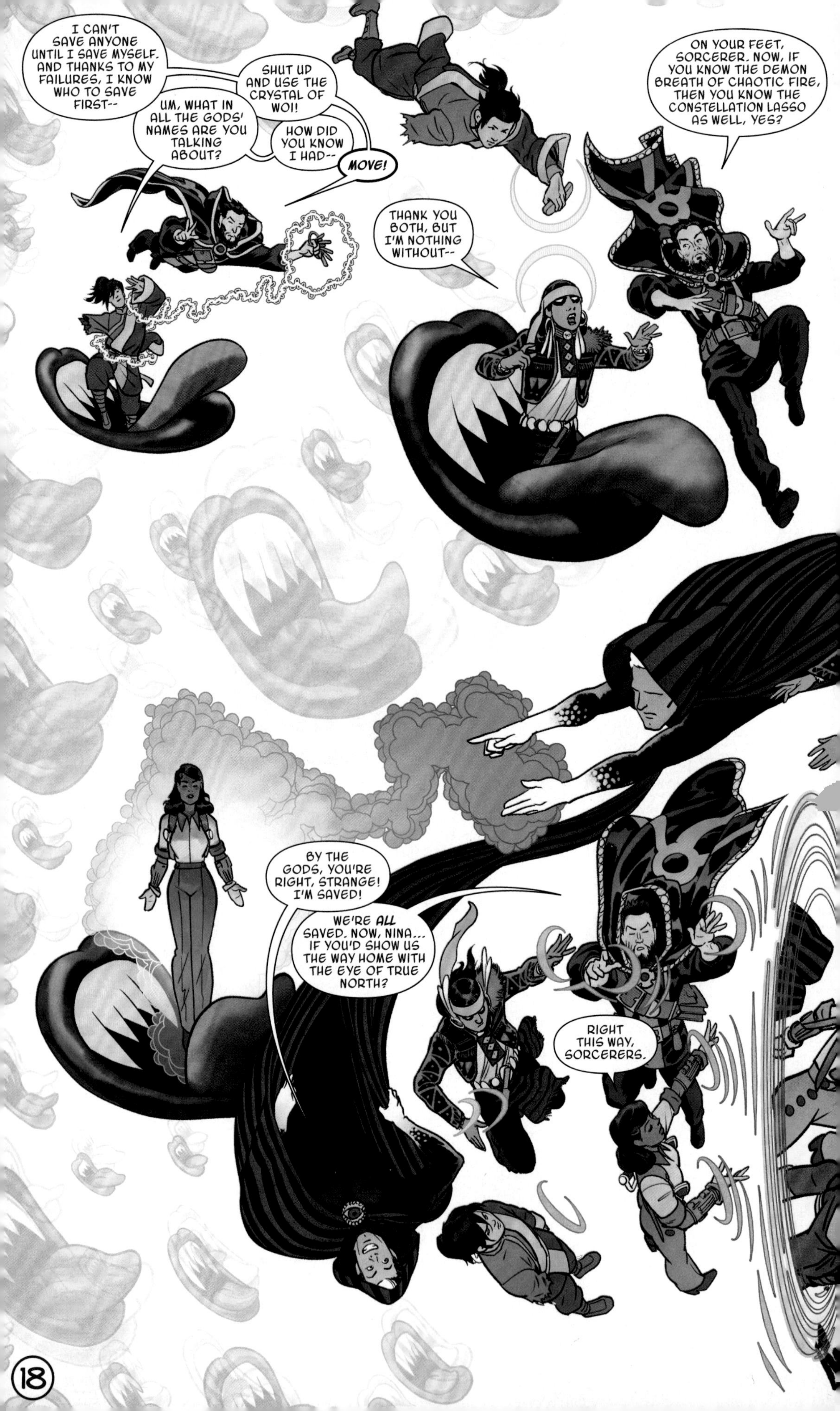
I CAN'T SAVE ANYONE UNTIL I SAVE MYSELF. AND THANKS TO MY FAILURES, I KNOW WHO TO SAVE FIRST--
SHUT UP AND USE THE CRYSTAL OF WOI!
UM, WHAT IN ALL THE GODS' NAMES ARE YOU TALKING ABOUT?
HOW DID YOU KNOW I HAD--
MOVE!
ON YOUR FEET, SORCERER. NOW, IF YOU KNOW THE DEMON BREATH OF CHAOTIC FIRE, THEN YOU KNOW THE CONSTELLATION LASSO AS WELL, YES?
THANK YOU BOTH, BUT I'M NOTHING WITHOUT--
BY THE GODS, YOU'RE RIGHT, STRANGE! I'M SAVED!
WE'RE ALL SAVED. NOW, NINA... IF YOU'D SHOW US THE WAY HOME WITH THE EYE OF TRUE NORTH?
RIGHT THIS WAY, SORCERERS.

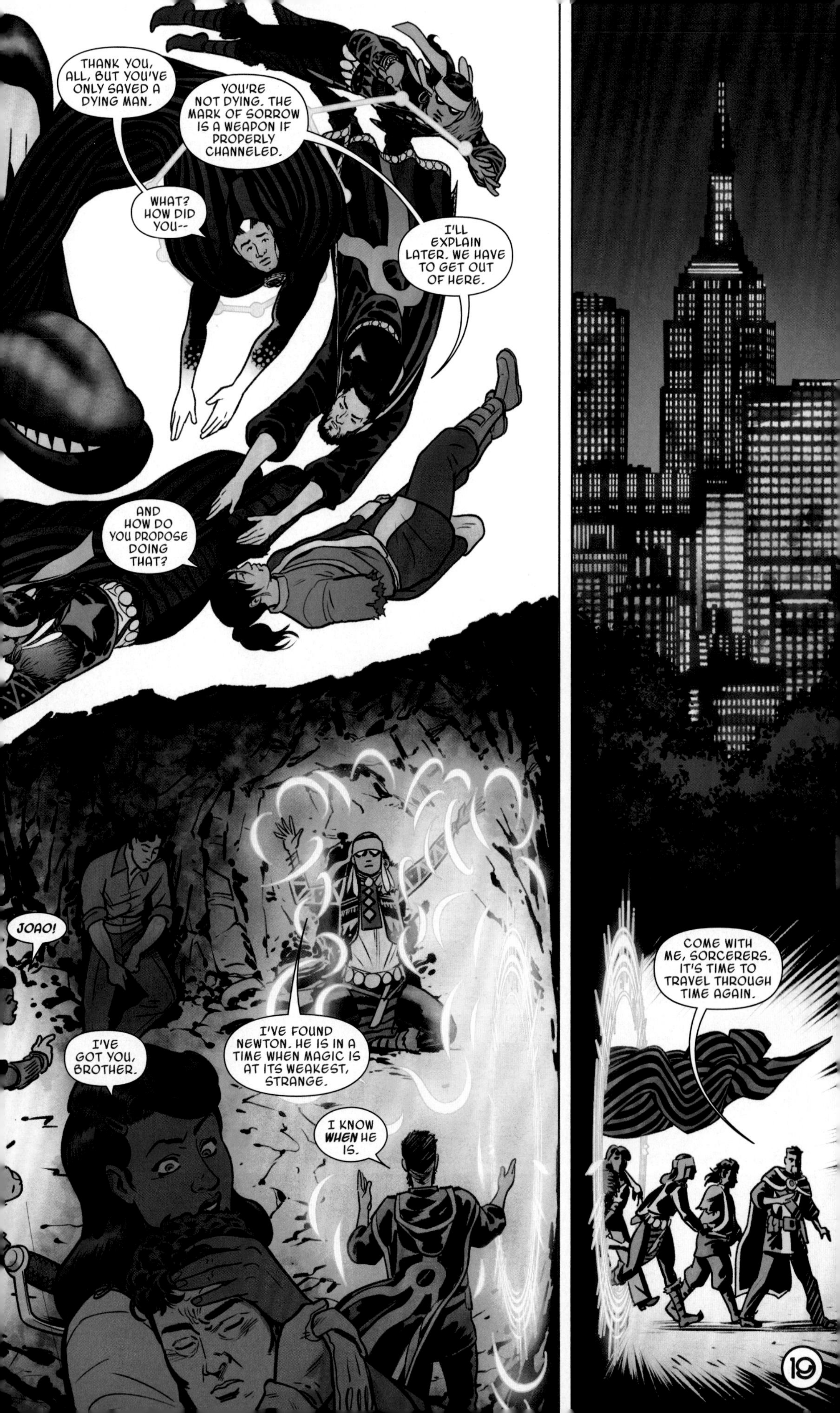
THANK YOU, ALL, BUT YOU'VE ONLY SAVED A DYING MAN.
YOU'RE NOT DYING. THE MARK OF SORROW IS A WEAPON IF PROPERLY CHANNELED.
WHAT? HOW DID YOU--
I'LL EXPLAIN LATER. WE HAVE TO GET OUT OF HERE.
AND HOW DO YOU PROPOSE DOING THAT?
JOAO!
I'VE GOT YOU, BROTHER.
I'VE FOUND NEWTON. HE IS IN A TIME WHEN MAGIC IS AT ITS WEAKEST, STRANGE.
I KNOW **WHEN** HE IS.
COME WITH ME, SORCERERS. IT'S TIME TO TRAVEL THROUGH TIME AGAIN.

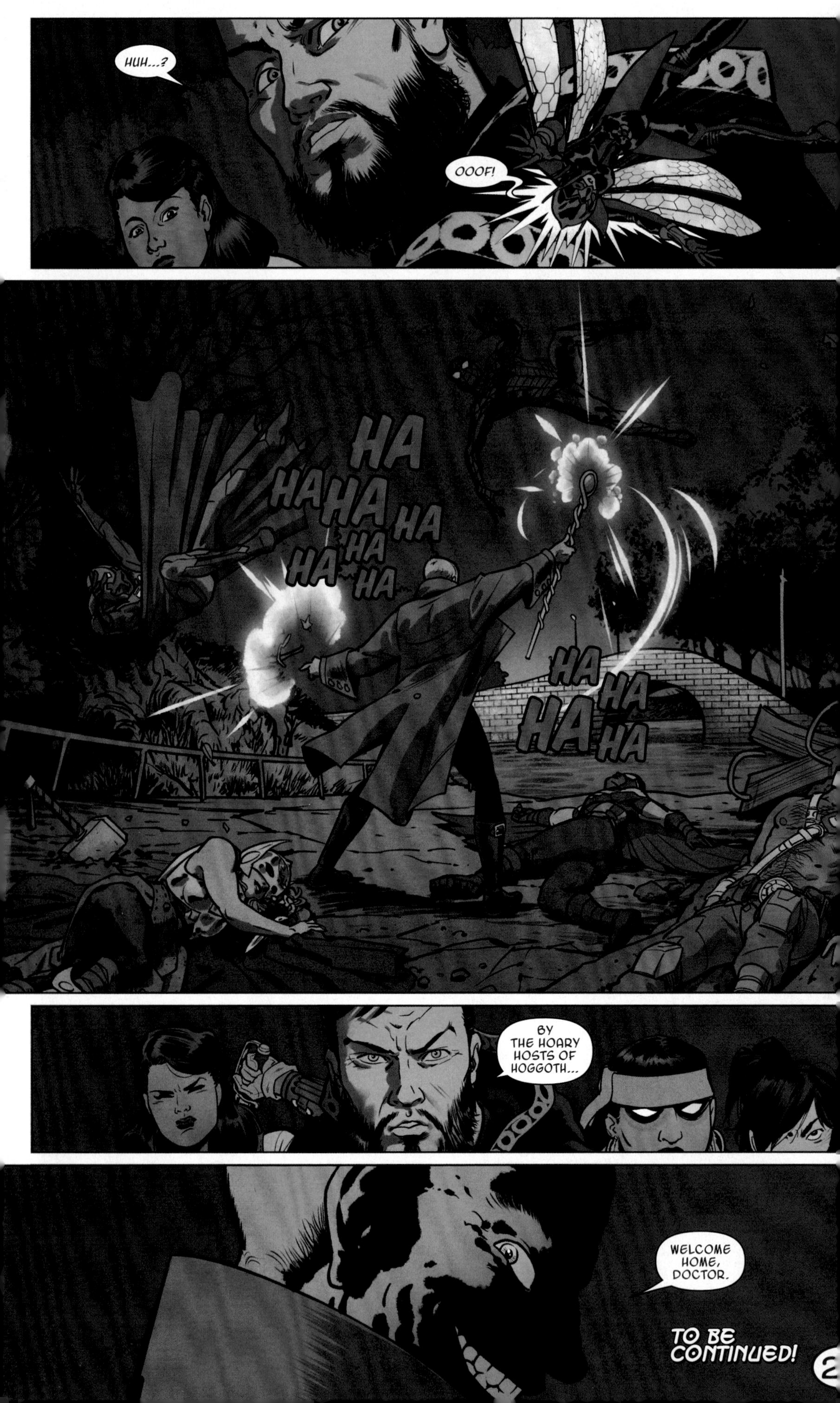
HUH...?
OOOF!
HA HA HA HA HA HA HA HA
HA HA HA HA
BY THE HOARY HOSTS OF HOGGOTH...
WELCOME HOME, DOCTOR.
TO BE CONTINUED!

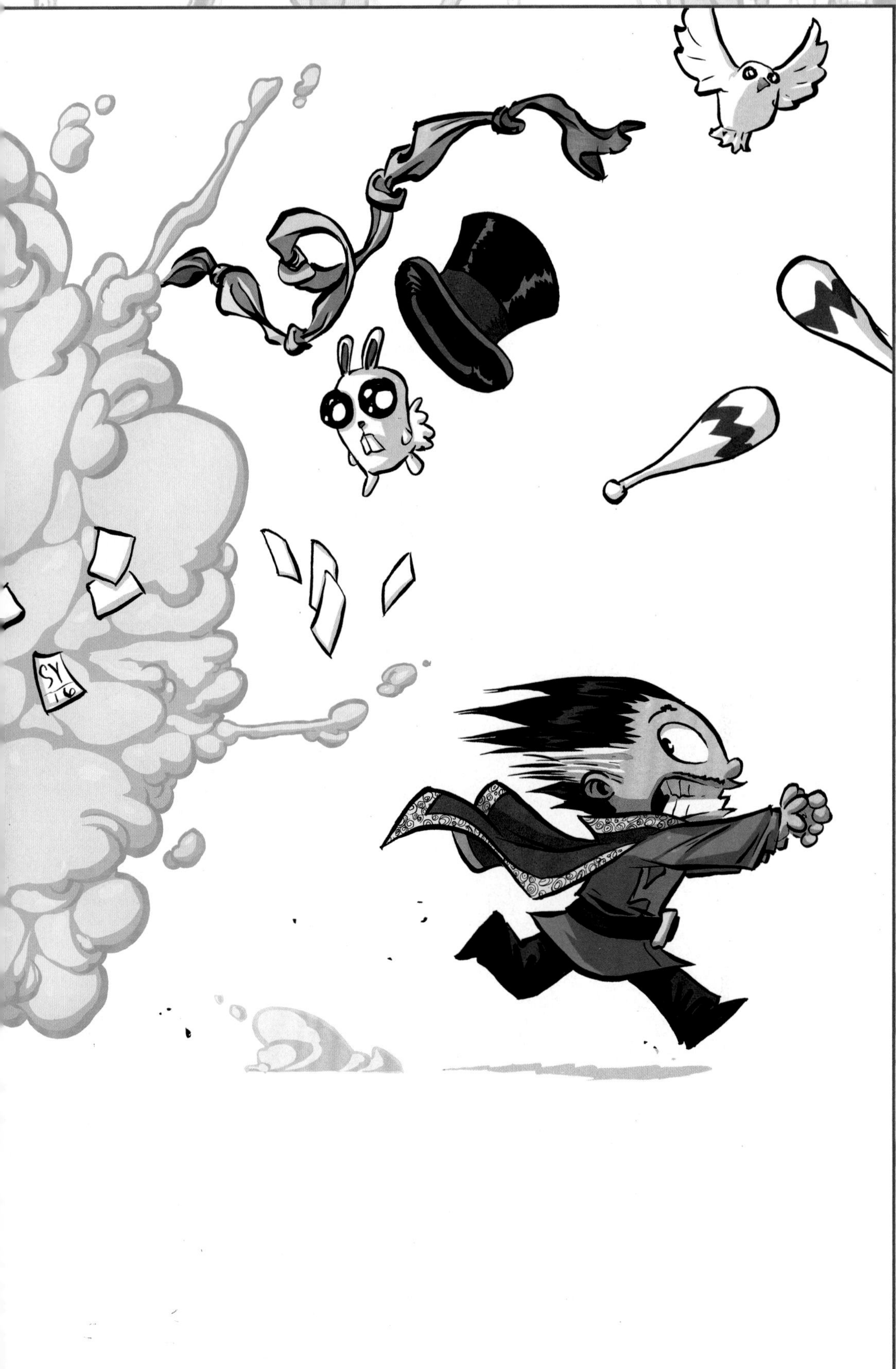
SY
16

NO. 1 VARIANT BY **SKOTTIE YOUNG**

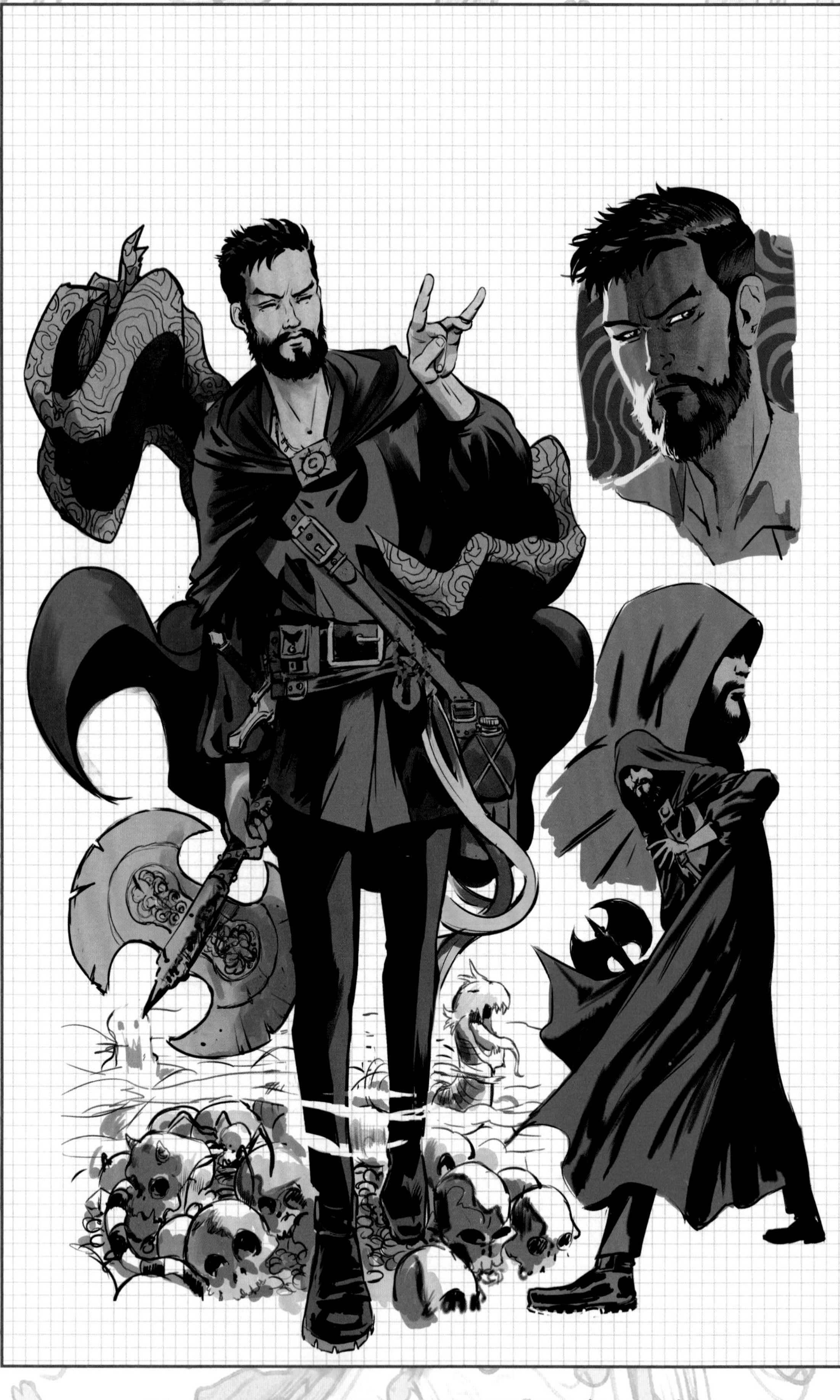

NO. 1 DESIGN VARIANT BY **JAVIER RODRIGUEZ & ÁLVARO LÓPEZ**

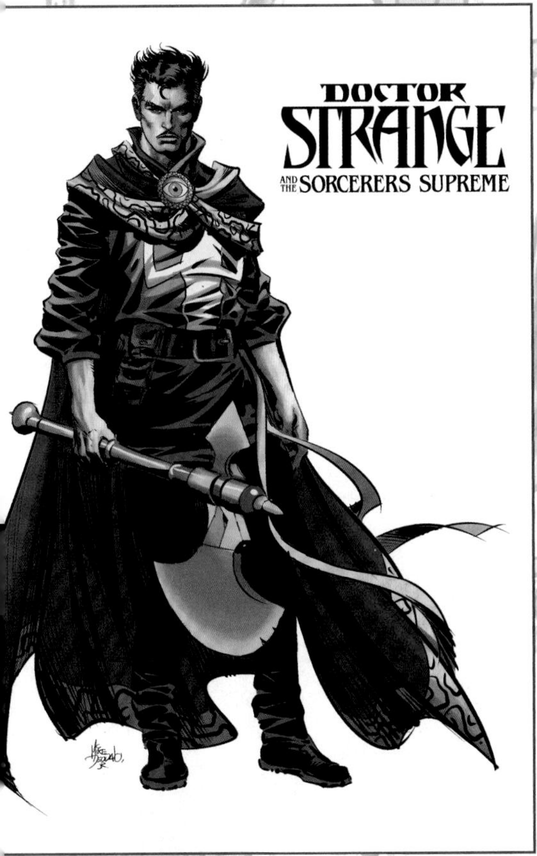
DOCTOR
STRANGE
AND THE SORCERERS SUPREME

NO. 1 TEASER VARIANT BY
MIKE DEODATO JR. & **FRANK MARTIN**

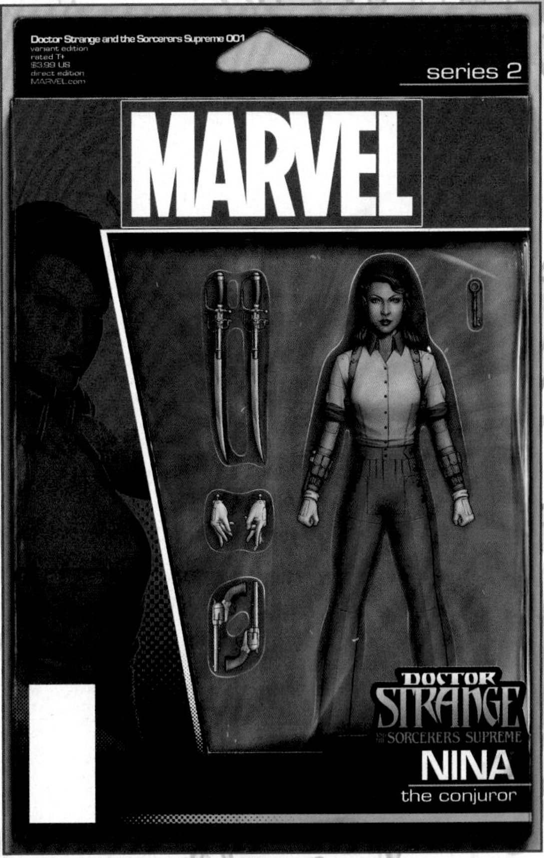
Doctor Strange and the Sorcerers Supreme 001
variant edition
rated T+
$3.99 US
direct edition
MARVEL.com
series 2
MARVEL
DOCTOR
STRANGE
AND THE SORCERERS SUPREME
NINA
the conjuror

NO. 1 ACTION FIGURE VARIANT BY
JOHN TYLER CHRISTOPHER

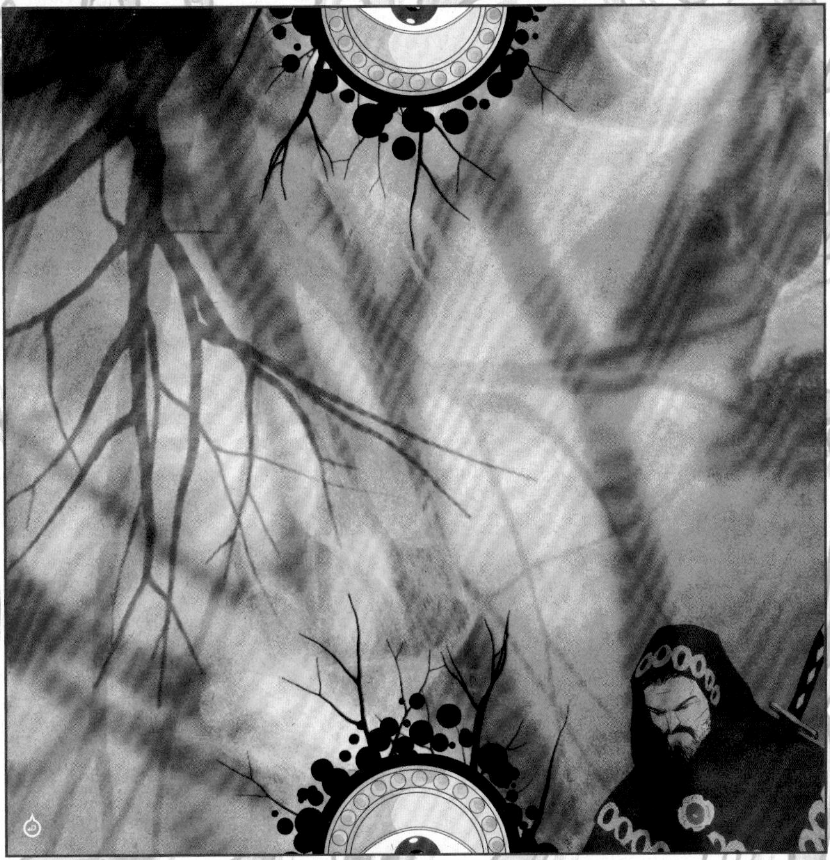

NO. 1 HIP-HOP VARIANT BY **JUAN DOE**

COVER SKETCHES

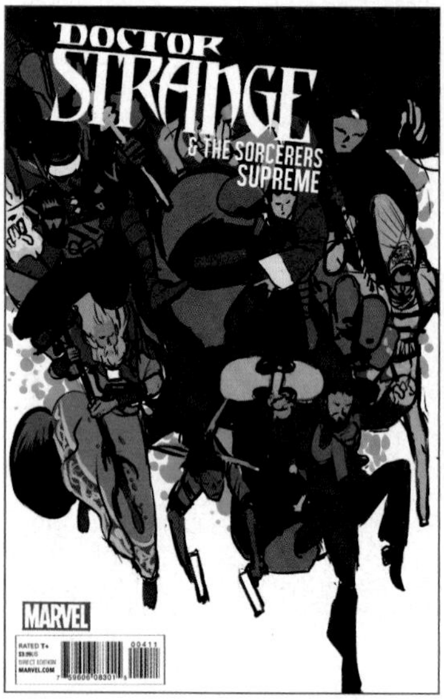
DOCTOR STRANGE
& THE SORCERERS SUPREME
MARVEL

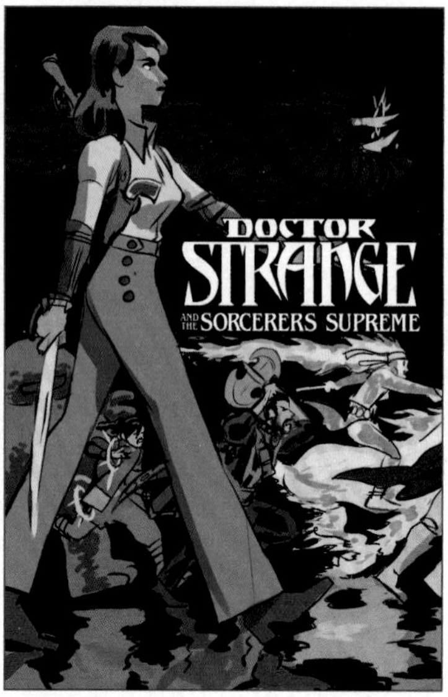
DOCTOR STRANGE
AND THE SORCERERS SUPREME

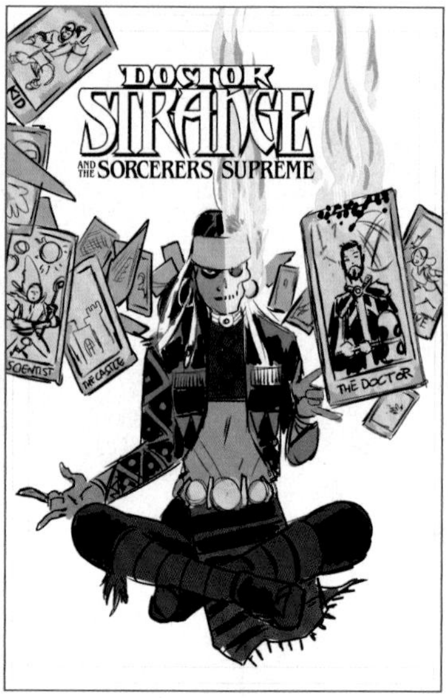
DOCTOR STRANGE
AND THE SORCERERS SUPREME
THE CASTLE
THE DOCTOR

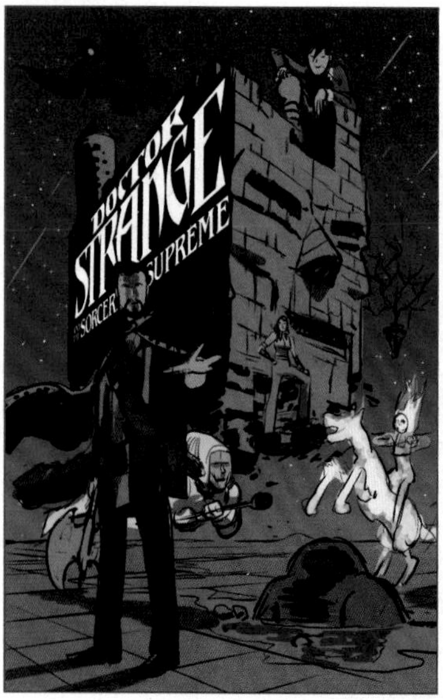
DOCTOR STRANGE
AND THE SORCERERS SUPREME

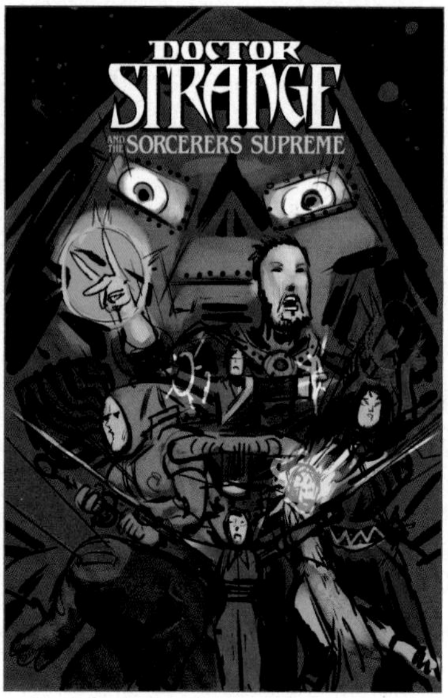
DOCTOR STRANGE
AND THE SORCERERS SUPREME

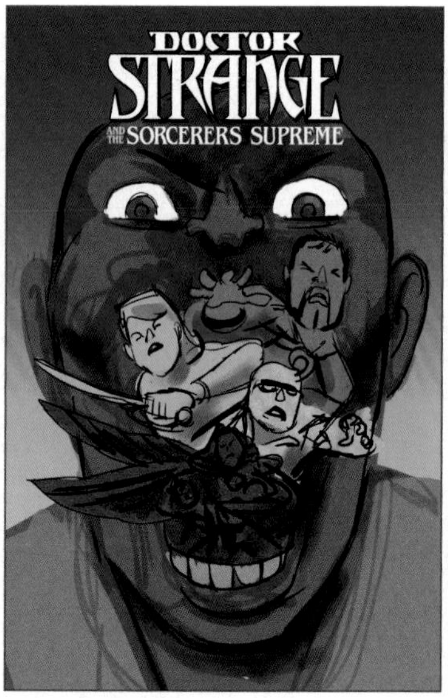
DOCTOR STRANGE
AND THE SORCERERS SUPREME

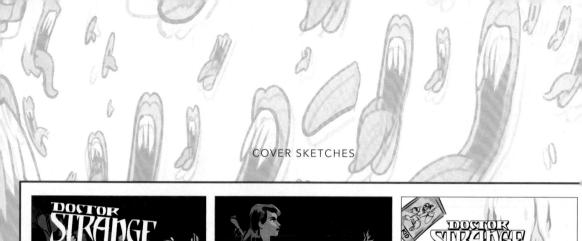